Ultimate FE Leadership and Management Handbook

Other Titles in The Essential FE Toolkit Series

Books for Lecturers

Books for Managers

Ultimate FE Leadership and Management Handbook

Jill Jameson and Ian McNay

continuum

Continuum International Publishing Group

The Tower Building   80 Maiden Lane, Suite 704
11 York Road   New York
SE1 7NX   NY 10038

www.continuumbooks.com

British Library Cataloguing-in-Publication Data
A catalogue record for this book is available from the British Library.

ISBN–10: 0–8264–9012–3 (paperback)
ISBN–13: 978–0–8264–9012–4 (paperback)

Typeset by YHT Ltd, London
Printed and bound in England by Antony Rowe Ltd, Chippenham, Wilts

Contents

Dedication

For Jill: this book is dedicated to Kevin, Imogen and my mum, Phyllis, with love and thanks.

For Ian: this book is dedicated to my students on leadership and management programmes, from whom I learned much. Thank you.

Acknowledgements

We thank all the interviewees, respondents, learners, teachers, leaders and managers who have helped in the creation of this book.

Series Foreword

THE ESSENTIAL FE TOOLKIT SERIES

Jill Jameson
Series Editor

In the autumn of 1974, a young woman newly arrived from Africa landed in Devon to embark on a new life in England. Having travelled half way round the world, she still longed for sunny Zimbabwe. Not sure what career to follow, she took a part-time job teaching EFL to Finnish students. Enjoying this, she studied thereafter for a PGCE at the University of Nottingham in Ted Wragg's Education Department. After teaching in secondary schools, she returned to university in Cambridge, and, having graduated, took a job in ILEA in 1984 in adult education. She loved it: there was something about adult education that woke her up, made her feel fully alive, newly aware of all the lifelong learning journeys being followed by so many students and staff around her. The adult community centre she worked in was a joyful place for diverse multi-ethnic communities. Everyone was cared for, including 90 year olds in wheelchairs, toddlers in the crèche, ESOL refugees, city accountants in business suits and university level graphic design students. In her eyes, the centre was an educational ideal, a remarkable place in which, gradually, everyone was helped to learn to be who they wanted to be. This was the Chequer Centre, Finsbury, EC1, the 'red house', as her daughter saw it, toddling in from the crèche. And so began the story of a long interest in further education that was to last for many years . . . why, if they did such good work for so many, were FE centres so under-funded and unrecognized, so under-appreciated?

It is with delight that, 32 years after the above story began, I write the Foreword to *The Essential FE Toolkit*, Continuum's new book series of 24 books on further education (FE) for teachers and college leaders. The idea behind the *Toolkit* is to provide a comprehensive guide to FE in a series of compact, readable books. The suite of 24 individual books are gathered together to provide the practitioner with an overall FE toolkit in specialist, fact-filled volumes designed to be easily accessible, written by experts with significant knowledge and experience in their individual fields. All of the authors have in-depth understanding of further education. But – 'Why is further education important? Why does it merit a whole series to be written about it?', you may ask.

At the Association of Colleges Annual Conference in 2005, in a humorous speech to college principals, John Brennan said that, whereas in 1995 further education was a 'political back-water', by 2005 it had become 'mainstream'. John recalled that, since 1995, there had been '36 separate Government or Government-sponsored reports or white papers specifically devoted to the post-16 sector'. In our recent regional research report (2006) for the Learning and Skills Development Agency, my co-author Yvonne Hillier and I noted that it was no longer 'raining policy' in FE, as we had described earlier (Hillier and Jameson, 2003): there is now a torrent of new initiatives. We thought, in 2003, that an umbrella would suffice to protect you. We'd now recommend buying a boat to navigate these choppy waters, as it looks as if John Brennan's 'mainstream' FE, combined with a tidal wave of government policies, will soon lead to a flood of new interest in the sector, rather than end anytime soon.

There are good reasons for all this government attention on further education. In 2004/05, student numbers in LSC Council-funded further education increased to 4.2m, total college income was around £6.1 billion, and the average college had an annual turnover of £15m. Further education has rapidly increased in national significance regarding the need for ever greater achievements in UK education and skills training for millions of learners, providing qualifications and workforce training to feed a UK national economy hungrily in competition with other OECD nations. The 120 recommendations of the Foster Review (2005) therefore in the main encourage colleges to focus their work on vocational skills, social inclusion and achieving academic progress. This series is here to consider all three of these areas, and more.

The series is written for teaching practitioners, leaders and managers in the 572 FE/LSC-funded institutions in the UK, including FE colleges, adult education and sixth form institutions, prison education departments, training and workforce development units, local education authorities and community agencies. The series is also written for PGCE/Cert Ed/City & Guilds Initial and continuing professional development (CPD) teacher trainees in universities in the UK, USA, Canada, Australia, New Zealand and beyond. It will also be of interest to staff in the 600 Jobcentre Plus providers in the UK and to many private training organizations. All may find this series of use and interest in learning about FE educational practice in the 24 different areas of these specialist books from experts in the field.

Our use of this somewhat fuzzy term 'practitioners' includes staff in the FE/LSC-funded sector who engage in professional practice in governance, leadership, management, teaching, training, financial and administration services, student support services, ICT and MIS technical support, librarianship, learning resources, marketing, research and development, nursery and crèche services, community and business support, transport and estates management. It is also intended to include staff in a host of other FE services including work-related training, catering, outreach and specialist health, diagnostic additional learning support, pastoral and religious support for students. Updating staff in professional practice is critically important at a time of such continuing radical policy-driven change, and we are pleased to contribute to this nationally and internationally.

We are also privileged to have an exceptional range of authors writing for the series. Many of our authors are renowned for their work in further education, having worked in the sector for 30 years or more. Some have received OBE or CBE honours, professorships, fellowships and awards for contributions they have made to further education. All have demonstrated a commitment to FE that makes their books come alive with a kind of wise guidance for the reader. Sometimes this is tinged with world-weariness, sometimes with sympathy, humour or excitement. Sometimes the books are just plain clever or a fascinating read, to guide practitioners of the future who will read these works. Together, the books make up a considerable portfolio of assets for you to take with you through your journeys in further education. We hope the experience of reading the books will be interesting, instructive and pleasurable and that experience gained from them will last, renewed, for many seasons.

It has been wonderful to work with all of the authors and with Continuum's UK Education Publisher, Alexandra Webster, on this series. The exhilarating opportunity of developing such a comprehensive toolkit of books probably comes once in a lifetime, if at all. I am privileged to have had this rare opportunity, and I thank the publishers, authors and other contributors to the series for making these books come to life with their fantastic contributions to FE.

Dr Jill Jameson
Series Editor
March 2006

Introduction

There is nothing to it. All one has to do is hit the right keys at the right time and the instrument plays itself.

Johann Sebastian Bach

The director was working peacefully one summer evening in the main building of a large further education (FE) college when, in a sudden commotion outside, gunshots rang out. Through the wide doors of the main college entrance, which opened out onto a busy street, ran a heavily-built, mature man of Middle Eastern appearance. He was yelling out loudly and bleeding profusely from the left wrist. Blood spattered crimson everywhere. Panic and fear was in his eyes. He didn't speak English, but the desperation was plain to see. The director was alarmed. The man had been shot in the main artery in his wrist. A large grey bullet was lodged there. She needed to act swiftly. It was clear the man would die quickly without help. He staggered towards her.

The director acted instantly. Fortunately, a capable security guard was on duty. She and the guard caught the man between them, sat him down, stopped the bleeding, supported his arm and reassured him, applying strong pressure to the wound. She continued to hold his arm tightly as the guard called the air ambulance rescue service. Her arm began to hurt from applying pressure, but she held on and did not give up. The ambulance arrived. She heard a thundering noise as the helicopter landed in a now-emptied street, and felt a strong gust of wind rush through the entrance. The man was still alive but very frightened. The ambulance crew took over. They immediately applied rescue treatment to save the man's life. Not a college student, but a Middle Eastern asylum seeker, the man had run desperately into the college to find sanctuary and safety. He had found it. She and the security guard were glad to help.

Afterwards, the director breathed a sigh of relief. They had managed the situation. All was well. She recorded the incident for the college log-book. The man had been shot by a local resident in a gang fight. He said he had done nothing to provoke it, but was an innocent victim. The director and security guard sent the lingering curious students on to their classes. They checked that the school-keeper and cleaners could cope with sorting out the mess. The director spoke to the local police, and wrote to the facilities manager and principal about the incident, alerting them to the gang shooting. She prepared an information briefing for college staff and a pre-emptive press release for the marketing manager.

She debriefed the security guard, thanking him for his actions. The wounded man had no known relatives to inform, but she recorded hospital details to ensure the facilities manager followed up the situation with local police and community services to avoid further incidents. She asked the security guard to write up his report, recommending future measures for any repeated situation. Lastly, realizing she was still covered in blood, she washed herself. She reassured her family later that she had no open cuts through which infection could arise.

The above true story of an event in an inner-city FE college took place a few years ago. The story is repeated here anonymously, with the permission of the director, to illustrate that sometimes working in leadership and management in a college is anything but easy. Mostly, the day-to-day work of leading and managing further education institutions is not a life-and-death struggle for survival. But sometimes it can feel like it, and sometimes it actually is. The task of looking after the learning and teaching opportunities, curriculum needs, budget, quality, facilities, well-being and safety requirements of further education institutions with thousands of students and staff is not an easy job, though it may be a rewarding one.

Sometimes, though, there is no overt reward for leadership tasks. In the above story, the director was not thanked or praised for her efforts. Once the immediate problem was sorted out with no negative outfall, no one really noticed much else.

Certainly no one noticed the way college leadership had handled it: there was no debriefing for the director. Yet, if the incident had been handled incorrectly, it would have been in the local (or possibly even national) headlines the next day. When the mess was sorted out, it was more or less ignored.

Responding in a 'real and authentic and useful' way (Jameson, 2006) to deal with this kind of situation, sometimes without any reward or recognition – just coping with the relentlessly ordinary, usually unrewarded tasks of day-to-day leadership and management in FE – is a difficult and sometimes lonely but necessary task. The best leaders and managers in colleges do it all the time. Those who fail in one way or another can easily become part of the statistics on UK leadership and

---

Learning from failure

In 2006, *Training Magazine* reported the findings of research by Ken Blanchard Companies, which investigated failure in leadership, asking 1,400 executives for their views on the top ten leadership mistakes leaders make. The results were:

1. Failing to provide appropriate feedback, especially praise and redirection.
2. Failing to involve others in processes.
3. Failing to use a leadership style appropriate to the personnel, task or situation.
4. Failing to set clear and understood goals and objectives.
5. Failing to train and develop their staff.
6. Inappropriate use of communication, especially listening, and a tendency to ignore alternative viewpoints.
7. A tendency to give too much or too little supervision, direction or delegation.
8. A general lack of management skills, such as problem solving, decision making and consensus building.
9. A tendency to provide too little or inappropriate support.
10. A lack of accountability, especially in holding staff accountable for agreed goals and behaviour.

(*Training Magazine*, 26 July 2006)

Figure 1: Learning from failure

management failures reported in the Figure Introduction .1. Some of these, disheartened, demotivated or simply exhausted, leave the profession. Others pluck up their courage, stay on, and learn from past difficulties of one kind or another, gradually turning prior misunderstandings or weaknesses into strengths, transforming themselves and their institutions in the process. Let us be honest and clear about this. There are very few leader-managers who are so gifted that they always get everything right and are always successful. Most of us fail in one way or another occasionally. In the first years of carrying out duties in leadership and management, some of us may feel we are failing most of the time. But hold on a bit before condemning that too much. Many of the most successful leaders are those who have recovered from occasional mistakes. Let's think about this a bit more.

Sometimes, leaders famous for their later achievements have built success on earlier recovery from errors, bad luck, misjudgements or criticism by others. What distinguishes truly successful leaders from the norm is the way in which such people respond to failure. As Elisabeth Kübler-Ross said,

> People are like stained-glass windows. They sparkle and shine when the sun is out, but when the darkness sets in, their true beauty is revealed only if there is a light from within. (Kübler-Ross, 1985)

To fail sometimes, especially when you are new or tasks are unfamiliar, is not the end of the world. Nor need it be the end of your career, unless you interpret it that way. The 'light' that Kübler-Ross is referring to we would interpret as the spirit and strength of character that can be developed from failure, as we learn from our mistakes, pick ourselves up and change our behaviours and actions in order that we can succeed the next time around. As John Dewey observed: 'Failure is instructive. The person who really thinks learns quite as much from his failures as from his successes'. (Gallian, citing Dewey, 1998)

In celebration of the freedom to respond positively to setbacks, and to build on the potential for changing and improving ourselves and our situations, this book proposes that the 'ultimate' task for leader-managers in FE is not to give up in the

face of difficulty, but to value your professionalism and contributions to education. We propose that people working every
day in FE should be encouraged to have faith in their work, to
persevere and hold fast to the vision that, not only is there merit
in much that is done every day in FE, no matter how 'ordinary'
this work seems, but also good things can be achieved through
staying the course and responding to the real needs of students
in colleges, making beneficial changes where appropriate. Such
changes are not easy: they are in fact an intrinsic part of the
essential role of education, as Dewey advised us in his 'pedagogic creed' more than a century ago. His words are still
relevant to the educational leader-managers of today: 'The aim
of education is to enable individuals to continue their education
... [and] the object and reward of learning is continued capacity
for growth'. (Dewey, 1916, Ch. 8)

Let's get this straight. We are not condoning repeated failures, laziness or inattention to the job of leadership and management. We are saying that sometimes failures may occur for
all kinds of complex reasons and that leader-managers can grow
and learn from mistakes to ensure continued success in the
future. All of the successful leaders interviewed for this and
previous works have admitted, quietly or not, that sometimes
they have had to cope with problems and/or failures of one sort
or another. People are not human without this: some of the
best inventions in the world would never have happened if
their creators had been successful the first time, and some of the
most successful leaders got that way through learning from
mistakes.

'With my sleeves up, brushing the steps'

When I went to interview Dame Ruth Silver, DBE, Principal
of Lewisham College, about leadership in FE in 2005, Ruth
alerted me to the need for leader-managers to adjust their
perspectives to changing realities between our ideal expectations of what leadership is and what it actually turns out to be,
in practical reality. She thereby encouraged people facing
challenges in leadership not to lose heart if things were difficult,
but to gain instead a new purpose and mission, adjusting to new

realities. In response to my question about whether she had changed her views about leadership and management over the years, Ruth said:

> I would have started off really like most people, with a kind of external view of leadership. So, when you become a Principal [you think], 'this is how you have to behave'. And it's very much like growing up, I guess ... you have an idealized version of yourself and then life does things to put it in its place ... The biggest changes in me came on the whole from the changing world ... So those kind of circumstances – you remember that lovely Buddhist phrase, you know, *obstacles are our teachers* ... All of those are the tools of sculpture, I think, to take the idealized version of yourself and make it real and authentic and useful. So from a view of kind of 'hands off' leadership that I may have started with, to find myself a year later with my sleeves up, brushing the steps, you know, that kind of stuff. And so I've learned that *leadership is about doing what has to be done, but in an ethical and related way.* (Dame Ruth Silver, interview on leadership (Jameson, 2006))

Sometimes, what leaders need to do is simply to carry the can, without reward, recognition or praise. As Ferreday, Hodgson and Jones (2005: 4) point out, leadership in FE can be 'a fairly lonely job'. Ferreday *et al.* report the words of an FE principal about his/her role, but in fact the loneliness of senior leader-manager positions in FE can be felt to some extent at every level, including that of directors, security officers, curriculum and administrative staff. Ruth also reported on this difficult element of her role as a principal, saying, '... it's a lonely thing, leadership. No, being a leader is lonely' (Jameson, 2006), going on to outline the vital need for ongoing support for and supervision of leaders in FE at all levels.

The intrinsic rewards of leadership actions in our story of the college director were plain enough: the man lived, the situation was sorted out; there were no further incidents of this kind during the next several years. That was reward enough, in a way. In addition, the director was pleased that the man had seen the college as a place of sanctuary, providing help and support for local people in need. The story reports a somewhat extreme version of the kind of community support role FE colleges often play, though one too little recognized and appreciated.

Learning from stories of leadership and management

What is important about this story for leadership and management in FE? Well, for a start, this was an unexpected occurrence – unplanned, unusual, needing instant action. As a leadership situation, it required immediate clarity of mind, effective communication and swift action by the director and security guard. There was no way to think through strategy on this one!

The director and security guard implemented a series of immediate actions to ensure the man's life was saved and the college students and environment were protected from the incident. They pulled together college resources to restore safety to the victim and ensure there was no negative outfall for students, staff or college facilities. They communicated to all, reassuring, reporting the incident, controlling the situation in a professional way. The director supported the guard's actions, recognized his strengths and delegated tasks suited to his role. They acted as a team instinctively, pulling resources together in a mutually respectful way to cope with this emergency.

Later, the director built on the lessons emerging from the incident to set up an environmental task force. This group, supported by the principal, tackled longer-term issues affecting the college from its challenging local situation in a strategically planned way. They inspired a new vision for the buildings and environment, gaining special funding with support from the finance director. These new funds refurbished and enhanced the canteen, entrance and meetings rooms, installed new security locks and purchased greenery and paintings for main areas. It was a successful initiative with students, who reported positively on benefits gained in the annual local student survey.

Leadership actions here demonstrated professional behaviour in handling an emergency incident, negotiating with police and air ambulance services, strategic planning, envisioning, effective coordination of relationships with staff, appropriate communication, funding generation and 'thinking outside the box' to refurbish the environment. In short, the director recognized and did the 'right things' as a leader.

As a manager, the director ensured the overall incident was effectively handled through college systems, using her position of authority to delegate tasks to the guard, who demonstrated skilled first aid and emergency organizational skills. She put in place follow-up actions to protect students and staff from the incident and from publicity about it. From a management point of view, the situation required practical, well-organized, coordinated actions. Management actions included supervision of staff, use of procedures for emergency incidents, risk aversion, site management of students, premises and security, authoritative debriefing of staff, handling publicity and communications. In short, as a manager, she did things 'in the right way'.

Differentiating between leadership and management

The difference between leadership as 'doing the right things' and management as 'doing things the right way' is not particularly highlighted in this example. Leadership and management duties here overlapped. However, such differentiation does have a point, which is that leadership can be envisaged at any level, regardless of institutional hierarchies, whereas management is linked to positional hierarchy. Leadership is more about 'who you are', your vision and influencing power, as distinguished from management, which is more about 'what position you occupy and how you effect management tasks'. Both the director and security guard used effective leadership and management skills to ensure this situation was properly dealt with. But since the guard was a day-to-day security manager without supervisory responsibilities, it was up to the director to shoulder responsibilities for senior management tasks. We explore some of the key differences between leadership and management more fully in Chapter 1 and elsewhere in the book.

The true situation described above took place in a 'beacon'

inner city college. Such an incident had never happened previously on college premises. Another situation of exactly this kind has never happened since in this college. However, the director explained to us afterwards that the experience this incident provided about leadership and management in FE affected her deeply and she reflected on it many times. She recognized the situation was a useful one for leaders and managers to reflect on. (It's one that lends itself neatly to a role-play as part of training, as long as no one plays the victim too realistically!) However, the director also observed that leadership and crisis management in such traumatic situations can be very different from the more ordinary day-to-day experiences most management staff experience in FE colleges. As Kelly, Iszatt White, Randall and Rouncefield (2004) observe, leadership in further education is more often about the ordinary day-to-day grind of 'mundane work' than about crisis management.

Leadership in crisis situations like this in FE can be, ironically, both more challenging and in fact easier than in routine college life. When there is a crisis, people tend to fall in line more readily: authority emerges and often operates through necessity quickly and decisively, for better or worse, as John Adair notes:

> The tendency of people to follow a leader who knows what to do, observed Socrates, is strengthened in a time of crisis. . . . . such a crisis should be more to an effective leader's liking than a period of ease and prosperity, for it is easier to make things happen. (Adair, 2002:18)

Sometimes, leadership demands immediate action in unpredictable situations which are difficult, challenging, even traumatic. Sometimes, there is no rule book to help you and no time to consult anyone. This can be stressful. However, if in the longer term college leaders apply dedicated efforts to the more routine tasks of strategic planning and operational management, nurturing the talents of teams they work with and building long-term trust and collaborative working relationships, they can get through most situations, including emergencies like the above incident, successfully.

Behind the scenes of the above story above, there was,

within this college, good senior management planning in place and a team of people with capable operational skills, who also worked hard, with passion and consideration for students, carrying out dedicated actions to ensure the college operated as effectively as possible. Placing the well-being of students and staff foremost in your priorities as a college educational leader and manager in more ordinary, ongoing daily work is of primary importance. This is a priority that shapes leaders and managers alike, as well as inspectors, and it is one that we will continue to stress throughout this book.

Reasons for writing this book and why it's an 'ultimate' handbook

Why are we writing this book on leadership and management in FE institutions? The task of leading and managing FE institutions has assumed increasingly greater importance during the years since the incorporation of FE colleges in 1992–93. The two authors of this book have, between us, a somewhat scary 65 years' experience of leadership and management in post-compulsory education and training (PCET) including, in the case of one author, specific leadership and management experience in FE. We wanted to share some of the reflections arising from that knowledge and experience with practitioners in leadership and management in colleges. Our background includes formal and informal knowledge of strategic leadership and operational management at governor, college executive, directorate, assistant directorate, head of department and programme leader levels in further and higher education during the past 30 or so years across several FE and HE/FE institutions and regions in the UK and abroad.

This book draws on accumulated years of knowledge from PCET teacher training, authoring and consultancy on leadership and management, research and staff development in FE. It draws on data from interviews carried out with principals and other senior post-holders in 2004–05 and on survey results on leadership in the learning and skills sector in 2006. It builds on experience of trustee board membership, networking events, QAA HE in FE audit with FE colleges, as well as ten years of governorship experience in five institutions. It draws on work authoring and editing journals and books on FE in the UK and internationally, and, most of all, remembers the many students and staff we have worked with and for.

The 'ultimate' aspect of this book, reflected in the title, is therefore about telling a story of long-term survival through many trials and worries in leadership and management in FE. We tend to subscribe to the views of the Centre for Excellence in Leadership (CEL) regarding 'passion for excellence', one of the key areas listed in the CEL *Leadership Qualities Framework* (CEL, 2004). In the longer term, the FE system will not be supported in the development of sustainable knowledge and skills for excellence in leadership and management without greater attention being paid to cumulative knowledge and evidence from the experience of people who have gone before. In this, we count the many people who have participated collaboratively with us in teaching, learning, research, scholarship, institutional and governance activities.

Having recovered a bit from experiences at the hard coalface of working life in FE/HE (during two careers that started around the time Professor Ted Wragg was still a dashing young academic making his mark at Nottingham), we decided to write this book. We did *not* call it '*Phew!*' but were persuaded by the publisher to use instead the title, *The Ultimate FE Leadership and Management Handbook*. The 'ultimate' part is, as we've explained above, merely with regard to joint longevity and long-toothed quality in survival terms, and breadth of experience across many areas of PCET operations, as well as the provision of an overview of aspects of leadership and management both within the series and from interviews and other research carried out in the sector. We would not claim to 'ultimate' status in any other way! It is 'ultimate' in the sense of meaning – 'We've survived so far! We made it through all that and are still here to tell the story . . .'

What this book is about

This handbook provides an overview of strategic and operational leadership and a range of management theories underlying effective practice in further education. It provides a commentary on the practical implementation of leadership and management in FE institutions in the UK. The book aims to help readers to understand important factors to take into consideration when planning for effective strategic and operational leadership and management of FE institutions. Consideration is given to the new *National Standards for Leadership and Management* and the *Principals'/CEOs' National Standards* currently being revised by Lifelong Learning UK (LLUK), with the Centre for Excellence in Leadership (CEL), based on the prior standards established by the Further Education National Training Organization (FENTO), now part of LLUK.

Consideration is also given to the CEL *Leadership Qualities Framework* (LQF) and to the views of a range of staff and agencies in the sector. In addition, we reflect on the importance of prior research on leadership and management in FE and on the role of government policy in such initiatives as the Foster Review (2005) and the government White Paper on further education: *Further Education: Raising Skills, Improving Life Chances* (DfES, 2006a).

A 'how to' guide to some key tasks for leader-managers is outlined across the chapters to ensure a clear focus is maintained on learners, staff, high-quality provision and good standards in leadership and management, while meeting inspectorate and external audit requirements. We are particularly interested in the role of values-based, collaborative and distributed leadership to assist in taking forward planned achievements and succession strategies for the sector on a wide scale. We envisage that leadership development is relevant to staff at every level, not only those at the top tiers of management. We also highlight the importance of using ICT/ILT, network management leadership (Ferreday, Hodgson and Jones, 2005) and social software where possible and appropriate for collaborative working right across the FE system. We echo the views of CEL researchers Ferreday *et al.* (2005) that there is a profound need to move away from the 'loneliness' model in which senior leaders at the top of the institutional hierarchy carry all the burdens for leadership.

We observe, with Dr David Collins, Principal of South Cheshire College, that appropriate distributed leadership development is needed at all levels of FE to ensure that everyone in the college takes responsibility for its survival and progress:

> I'm definitely a firm believer in distributed leadership although in my opinion, the overall responsibility for leadership can never be delegated. For real empowerment to occur, there's got to be a recognition that power, skills and responsibility, wherever they lie, must match, otherwise all that's likely to be distributed in my view is stress and confusion. This points to the need for personal skills development at all levels in a learning organisation. I would go even further than that. Without some form of distributed leadership, the *institution is very vulnerable to being too dependent on an individual or small group for its survival and progress.* (Dr David Collins, CBE, interview on leadership (Jameson, 2006))

We regard 'leadership' as a field of relationships and interactions between people, in ways that move within and also outside traditional management hierarchies, building on prior leadership work by Warren Blank (1995), Keith Grint (2000, 1999), Peter Northouse (2004), Tony Bush (2003, 2006) and Margaret Wheatley (1999), and on specific earlier research studies carried out by others in the learning and skills sector, notably in FE (Collinson and Collinson, 2005a, 2005b; Briggs, 2005b; Gleeson, 2001; Lumby, Harris, Morrison, Mujis and Sood, 2005; Sedgmore, 2002; Simkins, 2005). We also reflect on and refer readers to other leadership and management books in *The Essential FE Toolkit* series, including especially those by David Collins and Ann Briggs.

What this book isn't about

This book is not a government document, policy paper, inspection handbook, or business guide to leadership and management in further education. It does not provide a multi-authored collection of chapters, articles or interviews from leaders and managers in FE. It is not a research report including the analysis of significant amounts of research data collected from leaders and managers in the FE sector. However, it *is* informed by data collected previously from leaders and managers in the sector in research projects on leadership and management and by data collected from part-time staff and research project managers in the sector.

Overview of the sections and chapters

This handbook is made up of four sections and twelve chapters (see Figure 2).

Leadership and management in FE

The Introduction provides an overview. In Section One, Chapter 1, the book examines the national leadership and management position in FE, the national audit of skills in this

---

Overview of book sections and chapters

Introduction

Section One – Leadership and Management in FE
- Chapter 1: The significance of leadership and management for FE
- Chapter 2: What is 'leadership'?
- Chapter 3: What is 'management'?
- Chapter 4: Governance, executive, senior and middle management
- Chapter 5: Problems: rotten managers and leaky leaders

Section Two – Models of Leadership in FE Institutions
- Chapter 6: Modelling leadership in formal and informal ways
- Chapter 7: Pointing out the naked emperor: leadership theory in practice

Section Three – Models of Management in FE Institutions
- Chapter 8: Measuring attributes of excellent management
- Chapter 9: Diversity and authenticity in management

Section Four – How to be a good leader-manager in FE
- Chapter 10: Some lessons from leader-managers
- Chapter 11: A guide to bring out the leader-manager in you
- Chapter 12: Conclusion

References and appendices

Figure 2: Overview of book sections and chapters

area, and current tensions and government priorities. A consideration of the differences and overlapping areas between 'leadership' and 'management' is outlined. The issue of 'professionalism' versus 'managerialism' is discussed, together with the cultural issues and conflicts arising from these differences. Going beyond the 'performativity' of a targets-based culture, the importance of process and systems-based perspectives is considered. Distributed and emotionally intelligent leadership and management are discussed in relation to the leadership and management of FE institutions. The creation of values-based organizations is proposed, as is the concept of 'eating the dinner, not the menu' in leadership perspectives. Staff perspectives on leadership and management in FE are considered.

Chapter 2 looks at leadership in terms of definitions and the elements making up good leadership. Perspectives on the way some outstanding leaders operate are considered, as is the concept of 'just in time' learning. The concepts of paradox, trust and cynicism are considered, and the book looks at the definition of 'greatness and goodness' in a post-heroic age. Quantum versus 'classic' models of leadership are explained, as is the way to deal with rapid change in further education. Staff perceptions of leadership in terms of diversity and authenticity are put forward.

Chapter 3 provides an overview of management in FE, including definitions of management and the elements of good management. Business systems and solutions applied to educational management, lessons and dilemmas for management are briefly analysed. The concept of 'organizational learning' in terms of single and double loop learning is outlined. Mapping current achievements with target goals for institutions is considered, as are staff perceptions of management in further education.

Chapter 4 outlines 'senior' versus 'middle' management, 'executive' roles in the context of senior management, and line management roles and duties. The concept of functional management is examined. The role of 'governance' versus 'leadership and management' is reviewed, as are links with national, regional and local leaders and managers.

Chapter 5 looks at problems with leadership and management and the identification of destructive trends to overcome problems. A guide for spotting rotten managers, leaky leaders and toxic bosses is provided. An analysis of failing colleges is given, including scandals, messes and scapegoats in the FE system. Loss of staff in constant restructurings is discussed, in relation to the concept of 'amnesiac organizations', when we need to cope with the loss of 'organizational memory'. Methods for defeating bullies, outlasting 'mobbing' and blame cultures are outlined. Ways of healing anorexic and paranoiac institutions and the creation of holistic transformations through good leadership are discussed.

Models of leadership in FE institutions

In Chapter 6 formal and informal models of leadership are put forward. Positional authority and formal hierarchical models are briefly explained. Formal models – structural, systems, bureaucratic, rational models – are outlined. Early leadership models, including trait, behavioural and situational theories, are noted and newer models, including transformational, distributed, team and ambiguity theories, are briefly discussed. Emerging models – servant leadership, creative and quantum leadership – are examined for their relevance to FE. To round off the chapter, informal models of leadership, including collegial, shared and everyday leadership, are discussed and analysed.

In Chapter 7 links between theory and practice are demonstrated in terms of leadership duties. The concept of 'pointing out the naked emperor' is discussed in terms of 'transformational' theories of leadership. The role of reflective practice is considered and examined in terms of whether intermittent navel-gazing can help leaders to develop their skills. Elements of effective leadership situations in practice are outlined in terms of their enigmas and some possible answers to these. Transactional practices in leadership are outlined, and some methods for identifying good leaders, with assessment techniques for learning leadership, are put forward.

Models of management in FE institutions

Chapter 8 analyses the importance of some management techniques in achieving excellent high-quality provision. Attributes of excellent management are discussed and the role of strategic planning, finance, audit, quality assurance and governance are outlined. The key importance of values-based ethical management is proposed. Tools and techniques for managers, including 360° feedback, 3 Cs and 7 Ps and 'guru' models of management are referenced for further reading. The question of whether inspections measure the difference between good and poor management is discussed.

Diversity and authenticity in management are considered in Chapter 9, together with intrinsic solutions which map skills to local goals and demands. We outline the development of authentic situation-specific management. Recognizing the need for diversity and the relative lack of this at senior management level in FE, we recommend the implementation of policies for greater inclusivity in FE. Facts on the representation of women, black and ethnic minority groups and disabled staff in leadership and management are considered. The question of authenticity in management and leadership is discussed in relation to local potential solutions for cracking this nutty problem.

How to be a good leader-manager in FE

In Chapter 10 lessons from outstanding leader-managers are put forward, as are leadership and management suggestions from leaders from a survey on leadership. Some points relating to good leadership and management are outlined in relation to general FE colleges, sixth form education, adult and community education, work-based and training organizations, prison education, and the role of national agencies such as the Centre for Excellence in Leadership (CEL).

A guide to bring out the leader-manager within you is presented in Chapter 11. Suggestions for developing situation-specific leadership and management skills are outlined in the context of challenges facing leaders and managers in the further education sector, drawing on experience and findings from the field.

Chapter 12 forms the conclusion, giving a summary of previous chapters and including a round-up of leadership and management techniques. A final 'rounding-up' section draws together the overall messages from the book. The References and Appendices provide further information to readers.

Finally, we hope that you enjoy reading this book, as we have writing it, for the benefit of learners and staff in the learning and skills sector, and we wish you good luck in all of your journeys in leadership and management in the sector!

Section One: Important Factors in Leadership and Management in FE

1: Leading and managing FE institutions

Education is the kindling of a flame, not the filling of a vessel

Socrates

What are the most important factors in providing good leadership and management in further education (FE) institutions, or, more broadly, in the learning and skills sector (LSS)? This chapter identifies some key issues relating to this question, situating this book in the context of a range of recent research reports and developments relating to the FE system. Although our focus is on leadership and management in further education, we consider also some overview issues relating to the wider learning and skills sector.

We answer the question above throughout this first chapter, beginning with a consideration of selected recent research findings on sectoral leadership and management. Whereas other books in the leadership and management Essential FE Toolkit series are focused on particular key areas (e.g. David Collins on survival skills for senior college leaders, Ann Briggs on the role of middle managers, Beulah Ainley on race equality in the leadership and management of colleges, Gareth Parry, Anne Thompson and Penny Blackie on managing the provision of HE in colleges), this book, as its title indicates, will give an overview 'helicopter' view of a wide range of issues, theories and questions about leadership and management in the FE sector. Rather than focusing only on abstract theories about leadership and management, we contextualize and summarize a range of theories in terms of their suitability for the sector and relationship with research in and on the sector.

Practical wisdom: phronesis

We base these theories also directly on 'real-world' experiences and knowledge about prior, current and potential future issues that concern leaders and managers in FE institutions, as well as on our own research findings, on research from the Centre for Excellence in Leadership (CEL) and elsewhere. Our way of viewing leadership is linked with the development of *phronesis* (from Aristotle, in Greek, Φρονησις) or 'practical wisdom'. We suggest that professional educators who are leader-managers at all levels can and do work in ways deeply tuned into both 'knowing in action' (practical skills) and propositional knowledge (facts and theories), based on the evidence of research findings about 'what works' in education. This builds on Donald Schön's concept of reflective practice, as well as its many advocates and critics. However, it also takes into account the need to *situate* reflection on practice within FE and to update this concept with a more nuanced awareness of the gender and diversity issues (Clegg, 1999) as well as the surveillance concerns of critics of what has become the 'reflective practice movement' in an audited society. We therefore propose that the practical wisdom of *phronesis* provides an opportunity for creative and critical engagement with leadership and management in ways that we explore throughout this book.

National leadership and management perspectives in FE

A 'think-piece' on leadership prepared for the Foster Review of FE in 2005 by consultant research experts (Fox, Kerr, Collinson, Collinson and Swan, 2005) noted some key external and internal factors for Foster's review team to consider. Notable external issues for FE leaders included the identification of pressures driving FE leadership from a perceived prevailing 'audit' culture. The review team found that meeting audit demands in FE soaked up precious staff time and expertise and distracted leaders from what they regarded as the equally important external demands of engaging with local employers, political agendas, partnerships, communities and businesses. By contrast, important internal factors the experts identified included concerns about the motivation of staff, recognition by funding bodies and major issues about identity:

> A key internal issue concerns staff motivation and the identity of the sector, especially as it looks to the future. Staff are hugely committed to the learners and their achievements, and are committed to widening participation, but the funding regime does not appear fully to reward these commitments. (Fox *et al.*, 2005:1)

The same review team responded to the Foster Review question, 'What are the key challenges facing college leadership?', by listing the following:

- The complexity of the role of 'principal'
- Playing the auditing game and college self-presentation
- The strategic importance of local community and business politics
- The social justice and inclusion agenda
- The scale of the succession crisis and inadequacy of measures taken overall
- Equality and diversity
- National versus local accountability (Fox *et al.*, 2005:1)

We would concur in general with this list of challenges, but would add to them also our own concerns regarding the well-being and current relative de-professionalization of overworked staff in the FE system. It is our perception that the majority of staff at all levels in FE are, more or less, overstretched, under-funded and under-recognized, and that this systematic under-valuing of FE professionals is a vital issue affecting leadership, management, professionalism and the long-term effectiveness of the sector. This needs to change, as the *House of Commons Education and Skills Committee Report on Further Education: Fourth Report of Session 2005–06* (House of Commons, 2006) recently acknowledged.

Having contemplated briefly the above evidence from an expert group on leadership and management, reflecting also the complex diversity of local situations in FE, we can begin to arrive at an overview of some key important factors needed for the consideration of priorities for leadership and management in FE. The first guide for this is the Centre for Excellence in Leadership (CEL) Leadership Qualities Framework (LQF), developed in 2004. The framework identified the following four key areas for the development and practice of leadership:

- Focus to achieve
- Mobilize to impact
- Sustain momentum
- Passion for excellence

These areas are considered again and analysed in more depth in Chapter 8. For the moment, we discuss the external and internal demands on the sector, and its complexity and importance.

External demands: FE as 'the adaptive layer', the 'middle child'

There is a vast range of external demands on leaders and managers in FE. When I interviewed Ruth Silver, DBE, Principal of Lewisham College, in 2005 about leadership in the learning and skills sector, Ruth noted that she regarded FE as 'the adaptive layer' of the education sector: the stratum of education that continuously tends to shift and change to adapt to the demands of others. Building on Ruth Silver's definition, we note that Foster's image for FE (Foster, 2005) is that of the 'middle child' sandwiched between higher education and schools. When not being overlooked, the middle child tends to be pulled and pushed between the oldest and youngest siblings – their role is somewhat uncertain, always potentially contingent on others older and younger, requiring continuous adaptation to the demands of different age groups and situations. Whereas the youngest child tends to get special treatment as 'the kid' of the family, and the oldest child is often marked out by having greater responsibility, the middle child can have a difficult time establishing their identity.

FE institutions are subject to multiple continuous stringent demands by the national and local LSC, the government, public and private sector auditors, the inspection services, employers, institutional partners, and a host of other external monitoring agencies like awarding bodies and sector skills organizations. External demands on leaders and managers in FE also arise from potential, past and current students, parents, business clients and partners who are the 'receivers' of FE and training provision. It can seem sometimes to staff in FE that they are constantly under the gaze of external auditors, and continuously being scrutinized, as Fox *et al.* (2005) noted:

> A core theme . . . [in our research] is the detrimental effects of the 'audit culture' (Power, 1997; Strathern, 2000) on college life and leadership. There is, for example, immense pressure on colleges to achieve centrally-imposed short-term targets. 'Staff are distant and unable to influence strategic decision-making at LSC and Government department level' (Collinson and Collinson 2005b:9). Some senior managers state that the number of staff needed to provide the very detailed information to service and satisfy the audit requirements is extremely expensive and unsustainable. (Fox *et al.*, 2005)

The 'adaptive layer' of FE is one which seems continually to be stretched, pushed and pulled to meet external requirements and deadlines, to such an extent that it can be hard for colleges to establish an identity that is not constantly subject to surveillance. As in Jeremy Bentham's *Panopticon*, famously the subject of Foucault's comparative analysis with modern society, there is a continuing sense of being scrutinized:

> One of our studies (of both FE and Sixth Form colleges) suggests that in some successful colleges up to 50% of staff time is taken up with servicing the 'audit culture' in the sector (Collinson and Collinson 2005b:9). In one typical example the college was audited fifteen times in twelve months on different issues, often by external private sector auditors brought in by 'outsourcing' to conduct the audits. (Fox *et al.*, 2005)

The reason for all this auditing may be discerned as a direct result of the national place allocated for FE early on as a mass-production system for the factory of vocational education, as

Randle and Brady discussed in 1997, identifying 'a newly-found government commitment to FE as the source of a future highly skilled and flexible work force, the key to effective industrial and commercial competition' (Randle and Brady, 1997: 122, citing also McGinty and Fish, 1993).

To add to this routinized 'serviceability', the FE system was also for years marginalized and rendered invisible, as these authors also pointed out in 1997, citing an earlier article in the *Guardian*:

> ...the UK further education (FE) sector has been largely ignored. There has been virtually no independent work published based on research in the area ... but it has been noted in the press that whilst the sector appears all but invisible, it costs the taxpayer more than £2.5 billion a year, provides work for more than 100,000 people and has two and a half million clients. The workers are revolting, the customers are complaining, the police are investigating and 100 of its chief executive[s] have suffered votes of no confidence. It is a big business in big trouble, but no-one seems to care. Last week it was rocked by strikes and hardly anyone noticed. We are talking about further education – the Cinderella service that caters for more of the over 16 population than all the schools and universities put together (*Guardian*, 12 March 1995: 11). (Randle and Brady, 1997: 121–2)

The role of FE was linked to its undervalued status as the key provider of vocational education and training:

> The FE sector has traditionally provided the bulk of technical education and vocational preparation within the UK system, and it has been suggested that the academic value system has accorded this type of education little attention and low priority (McGinty & Fish, 1993). This may go some way towards accounting for the 'invisibility' of the sector. (Randle and Brady, 1997, *op. cit.*)

Internal demands on leaders and managers

In addition to the pressures of external scrutiny, perceptions of low status and a lack of autonomy, there are a multiplicity of internal demands on FE leaders and managers from governors, college curriculum and administrative staff, students, and a plethora of other clients and customers within colleges. The FE sector is possibly the most complicated and demanding of all education sectors to manage, in terms of its overall profile, qualifications, funding system and the size and variety of institutions involved. Diverse, continuing internal requirements on leadership and management from staff and students require leaders to play key roles in management, financial affairs, programme organization, marketing and operations, quality assurance, resource provision, ethos, estates and environment, health and safety, and a variety of other crucial areas, such as developing staff training and professional skills.

Given such external and internal pressures on college leaders and managers, how relatively important are issues of leadership and management in FE, in terms of their wider impact within the UK? What sort of numbers are we talking about, in terms of institutions, learners and staff in the FE system and the learning and skills sector as a whole? Surely this is just a limited issue affecting a few colleges in a few places, you might ask? Well, no – it isn't a limited or insignificant issue. Let's look firstly at the complex nature of the further education sector, and then at the numbers of staff and students involved overall in both FE and in the learning and skills sector.

The complexity of the further education sector

The sectoral complexity of further education is acknowledged within the *Foster Review* (2005), the government White Paper on FE (2006) and the *House of Commons Education and Skills Committee Report on Further Education Fourth Report of Session 2005–06* (House of Commons, 2006). The last publication is particularly illuminating for its understanding and refreshing approach to further education, highlighting key areas of concern not addressed either in Foster (2005) or the government's

FE White Paper (2006). Commenting with intelligent under-standing on the difficulties that have beset the sector for many years, the parliamentary report reproduces a structural diagram from the Leitch Review Interim Report (Leitch Interim Review, 2005), which summarizes the structural complexity of the 'organisational overlay' of 'bodies which oversee, direct and audit' the FE system (see Figure 1.1).

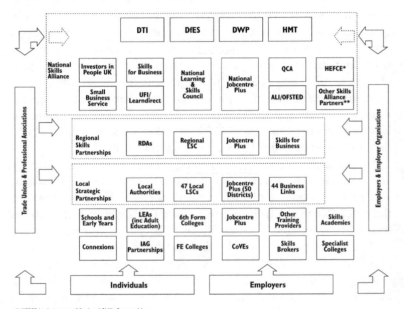

* HEFCE is also a part of Regional Skills Partnerships.

** The Skills Alliance also includes the Small Business Council, Connexions, TUC, CBI, National Institute of Adult & Continuing Education (NIACE), the Association of Colleges (AoC) and the Association of Learning Providers (ALP).

Figure 1.1: Organizational structure for FE and skills in England (Leitch Interim Review, 2005).

Figure 1.1 in itself is enough to give the reader a headache. Contemplating it, we note that, assuming staff do understand circuit board-type intertwining relationships, a tortuous com-peting morass of priorities and policies within the FE system makes for a repeating nightmare of multiple local, regional and national accountabilities. The *House of Commons Education and Skills Working Group Parliamentary Report*, noting this structural jumble affecting FE, has therefore sensibly requested that 'the

Government to carry out an urgent review of whether the organizational, planning and funding frameworks for further education and skills, viewed as a whole, constitute a coherent system' (House of Commons, 2006: 22). Such a review is long overdue. Recognition of this unhelpfully over-burdensome complexity to which FE colleagues are constantly subjected and accountable is most welcome. However, in addressing this, it is important that the baby is not thrown out with the bathwater: in other words, the strengths of FE, in which we include more generally adult and community and work-based learning provision, need to be retained. As the National Audit Office notes of the learning and skills sector:

> The learning and skills sector is very complex, comprising the further education sector (further education colleges, sixth-form colleges and specialist colleges), school sixth forms, adult and community learning and work-based learning. Learners and employers can go to a wide range of providers – colleges and providers in the private, voluntary and community sectors. The complexity creates obstacles – to potential learners wanting to understand how to access the right course for them, and to those trying to manage the sector in a simple and effective way. But it is also its strength, because of the innovation and variety of provision available. (NAO, 2005: 3)

This important point – that the complexity of FE is also a strength – has somewhat been lost in the drive to focus on vocational skills following the Foster Review, the government White Paper on FE, and new Bill on FE. While it is undeniable that FE will benefit from greater clarity in its organization, provision and from enhanced status, the focus on mission needs to be more widely envisaged.

Provider numbers in learning and skills

The LSC's 'Provider Information Management System' (PIMS) reported that there were 5,928 providers supplying education and training in England (October, 2005) on behalf of the LSC (LSC, 2005). These wide-ranging types of providers include

Table 1.1: Education and training providers in the learning and skills sector (adapted from LSC Provider Numbers Summary Report – Organisation Types (February 2005)).

National Level

Org Types

	Business Link	Chamb of Comm / Trade	Charit	Dance and Drama School	Former Ext Instit	General FE College incl Tertiary	HE Org (with FE Provision)	Independ school or college	Local Author	Local Education Authority (LEA)	Non-Charit	Org in Business in own right	Other Local Author	Other Private Org	Other Public Org	Other Vol Org	School Sixth Form (not college)	Sixth form college	Social Services	Special college - Agric and hortic	Special college - Art, design & perf arts	Special learning needs establ	Specialist college	UFI Hub	Total
Total	31	45	627	30	131	261	82	39	56	155	6	1,451	85	491	190	209	1,785	103	15	19	4	3	13	97	5,928

The original report is available at: www.lsc.gov.uk/National/Partners/Data/Statistics/HeadlineStatistics/ProviderNumbersbyOrganisationandFundingType+.htm (accessed 14 May 2006)

institutions and organizations of all sorts, such as charities, local education authorities, private businesses, higher education institutions and training organizations (see Table 1.1).

The numbers of FE colleges, sixth forms and specialist colleges within the LSC sector are significantly smaller than this overall number, but still very numerous. Statistical first releases for the UK Learning and Skills Council (LSC) in November 2005 and April 2006 confirmed that there were 5,928 LSC-funded organizations, with around 522 institutions in the FE sector, of which 261 are general further education colleges. Overall, according to LSC data, there are 385 FE colleges, including 102 sixth form colleges and 23 specialist colleges (though note that the NAO reported that there were 397 colleges with 103 sixth forms and 39 specialist colleges – see NAO, 2005). Since 1997, the number of post–16 learners has grown from around four million to six million, while investment in colleges increased by 48 per cent between 1997 and 2006 (DfES, 2006). The LSC now provides funding for the education of around six million post–16 learners in England, including some 5.4 million learners in FE colleges (LSC, 2006a, 2005).

The Council has an overall funding budget of £10.4 billion in 2006/07 (LSC, 2006b), including approximately £5,073 million spent on 16–18 and £2,999 million on adult education and training for 4.21 million students. Figure 1.2, from the National Audit Office report on *Securing Strategic Leadership for the Learning and Skills Sector* (NAO, 2005) and Figure 1.3 from

Of the Learning and Skills Council's £8.8 billion budget for learning and skills in 2003-04, more than half went to the 397 colleges comprising the further education sector in England.

Source: Learning and Skills Council Accounts 2003-04 and Department for Education and Skills Annual Report 2004

Figure 1.2: LSC funding of FE compared with total education funds 2003–04 (NAO, 2005:5)

Table 1: Education expenditure (revenue and capital funding), by sub-sector, 2000–01 to 2005–06, England.

	2000–2001	2001–2002	2002–2003	2003–2004	2004–2005	2005–2006	Change 2000–2001 to 2005–06
Schools (DfEs)	4918	5870	8849	9344	10151	10981	+123%
FE, Adult	5674	6587	7104	7773	7927	8394	+48%
Higher Education	6541	6545	6680	6959	7191	7529	+15%
Other	1258	1754	2339	2657	2467	2801	+123%
Total (DfES)	18389	20756	24572	26733	27736	29705	+52%
Total (all education)	39837	43741	45438	49686	52419	55021	+38%

Adapted from HM Treasury (2006) Public Expenditure Statistical Analyses 2006, CM 6811, table 3.1.

Figure 1.3: Educational Expenditure by sub-sector in England 2000–1–2005–6 (House of Commons Education and Skills Committee, 2006:7).

the Education Select Committee Report (House of Commons, 2006) illustrates the expenditure of the LSC and DfES respectively in 2003–4 on the further education sector in England, relative to total education funds. Of the £8.8bn budget of the LSC in 2003–4, more than half went to the 397 colleges comprising further education in England.

In 2004–5, the LSC sector employed 246,005 staff, including both full and part-time teaching and support staff. These are massive numbers. The LSC sector is in fact the largest education and training provider in the UK. Figure 1.4 from the DfES (2002) demonstrates the areas of management and governance covered by the LSC. These areas include both sections marked 'Further Education Institutions' (16–17 and 18+), that for 'Other learning' and 'Distance learning', as well as areas in secondary schools offering provision to ages 16–19. Everything that is part of English government-funded public education in the age ranges 16+ that does not take place in the 'Higher

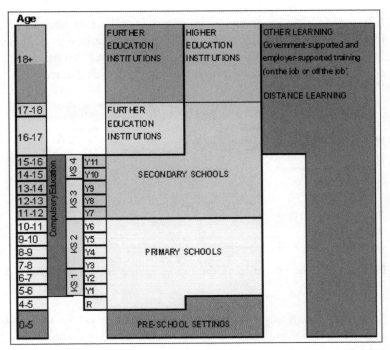

Figure 1.4: DfES: 'Chart A – Education and Training Structure' (DfES, 2002).

Education Institutions' area of the chart is funded by the LSC. Provision for 14+ schools students engaged in vocational training is now also increasingly delivered within FE colleges. The LSC sector is huge in size and financial power and very diverse in its operations. Leading and managing the delivery of this vast education and training provision effectively across England is a major challenge.

Therefore, leadership and management issues affecting the LSC sector have considerable importance in terms of their knock-on impact across society as a whole. Table 1.1 illustrates this overall complement of numbers in education and training. What makes things particularly complex is that, within this vast range of providers, there is also a massive variation in the size of further education institutions, which vary from under 10 part-time students to 92,000 part-time students, and from under 100 full-time full year students to 7,400 full-time full year students.

Institutions also massively vary in terms of budget allocations, from £1.2m for the smallest to £51.3m for the largest in the year 2002–3. This variation is illustrated in the NAO report extract reproduced here for the information of readers as Figure 1.5.

3 The size of colleges varies widely		
	Minimum	**Maximum**
Number of full-time full year students (2003-04)	Several colleges under 100 (with 80 – 1,000 full-time part-year and 400 – 3,700 part-time students)	7,400 (with 1,800 full-time part-year and 19,500 part-time students)
Number of full-time part year students (2003-04)	Several colleges under 10 (with 400 – 2,000 full-time full-year and 350 – 1,900 part-time students)	8,200 (with 3,800 full-time full-year and 26,000 part-time students)
Number of part-time students (2003-04)	Several colleges with under 10 (with 800 – 2,200 full-time full-year and zero to 20 full-time part-year students)	92,000 (with 35 full-time full-year and 1,500 full-time part-year students)
Income 2002-03[2]	£1.2 million	£51.3 million
Source: Learning and Skills Council		

Figure 1.5: Large variation in the size of further education colleges (NAO, 2005:5).

All this variation means that there is a great need for specialist sectoral training and many well-qualified staff. There are, indeed, considerable numbers of staff in the sector. In the post-compulsory and higher education sectors more generally across the UK, there are currently some 744 Principals/Chief Executives and some 3,364 top-level directors. Within the Learning and Skills Council-funded (LSC-funded) sector in England and Wales, there are a total of 71 Beacon institutions, of which 12 are general FE colleges, while the highest number, 23, are sixth form colleges.

However, nationally, a 'succession crisis' imminently looms, in view of the large numbers of managers due to retire in the learning and skills sector during the next few years and the current difficulties with recruitment of principals (Collinson, 2006). Key priorities are to investigate and establish more fully the national audit of skills in leadership and management in FE, as well as current issues and tensions in provider institutions in implementing effectively the targets imposed by government policy initiatives. A further priority is to develop professionalism across the LSC sector and FE system. Let us examine some of the issues relating to the differences between leadership, management and professionalism in practice in FE.

Professionalism versus managerialism: cultural issues and conflicts

The issue of 'professionalism' versus 'managerialism' is a key one for FE institutions in which so many staff in both teaching and administrative roles are qualified with more or less advanced professional status in a variety of occupations. Managers can sometimes be at odds with professionals. While some professional managers easily resolve any such conflicts by regarding themselves as simultaneously professionals and managers, the potential differences between the two roles can be of such a nature that cultural issues and conflicts inevitably arise. Managers tend to be more concerned with authoritative control of systems, staffing, processes, quality assurance mechanisms, income generation, institutional loyalty, financial and resources management to implement strategy planned by senior leadership. By contrast, teachers tend to be more concerned with pedagogy, learners in the classroom, an ethos of public service accountability, the maintenance of trust and tactic professional knowledge in peer-group networks, professional standards and autonomy, as Randle and Brady (1997a) identified about a decade ago (see Figure 1.5).

Both groups can therefore regard themselves as being at the 'top of the food chain' of employment, in ways that can lead to irresolvable clashes. Managers within institutions tend to be driven by loyalty to the organization, a sense of duty to achieve the requirements of external funding agencies such as the LSC, and to effective, efficient achievement of outputs, outcomes and budgetary control. FE managers tend to regard lecturers and administrative staff as resources to be managed, deployed and 'controlled' to achieve efficient quality outcomes for the organization.

Professional lecturers and, to a somewhat lesser extent, some specialist, technical and administrative staff, however, tend to regard themselves as mainly accountable to the recipient group for their professional services (whether these are students, business clients or other staff), and to national or international professional standards extending well beyond the walls of any one institution, linked perhaps to the 'community of practice'

Professional paradigm	Managerialist paradigm
Goals and values	
• primacy of student learning and the teaching process	• primacy of student throughout and income generation
• loyalty to students and colleagues	• loyalty to the organization
• concern for academic standards	• concern to achieve an acceptable balance between efficiency and effectiveness
Key assumptions	
• lecturers as funds of expertise	• lectures as flexible facilitators and assessors
• resources deployed on the basis of educational need	• resources deployed on the basis of market demand and value for taxpayers' money
• quality of provision assessed on the basis of input	• quality assessed on the basis of output/outcomes
Management ethos	
• collegiality; 'community of practice'	• control by managers and the market
• professional autonomy/the trust principle/accountability to peers/tacit knowledge	• management by performance indicators and surveillance
• pluralism	• unitarism

Figure 1.8: Randle and Brady's (1997) table identifying the managerial-professional conflict in FE

(CoP) of a professional network (Wenger, 1998). The allegiance of professionals is usually more strong tied to colleagues, students/clients and to the relevant professional body than to any one institution. Randle and Brady (1997a) discussed this clash between 'managerialism and professionalism' in relation to further education.

Managerialism in FE post-incorporation 1992: cultural issues and conflicts

Following the incorporation of FE in 1992, 'harder' styles of management in FE were identified and frequently described as 'managerialist' by critics. A number of studies emerged investigating and criticizing the corporate leadership and management styles adopted in FE during this period (Elliott, 1999; Leader, 2003, 2004; Randle and Brady, 1997a). Leadership and management were criticized for many faults during the post–1992 incorporation era, including behaviours regarded by critics as 'macho', bullying, hierarchical, dictatorial, controlling, overly business–driven and autocratic. Power was seen as residing almost exclusively at the top of organizations, specifically in the role of the Principal, now often called a 'Chief Executive'. It was perceived that a business–like ethos prevailed, in which a small number of top managers seemed to hold most authority and power driven by sectoral demands. A clash between the business–like approaches of management and more pedagogically–centred teacher professionalism lingering from earlier eras amongst echelons of staff lower down in the hierarchy was observed by Randle and Brady (1997a), although their work was based only on a limited case study. A concomitant clash was described between the values of teacher professionals and the more economically–driven orientation of controlling senior managers.

Critics noted that lower echelons of staff and students in FE rarely, if ever, seemed to have a real say in the running of the institution. The investment of greater levels of power at the top of further education institutions set up divisions from staff operating at other levels. A new, more formal dress code for FE managers in the post–1992 era gradually emerged in contrast to pre–incorporation styles. Managers, male and female, would, in our recollections of that era, invariably be dressed smartly in business–like suits and would behave in ways that could be interpreted as signifying that they thought they were more powerful and important than other staff, reversing earlier trends in which dress codes were more relaxed and egalitarian. Reserved spaces in the car park for management would be provided, secretaries would service managers' needs and direct telephone calls would be re–routed through personal assistants. A 'them' and 'us' culture emerged, based on new managerialist audit implications of 'strategic planning'.

Successive waves of post–incorporation restructurings, the setting up and growth of the Learning and Skills sector under the LSC in 2001, the establishment of CEL in 2003, combined with an increased emphasis on FE in government policy following the election of the new Labour government, changed the situation. In 1999, Gleeson and Shain critiqued an over-deterministic simplification in the concept that a managerialist imperative was of necessity dominating the culture of the FE system (1999: 462). They observed that the situation was more complex. Writing in 2000–2, Simkins and Lumby again noted that a more complex, differentiated analysis of leadership and management in the sector was necessary (Simkins and Lumby, 2002; Lumby, 2000).

Although the call for fuller and more differentiated analysis has still not fully been met, research findings indicate that trends from earlier periods of post-incorporation marketization and scrutiny still permeate the FE system. A key emphasis is still placed on accountability and external measurement to benchmarks, though a disjunction between the kind of measurement required in institutions and the actual goals set forth by government policy has been noted by CEL researchers (Fox *et al.*, 2005: section 2.1). To address this kind of disjunction between the imperatives of government and the actual work being done in colleges, Fox *et al.* put forward the mission of the research carried out by Centre for Excellence in Leadership:

CEL's research begins from a focus on what it is that people in leadership positions in FE colleges actually do. This contrasts with models of leadership which are often decontextualised. Such examples include recent concerns with transactional, heroic, transformational and distributed leadership; models which remain popular in leadership literatures, but which lack a substantial empirical understanding of how they are adopted and used in practice. From our research perspective, we have found that leadership work in FE colleges is less about the work of a few talented individuals and more about the successful organization of a complex network of situated leadership practices involving staff from across the organization. (Fox *et al.*, 2005: section 2.2)

Going beyond 'performativity'

Within an environment of measured 'performativity', in which, as Michel Foucault might say, 'Inspection functions ceaselessly. The gaze is alert everywhere' (Foucault, 1977), how can we move beyond this feeling of 'being watched' in the kind of targets-based panopticon culture of audit and surveillance described above? Well, our own answers to this, having worked as leader-managers in the FE sector for more than 20 years, and being, like many readers, subject to inspection, audit, constant reporting and scrutiny by what seemed like everyone for everything more or less all the time, is, 'if you can't beat 'em, join 'em'. In other words, cautiously welcome this tendency in FE to want to measure performance, for the sake of the more positive aspects of it – i.e. improving achievement and quality for students and staff – and take control of this, to the extent that that is possible, by doing some scrutiny yourself, not only of the performance targets involved, but of the system and mechanisms used in measurement and recording itself.

Process and systems-based perspectives: gaining some liberty and agency

To take control of the situation of feeling constantly as if your institution, yourself and your teams are being 'watched', we would recommend that the function of liberty and agency in this instance may be to accept that this is indeed the reality – you *are* being watched (we all are: the UK is the most surveilled country in the world). The best thing might be to accept that there are some positive reasons for this UK-wide scrutiny for the sake of learner achievement and public accountability and to work with this in a productive way, through strategic selection (and de-selection) from the menu of possible actions, to gain control of the data being fed into the scrutiny machines and to turn some of the cameras back on the watchers. Be watchful of what is being required of you, why, by whom and when, and ensure that this measurement and reporting is always appropriate, necessary and in the best interests of your institution and its students. Aim to *lead* the processes involved in audit and inspection by being proactive, being early to meet deadlines, requesting advance information and follow-up feedback from inspectors and auditors about the reasons for and processes involved in measurement of your institution, the results, reports and publicity involved, and the ethical guidelines and permissions followed.

Aim to get an overview of all annual monitoring of your institution by external agencies in terms of dates, times, arrival and departure points for external scrutineers. Ensure that all inspectors and auditors are appropriately welcomed in a friendly way, and that suitable staff are well briefed in advance to handle all the processes involved in audit and inspection. Be proactively and energetically cooperative to ensure your institution gains the best possible results from external scrutiny in every single case, and react quickly and decisively to challenge results that you feel are unfair or lack a sound evidence-base. Beat any particular scrutinizing agency that people are worried about at their own game by being super-efficient, welcoming and helpful in meeting all demands you consider to be appropriate and necessary, and querying those that are not. Make sure your own internal systems of measurement and data monitoring are better than those of external scrutineers, so that data is ready and immediately available in accessible formats in ways that directly meet and, if possible, surpass the requirements of inspectors and auditors.

A helpful example of this kind of excellence in measurement and recording of student and institutional progress is demonstrated in the leadership and management work of Farnborough Sixth Form College. In 2005, I went to interview Dr John Guy, OBE, Principal of Farnborough College, about leadership in post-compulsory education. The college was rated by Ofsted in 2002 as the sixth form college with the 'best teaching in the entire country'. The college has frequently been singled out for praise by government ministers as a sixth form institution with 'outstanding' teaching and learning provision, and 'outstanding' leadership and management.

John talked to me about the internal Farnborough quality assurance and data collection system for measuring ALIS (Advanced Level Information System data, measuring the distance travelled by learners between the start and end of a course) value-added data on achievement for every department each year against the targets achieved from the previous year, and the way this had affected inspections by Ofsted:

> JJ: So you're about as rigorous to the college inside as Ofsted would be to you from the outside?

> John: I think more rigorous. . . . When Ofsted came and saw we'd done this, [they said], 'Oh, we've never seen that before', because it's a very good management technique, actually, because it's transparent . . . (Dr John Guy, interview Jameson (2006)).

So, we could aim to be like John and his senior team at Farnborough Sixth Form College, taking control of the process of quality management and internal data collection and analysis to such an extent and in such good quality ways that external scrutineers are impressed, change their views, and learn from what we do internally.

Or, if we find this to be too much of a hurdle straightaway, we could begin the process towards achieving excellence in performance management by being ready, willing and prepared to take ownership for processes of data collection for external scrutiny, being transparent about sharing data appropriately and not overly worried about external auditing. We could aim to regard inspectors and auditors as helpful, just trying to do a necessary job, mostly as human and sympathetic as the rest of us (indeed, sometimes more so) but finding themselves necessarily trapped into the requirements of corporate state bureaucracy. The importance of implementing good processes and systems-based perspectives in meeting the demands of external scrutineers is outlined in more detail in Julian Gravatt's book on financial management and in David Collins's book on senior leadership of colleges in *The Essential FE Toolkit Series*.

'Eating the dinner, not the menu': creating 'values-based' organizations

The idea of 'eating the menu not the meal' is derived from an analysis of Zen Buddhist meditation by Chuan Zhi Shakya (2005), to describe what happens when a practitioner of meditation mistakes the controlling processes involved in initiating meditation for the thing itself. Lesley Prince high-lighted attention to this for the field of leadership studies in an article on the Tao and leadership (Prince, 2005). Prince's article describes the way that, in Western culture, we sometimes pay a great deal of attention to the hierarchical and controlling aspects of leadership rather than to such Taoist concepts as the:

> . . . fluid set of interrelations co-ordinated with a natural order as it is, emphasizing co-ordination, location and con-nection with environmental contexts, rather than modifica-tion of the environment in line with an intellectual idea of what we would prefer it to be. Whereas for the West lea-dership is about active and shaping control, for Taoism it is more about engagement, understanding and co-ordination. (Prince, 2005: 105)

Certain aspects of Prince's article ring true in terms of trends affecting recent leadership initiatives in the learning and skills sector. A great deal of interest has been expressed in the col-laborative, networking and engagement aspects of leadership, and the importance of partnership and team working. Less of an emphasis is now being placed on hierarchical top-down management, partly in reaction to the history of post-incorporation FE 'micro-managerialism', which was generally seen as destructive. For this, the creation of a values-based organization, i.e. one guided by a coherent set of commonly shared values through which the organization operates, is increasingly important. We devote more attention to this concept of 'values-based' leadership in Chapter 2, and then again in different ways in a number of chapters later in this book. The concept of 'eating the dinner, not the menu' in leadership perspectives is therefore used here to signify the importance of leaders giving detailed attention to coordinating and understanding the living and the lived environment, the people, relationships, contexts, needs and daily actions of staff they work with, rather than acting remotely as controlling managers issuing a series of orders from 'on high' to the troops below. Kelly *et al.* (2004) discuss this trend in relation to their own leadership research studies in the sector:

The traditional notion of leadership as 'leading from the front' is therefore not nearly as important in FE colleges as gaining the trust of organizational members as followers and gaining their permission to be led (Iszatt White *et al.*, 2004; Kelly *et al.*, in press). Thus, leadership depends on gaining legitimacy. This gaining of legitimacy is often through relentless attention to a multitude of varied, and what might sometimes be called 'mundane' tasks. (Kelly *et al.*, 2004.)

The *'gaining of legitimacy'* through engagement in everyday, authentic actions might be called 'living leadership' (Binney, Wilke and Williams, 2005), in contrast to the inert or passive controlling management of those who sit back and run the show from behind closed doors. It involves the kind of 'leadership work' Ruth Silver described in when she talked about enacting a principalship role 'with her sleeves up, brushing the steps'. The use of that metaphor applies sensitively in living contexts – i.e. the leader steps in with mindful engagement to do whatever needs to be done in ways that are crucially important, swiftly, effectively, in an engaged and relevant way, with skill.

Distributed and emotionally intelligent leadership and management

Linked directly to the perspective of 'living leadership' in the reality of daily life within FE institutions, the idea of 'distributed leadership' is a model of leadership which conceives and locates leaders at a range of different levels in the hierarchies of institutions. Within the perception that leadership can effectively be distributed, not as an ultimate reality in terms of final authority, but as 'the deployment of discretion' on a shared basis throughout an institution (see Ruth Silver's unique concept of this in relation to distributed leadership in Chapter 7, Figure 7.1), the role of emotional intelligence is of crucial importance.

Gardner's (1975) work on 'multiple intelligences' was followed by Goleman's (1995, 1996) development of the concept of 'emotional intelligence' or 'emotional intelligence quotient' (EI or EQ), which includes these five aspects of ability:

(1) to know your emotions, being able to identify and name these and understand the link between emotions, thoughts and actions;

(2) to manage your own emotions, being able to shift negative emotional states into more adequate ones;

(3) to enter into emotional states at will, e.g. to motivate yourself;

(4) to recognize and understand other people's emotions, to be sensitive to and influence these; and

(5) to manage relationships, ie., able to sustain effective inter-personal relationships.

Evidence informs us from the work of Goleman (1995, 1996) and other theoreticians and researchers on EI/EQ that emotionally intelligent people are more likely to succeed in life in general, and that no matter how many qualifications you have, how many years' experience, how intelligent, expert and skilled you are in a range of areas, if you are not also gifted with emotional intelligence, it is hard to influence people effectively. Those who handle their emotions well and are also sensitive to the needs of others often go further in life and in their careers than those who are not. It can be as simple as that. Emotional intelligence is of paramount importance in leadership. The good thing, however, is that this quality can be developed: we can learn from our mistakes if we are open to feedback to others and to the potential for change.

Staff and student perspectives on leadership and management in FE

Staff perspectives on leadership and management in FE were gained from the online leadership survey set up in 2005–6, to inform this book. The results of this survey are implicit throughout the text and are reported in detail in Chapter 10. Student perspectives can be gained from a brief consideration of the highlights of the results from the 2004/05 *National Learner Satisfaction Survey* (NLSS) published by the LSC (LSC, 2006). For the latter survey, the LSC contacted a sample of over 43,000 learners in 2005 and interviewed them about their experiences of education and training in the learning and skills sector. The students were questioned about their satisfaction levels regarding all aspects of learning. Student satisfaction rates are generally very positive for further education and work-based learning, for which the percentage of learners who said they were 'extremely', 'very' or 'fairly' satisfied with their overall learning experience was 90 per cent. The news was even better for further education delivered by adult learning providers and non-accredited adult and community learning, with 93 per cent and 94 per cent satisfaction rates respectively. These are generally very good results. Building on this picture, we now move to consider leadership in FE more generally in Chapter 2.

Summary

In Section 1, Chapter 1 we examine the national leadership and management position in further education, the national audit of skills in this area, and current tensions and government priorities. Issues of 'professionalism' versus 'managerialism' are discussed, in the context of the cultural issues and conflicts arising from these differences. Going beyond the 'performativity' of a targets-based culture is recommended. The importance of process and systems-based perspectives are considered in leadership and management in FE. Distributed and emotionally intelligent leadership and management is outlined briefly with reference to the need for this for the effective leadership and management of FE institutions. The creation of values-based organizations is highlighted, as is the concept of 'eating the dinner, not the menu' in leadership understanding and implementation. Staff and student perspectives on leadership and management in FE are briefly mentioned and a reference to Chapter 10 is made for more detail on staff perspectives.

2: Leadership in FE

The first responsibility of a leader is to define reality. The last is to say thank you. In between, the leader must become a servant and a debtor.

Max De Pree

Most important, leaders can conceive and articulate goals that lift people out of their petty preoccupations and unite them in pursuit of objectives worthy of their best efforts.

John Gardner

What is leadership?

What is leadership? Max De Pree envisages leadership to be 'service'. Lao-Tzu, ancient Chinese philosopher, also thought that to lead effectively was to serve people with humility in a respectful way: 'To lead the people, walk beside them.' Would you agree with these definitions of leadership? What does this kind of 'service' mean in practice? If it is just 'service', why is leadership important, and how is it different from any other kind of service? What other aspects of leadership are there? We explore here some definitions to answer these apparently straightforward yet also riddling questions. The chapter will define key characteristics outlined by some who have theorized and practised leadership effectively, notably in or for further education in the UK and beyond. The chapter will also build on the differentiation between leadership and management and other characteristics of leadership already briefly identified in Chapter 1, while being aware that both leadership and management are needed throughout all educational institutions.

Let's look, first of all, at the 'official' definition of leadership and management in the recently re-issued *National Occupational Standards for Leadership and Management in the Post-Compulsory Learning and Skills Sector* (Lifelong Learning UK, 2005). These generic standards (often summarized as the NOS) are currently under review. However, they give us a useful initial differentiation between leadership and management in the learning and skills sector:

The cross sector leadership and management board of the Sector Skills Development Agency (SSDA) defines its basic leadership model as:

'the process of moving a group (or groups) of people in some direction, by being clear about the direction they want to go, by getting this message over clearly, and getting the staff energetically to support the process to achieve this change'.

The SSDA board defines management as broadly being:

'concerned with planning, implementing, controlling and using resources, typically on a day-to-day basis'. (Lifelong Learning UK, 2005: 6)

Building on this definition, we include here also a summary of the values and assumptions behind the NOS (see Figure 2.1), which enables us to situate these standards within the generic expectations of the SSDA and LLUK, and to differentiate between 'leadership' and 'management' as we explored briefly in the Introduction.

The paradoxical complementarity of leadership and management

We also need to observe that 'leadership' and 'management' are, in effect, however, paradoxically simultaneously different and conjoined in institutional practice at all levels in further education across the UK. The presence of leadership and management at every level in the positional hierarchy is signified in the concept 'distributed leadership' and 'distributed management' in institutions, as we will discuss in the viewpoint from

Centrality of learner success
All management activity in the learning and skills sector should reflect the centrality of learner success. For example, under the English government's 'Success for All' agenda, learner success drives the learning and skills sector.

Equality, diversity and inclusion
The drive for higher standards in the post-compulsory learning and skills sector includes questioning complacency, changing attitudes and removing barriers to success, which prevent the sector from drawing on and developing all the potential available to it. The sector needs to create a more diverse workforce, building on all existing skills, nurturing and developing new talent...

The Race Equality in Employment Standard (REES)
The recently-launched Race Equality in Employment Standard, to be piloted in England in 2005, provides learning and skills organizations with a coherent, consistent, national framework for promoting race equality that complements compliance with the Race Relations Act Amendment (RRAA), Ofsted/ALI inspection requirements, and the requirements of the LSC provider performance review.

Strategic thinking and creating a vision
Leaders and managers in the sector often have to work with ambiguity, uncertainty and conflicting pressures. They have the responsibility to think and plan strategically to determine the organization's strategic direction, taking into account the present, and yet being aware of future implications. This presupposes an excellent understanding of how the broader learning and skills sector works, and the local, national and international context within which it operates.

Collaborative working in the interest of learners
In England the government's 'Success for All' strategy signposts the ways in which the learning and skills sector needs to improve the quality of learning, teaching and training for all learners. This policy includes: widening participation; improving skills; developing the learning infrastructure and increasing flexibility; developing and maintaining effective partnerships. This requires closer and more complex collaborative working arrangements.

Performance management
Leaders and managers translate their vision into action. They challenge how things are done and take others with them. In order to achieve service improvement, appropriately stretching performance targets are set at organization, team and individual levels across the post-compulsory learning and skills sector.

Responsibility and accountability
The effective learning and skills sector leader/manager promotes the concept of the responsible and accountable organization. Responsibility and accountability are at organization, team and individual levels, with a clear and shared understanding of what this means. Leaders and managers in the learning and skills sector use public resources and must do so ethically and responsibly. They often need to be enterprising in securing resources.

Quality
Effective leaders and managers in the post-compulsory learning and skills sector promote a climate where quality is everybody's business within the organization. Learner achievement is at the centre of their quality arrangements.

Selected extracts only. See LLUK, 2005: 12–16, for the full original document.

Figure 2.1: Viewpoint: Values and assumptions behind the *National Occupational Standards* (NOS) for leadership and management in the post-compulsory learning and skills sector: selected key extracts

Ruth Silver in Chapter 7. David Collins also commented on the interweaving of these two functions in the constantly oscillating dance between leadership and management in 2005, saying:

> Within a college, pretty well all individuals, I think, will have elements or can have elements of both management and leadership within their role. And, in the better institutions, I would suggest that neither leadership nor management exist solely at the top. (Dr David Collins, CBE, interview (Jameson, 2006))

We note, though, that some leaders do not act effectively as managers in further education, and vice versa. Skills and knowledge are needed in both leadership and management for people to be effective in positional levels in FE institutions. The competency diagram for this is illustrated in Figure 2.2, in which the ideal rôle model for those with positional responsibilities in FE would be that of a person who attains the leader-manager position at top right. However, we note that there do exist some effective informal leaders who do not have management functions but do a good job within their sphere of operations, contributing a great deal to FE institutions, whether this as a governor, front of house staff member, canteen or

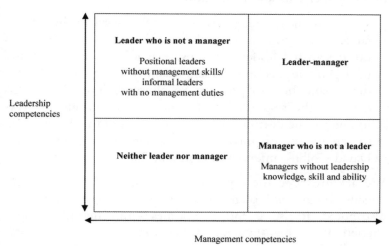

Figure 2.2: Leader–manager competencies

crèche worker, business leader, technical staff member, sports leader, volunteer, entertainments leader, student leader, parent leader or learning assistant. The connected local communities in which FE institutions tend to operate mean that sometimes these people are well known locally to almost everyone, and perform important services, but may be recognized only at an informal level.

Since leadership can be, and in the best instances often is, distributed throughout colleges, then what is the point of having senior leaders and managers? What is the role of a principal, if everyone can share in both leadership and management? Ruth talked to us about the way in which the role of principal is essentially 'where the buck stops' – that is, no matter how much leadership and management are distributed to other people in the hierarchy of colleges like her own, ultimately it is the principal and the governing body who carry the final responsibility for the overall performance of the college.

We will explore these points regarding power and accountability throughout this book, but for now, let's listen to David further on this, remembering that he speaks from many years' practical experience as the Principal of South Cheshire College and also from senior leadership experience in a range of other further education institutions:

> What I think it comes down to, with regard to the importance of the 'top' ... is in the fact that the responsibility of the designated leader is to ensure that both leadership and management exist in sufficient quantity and quality to allow the organisation to prosper. So although it might be distributed, the responsibility for its distribution and the reasoning for the distribution, and the extent of the distribution, to achieve the organisation's aims, lies with the leader. (Dr David Collins, interview (Jameson, 2006))

We acknowledge these paradoxical tensions. Sometimes leadership ought *and* ought not to be, can *and* cannot be, distributed. It also is and, sometimes simultaneously, is not, aligned with management. Operating ambiguously, paradoxically, leadership both is *and* is not all of these things at the same time. Sometimes leadership seems to shift and change to suit the demands of the moment and tensions of the situation. We seek to find useful ways of exploring these paradoxes and the heterogeneous topic of leadership for the benefit of current and nascent leader-managers in FE.

At the outset, we need to recognize that the holographic, multidimensional subject of 'leadership' has such an elusive quality about it that there are no easy answers. The Chinese sage Lao-Tzu wrote, 'One who knows does not speak; one who speaks does not know ... the enlightened possess understanding so profound they cannot be understood. Because they cannot be understood, I can only describe their appearance ...' We are not suggesting that any one individual or another in the learning and skills sector is sage-like (!), as we don't tend to agree with 'heroic leadership' (actually, nor does Lao-Tzu – his writings propose that gentleness, frugality and humility are the highest virtues), but, rather, we suggest that the very concept and practice of effective 'leadership' itself is not only unusual, but also somewhat elusive and unquantifiable, embedded in unique, situated processes and actions in a myriad of different contexts. The vastness of what 'effective leadership' can be – and, in international contexts, actually is, around the world daily – eludes all of our definitions, while at the same time the situated practice of 'leadership' remains also very ordinary, even sometimes boringly dull, being about things like 'washing the steps' (in Ruth's terms), taking risks for the sake of the organization, sorting out difficult, grey areas of challenging decision-making no one else wants to touch or take responsibility for.

We speak here of 'leadership' in general practical and theoretical terms rather than suggesting that this quality denotes or is unique to any one individual. Paradoxically, when leadership is actually in operation effectively in institutions, it seems to be quite simple and ordinary and sometimes even goes unnoticed. When I saw her in 2005, Lynne Sedgmore, CBE, CEO of the Centre for Excellence in Leadership, described this kind of quality for us:

If you take some of the most 'present-aware', enlightened beings that you meet, you can also feel like they're the most ordinary, grounded, centred people – you know, they're not big egos, they don't have huge charisma, necessarily, but what they have is a 'presence' or sense of being able to 'be aware': 'self-awareness' ... awareness of your impact on others is a major element of leadership for me. But that can be quiet and that can be very facilitative ... I like the latest book on *Living Leadership* which is very much about ordinary heroes, if you like. ... I think it is a paradox, which is that the real – the really advanced, outstanding people don't need to tell everybody or don't need it to be exhibited. I think they can actually do it in such a way that they're also very ordinary, very approachable, very accessible and all those things. Do you see what I mean? And I want to get that across – it's that lovely paradox that they are actually quite outstanding, but they're actually also very ordinary, very real – and people just go, 'Oh yeah, but aren't they also – like you can talk to them, or you can be with them?' So it's that mix. (Lynne Sedgmore, CBE, interview 2005 (Jameson, 2006))

Effective leaders tend to place an emphasis on the people in their organizations, not so much on themselves, as Max De Pree writes:

The art of leadership lies in polishing and liberating and ena-bling the variety of gifts people bring. (De Pree, 1987: 9–10)

Warren Bennis also reminds us of this kind of quality in the effectiveness of good leaders, as it relates to our reactions to them at every level:

Good leaders make people feel that they're at the very heart of things, not at the periphery. Everyone feels that he or she makes a difference to the success of the organization. When that happens people feel centered and that gives their work meaning. (Bennis, 1994)

Effective leadership is sometimes easier to experience directly than to understand in abstract ways. Theoretical attempts at definitions of leadership are to an extent limited and partial. Here is another definition we could suggest for the FE sector: *Leadership exists in relationships of beneficial influence that motivate and challenge people to achieve clear goals.* While this is in some respects a useful definition, one missing element we could point out is the idea of context and situation, including location, place and culture. It is difficult to separate out leadership effectively from the contexts in which it operates and this definition does not contain anything about context. So perhaps a better definition would be: *Leadership exists in relationships of beneficial influence that motivate people to achieve clear goals within particular contexts of time, culture and location in further education.* There will, however, be much that can be challenged in this definition too, as the 'vision' and 'mission' aspects of leadership are not highlighted. So, perhaps it might be better to say: *Leadership creates a meaningful vision and mission, through values-based service in relationships of beneficial influence, within which people are empowered to achieve clear, challenging goals in particular contexts of time, culture and location.* A bit of a mouthful, but maybe this kind of rough definition will do for now.

Rather than try forever to achieve the best single and only definition of leadership in FE, which may have us all going endlessly round in circles, it might be helpful instead to stick with the rough definition above, and then envisage actual examples of 'leadership' in operation more vividly and practically through the achievements of leaders in FE ('by their fruits you shall know them'). Defining, contextualizing and researching leadership through the tasks it accomplishes is not an easy job, though, which is one reason why the Centre for Excellence in Leadership (CEL) was set up in 2003–4 to take forward a range of developmental and research work on leadership for the learning and skills sector. We examine briefly some of their work here.

The *Explicating Leadership* project funded by the Centre for Excellence in Leadership is focusing on researching the ordinary, everyday contexts in which people work in further education, rather than on abstract models that have little or no relationship to realities on the ground in the sector. Research reports from the project published by CEL, for example, concentrate on the idea of 'leadership as mundane work' (Kelly, Iszatt White, Randall and Rouncefield, 2004) in the ordinary daily tasks carried out by leader-managers in FE, eschewing grandiose, 'heroic' and abstracted glamorizations of leadership, which fail to take account of the fact that leadership exists in the daily practices of ordinary work:

> The work involved is routine, meticulous and unglamorous – mundane in every sense of the word – but its implications for every aspect of the college's wellbeing (funding, levels of provision, career prospects for staff, to name but a few) make its accomplishment a key role of the college leadership … Our findings show that leadership in the learning and skills sector is less about the work of a few talented individuals and more about the successful organization of a complex network of distributed leadership practices involving staff from across the organization … Our research clearly shows that leadership is neither mystical nor heroic, but consists of relentless attention to relatively mundane tasks and much of leadership is management. (Iszatt White, Kelly and Rouncefield, 2005)

As the above researchers point out, the separation of leadership from the actual everyday practice-based contexts in which it takes place can tend to result in 'second order' justificatory explanations that are *stories* about the process of leadership, rather than the work involved *in doing being a leader* (Kelly *et al.*, 2005), i.e. the thing itself. Useful as such stories can be for enabling meaningful staff development through 'teachable moments' (Kelly *et al.*, *ibid.*) about leadership, they also need to be contextualized within observations of the real-life contexts of leader-managers in order to understand what is actually occurring during the processes of leadership in action. Let's hear again from some leaders in the field. When I asked David Collins, Principal/CEO of South Cheshire College, one of the most successful FE colleges in the UK, to define how leadership operates, he said:

> Ideally, people share a vision about what they want to achieve. It is that sense of direction and movement that's essential to leadership, as distinct from the mechanics of management which is the best way of getting there and how you actually operate to get to where you are going. To do that, you've got to be able to free up people's thinking away

from the day to day. (Dr David Collins, CBE, interview (Jameson, 2006))

The idea that leaders have a vision, are able to inspire others to lift their eyes beyond 'the day to day' and are able to communicate that vision and share it with staff in beneficial ways, making meaningful coherence in situated ways for their staff, is a crucial distinction in the definition of leadership. When I interviewed John Guy, Principal of Farnborough College, one of the most successful sixth form colleges in the UK, John said, in similar terms:

> ...leadership is 'the vision thing'. It's about knowing what you want to do, where you want to go, and clearly articulating it .... that's not autocratic, that's about ... 'authoritative leadership'. I don't mean 'authoritarian', I mean, *a vision based upon knowledge of the reality and the need*. So, leadership is the vision thing ... doing the right things, and management is the way you do them ... doing things right. ... You see, you can be a very effective manager because ... you know what it is that has to be done, but, if you don't know what it is that has to be done, then you can't effectively manage it. ... It's that *clarity*, the *single corporate objective*, that's the vision. ... Now, what can we do to enable that to happen? Well, that's partly leadership as well, but the management is: OK, having decided to do that ... what's the best way of implementing it? I suppose, for me, the difference is that *leadership is able to transform and the management thing is about transaction*. (Dr John Guy, OBE, interview (Jameson, 2006))

As we discussed earlier in this book, the idea that 'Management is doing things right; leadership is doing the right things' derives from Peter F. Drucker. It is widely accepted as a distinction between leadership and management, which helps us to focus and narrow down our explorations about what exactly this mysteriously complicated yet obvious thing called leadership is or isn't.

Let's consider now two other views on definitions about leadership in post-compulsory education, to add to this growing rich picture. Lynne Sedgmore said this about the distinction between leadership and management:

I believe there are generic attributes, qualities, and skills for both leadership and management .... as well as specific contextual ones for post compulsory education. So, in a nutshell ... on a generic front, for me leadership and management is a spectrum or a continuum, with a leader more able, skilled, 'natural', even, perhaps, at visioning, engaging in the commitment of others, co-creating and bringing about empowering environments. Fundamentally for me a leader thinks, acts and impacts more in the 'meaning and purpose' realms. If you like, they win hearts and minds: they generate followers, they're highly relational. They live 'distributed leadership', they live 'learning', actually, they are in a constant inquiry, they believe in leadership at all levels, they ensure that the community, whatever it is, or that group that they work with, is doing the right things. Whereas I believe that managers are more focused on 'doing things right': systems, monitoring, operational realities, and that more kind of 'control' and 'environment'. (Lynne Sedgmore, CBE, interview (Jameson, 2006))

Ruth Silver distinguished between leadership and management in the following ways:

... at Lewisham, we have a collective way of thinking about this. It's ... part of our leadership development programme .... we define 'management' as 'getting things done through, with, and by others' and 'leadership' is 'developing the capacity to win hearts'. ... Our belief is that you cannot buy a heart, you cannot instruct a heart – that actually you really do have to *win hearts*, for the primary purpose of the organization, for the decorum, the professional decorum you want to see in there .... 'winning hearts' is what leadership has to do. ... I think you can *buy brains*. ... That's called 'being a worker, an employee'. And you can *instruct hands*, because that's part of the job description detail .... *but you cannot instruct a heart, and you can't buy a heart*. So 'brains' are the easy bit of it. ... But hearts are quite a different thing .... one of the notions I really believe in ... it's the task of leadership to breed this – is a kind of 'professional love'. We don't talk enough of that. We talk about, you know, interpersonal love – but actually there is a love of the task, of the organisation. That is in the hands of leadership ... People always say when you walk in through the door at Lewisham, you can feel a difference ... They feel a place where there is a – you know we don't always agree with one another – and *'winning hearts'* quite often means toe-to-toe differences. Resolving those, saying 'because it matters, we will argue for that' so the rule is that you fight for things not with people. And of course *the animation of ideas, that is absolutely the leadership's task, is where you start to win the heart.* So this college is about serving this community: absolutely honest public service, in its old sense, which is not the managerial kind. ... We have as you know, Beacon status and excellent performing reviews, financial grade A status: we have all of those dimensions. So management is kind of the least of our concerns. But hanging together, around this very needy and quite often difficult community, I think takes real work. It takes working with threads, and with the seams, of the many parts of this organisation. (Ruth Silver, DBE, interview (Jameson, 2006))

Having cited these formative views, we need to note that there are also many other thousands of definitions, explanations and theories for leadership, so that even the views above from leaders in the field and from the NOS are not adequate fully to define the concept of leadership. Probably if we interviewed all of the 397+ principals in all colleges in England, we would get 397+ different definitions of leadership, never mind all of the other principals in the UK, plus all of the views from the thousands and thousands of interviews with all staff at other levels, students and clients of FE we would need to carry out. Defining leadership in further education really adequately, taking into account all of these points of view, would probably take us several lifetimes to accomplish. Moreover, it would probably be like painting the Forth Bridge: it would take so long that everything would change before we reached the end, so we'd need to start again and would never, in fact, finish this unending task. So we need to work from a selection of views in FE which are partially representative.

In addition, moving beyond FE into wider definitions of leadership, numerous new books and papers on the subject of leadership more generally are published almost every day across the world. If we wanted to be truly accurate, we would also need to take into account all of these examples. The numbers of studies in the area of 'leadership' have grown exponentially globally in past decades: the numbers of search results on Google for the word *'leadership'* now stands at around 274 million, whereas a search for the phrase *'further education'* in Google currently attracts about 195 million results. Leadership is one of the most researched subjects in the world: its vastness increases daily. However, rather than bewilder readers with this excessively large array of information and resources, we will, instead, get on with the job of providing this handbook by using some reasonably well-accepted definitions of leadership and management and then specifying what this book will contribute to the field of leadership and management in further education and what it will not do.

In this book, we confine ourselves to the consideration of educational leadership in the UK learning and skills sector, specifically relating to further education, although we recognize that many elements of this work are applicable also in other educational institutions and in international contexts of lifelong learning and further education. It is helpful to have noted at the outset that there is no perfect answer to the question, 'what is leadership in FE?' and that attempts to find a 'one size fits all' answer to this question are unlikely to be successful.

In my interview with Dr Andrew Morris at the National Educational Research Forum (NERF) in 2005, Andrew made the above point effectively in relation to leadership in general. However, this also applies specifically to further education, in view of the enormous range and diversity of provision in the post-compulsory education sector. Andrew said he found 'one size fits all' approaches to leadership in post-compulsory education generally unhelpful, disliking the:

> ... tradition of 'gurus' publishing pulp paperbacks about 'ten tips for being a good manager' ... there's a kind of 'finger pointing' attitude. It puts you in a wrong position as a recipient

of somebody else's clever analysis. Which is almost entirely upside down from what you need: slowly growing towards understanding through, essentially, analysis of experience. So it seems to be diametrically opposite to what you need. (Dr Andrew Morris, interview (Jameson, 2006: 164))

By contrast, Andrew's suggestion is that people benefit much more from a 'slow growth towards understanding through analysis of experience'. I found this a useful statement for considering the ways in which to respond effectively to the complexity and diversity of individual, situated leadership contexts and demands within colleges. The concept of 'slow growing' towards some kind of 'practical wisdom' ('phronesis' – see Introduction), informed by theory carved out for ourselves as we learn, is appealing in education. We are familiar that students' learning, for example, has a particular developmental cycle that sometimes cannot be rushed and is deeply and importantly unique. Doris Lessing points out the crystallization process that occurs in deep learning: *'That is what learning is. You suddenly understand something you've understood all your life, but in a new way'* as John Guy also discussed in relation to the 'crystallization process' of learning in my interview with him (Jameson, 2006).

So, if we consider our college environments and individual leader-managers to be somewhat like students learning in their need for time, stimuli, support, nourishment, knowledge and skills, resources and good structuring, an 'organic' model of leadership emerges of a learning organization with the leader as educator and mentor. In this, care for growing and developing staff as both leaders and led takes precedence: sustained reflection on and examination of the 'fitness' of local situations for growth and support is prioritized.

Andrew would also agree that evidence-based theoretical perspectives on leadership are important to provide a background enabling leaders to frame what happens locally within a wider context. Individual analysis of experience is considerably aided by reading about approaches, methods and systems for leadership and management that others have tested and learned from in the past. So although we might not find 'guru' publications to be as directly relevant to FE as we'd like, the wider range of research literature on leadership and management is of tangible use in understanding the vast potential in this field. In this book, we provide a range of educational leadership theories and strategies, and refer you to a wider range of literature in the References section.

What research has been done on leadership in the learning and skills sector?

Many of the publications listed in our References relate to leadership in general, though a number are directly linked to and based on or within the learning and skills sector. Leadership in the sector is still relatively under-researched, although there were a number of past studies provided by the FEU (Further Education Unit – see, e.g. McNay, 1988, 1989). There are also a range of key studies that have emerged in recent years, amongst which is research work on leadership commissioned by the Learning and Skills Research Centre (LSRC) of the former Learning and Skills Development Agency (LSDA), as well as research work by the Centre for Excellence in Leadership (CEL). There are also a range of key journal articles and books on leadership in the LSC sector that have been published by individual academics with an expertise in this field. We summarize some of these in the *Appendices*.

In a recent report commissioned by the LSRC on leadership in the learning and skills sector, Lumby *et al.* (2005) found there was no single approach to leadership that prevailed across all institutions in their study of ten successful providers. The report by Lumby *et al.* confirmed the relative lack of research and development on leadership in the sector. The research team investigating leadership in this study found a 'mix of transactional, transformational and distributed styles . . . in operation'.

The team reported that 'though a transformational style is considered to be the most effective way to improve organisational performance, line mangers are more often seen as employing transactional approaches'. The researchers observed that distributed leadership operated at case study sites under investigation, but that real power was not allocated to lower levels, since 'distributed leadership is often distribution of operational responsibilities rather than a distribution of power'. (Lumby *et al.* 2005). The team concluded that further research and development on leadership was necessary, given the relative paucity of studies and the need for urgent capacity building across the sector to cope with a looming massive succession crisis.

What are the elements of good leadership?

There are as many different elements of good leadership in FE as there are individual characteristics within good leaders in the FE system. So it is impossible to have a hard and fast absolute list here of the definitive characteristics by which good leadership is manifested. However, there are some basic pointers that are more or less universally regarded as indisputably necessary for leadership to be effective. These comment on but are also differentiated from the values already listed in the NOS:

- Prioritization of student success as the core educational value of the sector
- Communicative clarity and coherence in influencing others
- A strong values-base
- Strategic thinking – big picture
- Capable of motivating others
- Capable of being people-centred/an emotionally intelligent leader
- Capable of authenticity
- Having passion and optimism
- Capable of teamwork
- Capable of building on and using others' perspectives
- Able to engage in self-development

We discuss this list of attributes again in Chapter 10, drawing in also some lessons from leader-managers in FE. At first, some of this list may seem daunting, but in fact it is possible to learn and to develop these attributes. Leaders need to develop themselves all the time, and we provide some guidance in Section 4 to suggest some ways in which this can be achieved.

Perspectives on the way some outstanding leaders operate: 'just in time' learning

Some leaders seem to operate with a fluency and immediate responsiveness that has the elements of unplanned improvisational expertise. This cannot be predicted, legislated for or bought. It sometimes just happens, serendipitously, arising from natural ability, just as expert intuitive musicians can pick up an instrument and improvise brilliantly with no preparation as a result of many years' prior experience of playing music. While we welcome this kind of brilliance from those who have the unusual skill and depth of experience to sense the wind of change and learn 'just in time' to adapt to new circumstances with intuitive success, for others, it is not so easy. In the development of leadership and management in FE, therefore, new research findings produced by CEL are increasingly valuing the 'teachable moments' derived from the stories of leaders who have this kind of depth of expertise derived from many years' practical work. Shön's (1987) definitive work on professional knowledge and reflection *on* action as well as the possibility of reflection *in* action has recognized the value of professional expertise that cannot be expressed or taught directly, but needs to be gleaned through observations of leadership in action, the practical wisdom of 'ways of knowing' in action.

Paradox, trust and cynicism – 'greatness and goodness' in a post-heroic age

There is much that is paradoxical and unknowable in leadership. Handy (1994) discusses the 'paradoxes of our times', identifying nine paradoxes that are the dilemmas of modern times: the paradoxes of (1) intelligence; (2) work; (3) productivity; (4) time; (5) riches; (6) organizations; (7) ageing; (8) the individual; and (9) justice. We can identify also some paradoxes about further education, i.e. seemingly contradictory statements that may nevertheless be true, as follows:

The paradoxical importance *and* insignificance of the sector

The learning and skills sector, notably FE, is still consistently under-funded, under-recognized, under-researched, under-valued and under-theorized. Yet it is the largest educational sector in the UK with the greatest number of students, crucial to UK and international economic success and to the well-being of millions of students, with a budget over £11 billion. If we state that it is 'important', we need to observe, simulta-neously, that its significance is, in illogical ways, almost totally under-recognized. It tends to be a sector that is taken for granted, yet also valued. As David Bell, Chief Inspector, Ofsted, put it: 'FE is vital to the economic, social and cultural life of a country but for many reasons it attracts much less public attention than schools. Many people do not understand the diverse and significant role of colleges in both academic and vocational education' (Bell, 2005: 1).

The paradoxical valuing *and* under-valuing of vocational training

While the government wants to expand vocational skills acquisition to higher technical skill levels to increase pro-ductivity and improve the competitiveness of the UK econ-omy, at the same time, vocational training continues to be regarded with low levels of esteem in comparison with more elite academic pathways. Increasingly there is criticism that professionals and employees at all levels are being de-professionalized and de-skilled within a bureaucratized and casualized workforce that is lower skilled than previously, while strategies for increasing higher skills levels proliferate. Voca-tional training is simultaneously valued and marginalized.

The paradox of mass entry to HE *and* elite selectivity

While the government has, since 2001, proposed a target of 50 per cent mass entry to higher education by 2010, during the same period, participation figures in HE have been negatively affected by higher student fees. With every new policy initiative to increase participation, actual participation figures attained across the UK seem to be affected by other factors. There seem

to be several reasons for this, among which is that elite selectivity into older, more highly rated institutions has sharpened
and fees for HE entry have tended to make it more difficult,
competitive and economically challenging to gain a degree
which is separated out from the masses by its exclusivity and
quality. While on the one hand we encourage mass HE participation, on the other hand we take this away, keep bostering
up the selectivity of elite institutions, and speak the rhetoric of
engagement in HE without following through on the practice.

The paradox of both training adults *and* denying them education

While the Foster Review (2005) and government White Paper
on FE (2006) encourage a key focus on vocational skills within
FE colleges, and acknowledge also the role of college provision
for social inclusion, including priorities for adult workforce
training, there is little emphasis on the role and importance of
adult continuing education in its wider forms (other than at
basic education levels and specifically for social inclusion). Yet,
at the same time, national student feedback on the quality of
ACE is the highest rated in further education (93 per cent) with
the best response overall for non-accredited provision (94 per
cent). The more adult education suffers yet another manifes-
tation of the oft-repeated threat to extinguish it, the more it
seems quietly to blossom and thrive beyond the reach of
auditors. The House of Commons Education and Skills
Committee report draws attention to this (House of Commons,
2006).

The paradox of the paperless *and* paper-full office in FE

While ICT admin and e-learning systems were meant to 'do
away with paperwork' when they were first introduced in FE,
as everywhere else, so that offices would become increasingly
paperless, in fact there is now more paper being produced than
ever in further education, as people now seem to need to have a
paper copy of everything that is online as well. We still talk
about e-learning enabling online information efficiencies, while
tending to continue to print out all major documents rather
than read them on the computer screen. When will we learn

that the 'paperless office' of ICT/e-learning and so-called economies involved are a myth?

The paradox of both widening *and* narrowing participation

While the government has proposed widening participation initiatives to increase the numbers of students from lower social classes in HE, in the same period, participation figures from lower social classes have stayed the same or dropped. Despite every new policy initiative to increase participation from social classes D and E, actual participation figures attained across the UK seem to stay at the same level, or drop further, due to the effect of other forces (for example increasing fees for HE entry). Researchers have recently discussed the concept of 'narrowing participation' to describe this phenomenon (NIACE, 2006), yet at the same time there are still major government priorities on widening participation, with funding attached.

Growing trust

Given these kinds of paradoxes and dilemmas affecting leadership and management in FE/HE, how far can we trust the continuing rash of new government policy initiatives? There has increasingly been a cynical response from some FE staff in reaction to the multiplicity of policy initiatives affecting lifelong learning during the past decades. It seems that levels of trust in the 'powers that be' have been low, and cynical responses to policy initiatives have increased. An online Eword Blog initiative was set up in May 2006 by the *Times Educational Supplement* (TES) with the Centre for Excellence in Leadership and Policy Uplugged to allow aspiring leaders in FE to contribute to a debate in answer to the question, 'What one key thing would YOU change about college leadership?' The following responses (taken from the TES (2005) e-word symposium, FE Focus) highlight some of the concerns staff feel about ongoing ever-changing policy initiatives in FE, and the fact that college leadership can become 'puppets' of central government:

> The one key thing in the management of FE I would change would be to stem the flow of constant changes to the Sector,

for example planning and funding arrangements. This has a significant impact on the management of Colleges and the stability of the workforce. Too much time and effort is spent keeping pace with changing requirements and the inevitable bureaucracy that comes attached. More time is needed to embed, review and evaluate regulations and initiatives. (Karen Mitchell, Head of Quality, Learning and Professional Development, Aylesbury College)

I would change the FOCUS of management. Instead of being puppets of government initiative with a business mentality, I would want an SMT that leads the way in contributing to a debate on the nature of vocational education in the 21st century and demands quality and high standards of teachers and students; leaders in education not stocks and shares. (Liz Thomas, Lecturer in Education, Nottingham Trent University)

I would stop changing things. Strategic change at top level and the consequential competition for the varied funding of it requires more management and therefore misplaced resources. The LSC has been entirely created by government to implement change. We do not need more strategies. Prioroties [sic] are already clear and we have inspection and audit to ensure that they are met. Colleges should have sole responsibility for achievement and single-stream funding to provide stable provsion [sic]. (Josie Pederson, Widening Participation Manager, Boston College)

The concepts of 'greatness and goodness' in policy-driven leadership in a post-heroic age have been hard to maintain in the face of the paradoxical nature of apparent 'progress', which actually sometimes has resulted in declining situations of increasing overwork and stress for staff on the ground. Practitioners distrust empty sound-bites and rhetorical phases used by some leaders: who can be trusted anymore? In the *Essential FE Toolkit* book *Everything You Need To Know about FE Policy* for leaders and managers by Yvonne Hillier, some useful ways to understand and cope with this kind of policy battleground in FE are discussed in greater detail. In this book, we recommend that leader-managers develop their own 'philosophy for all seasons', their own sense of professionalism and trust within pedagogy, scholarship and ongoing values of student-centred education, to guide us through all the tricky short-termism of policy changes affecting FE. Leader-managers need to situate and locate this within their own institutional frameworks.

'Quantum' versus 'classic' leadership – dealing with rapid change in FE

Continuing the theme of the paradoxes which affect FE leadership discussed earlier in this chapter, we observe that quantum physics has radically changed scientific understanding of the nature of reality during the past century, as a result of the findings of theoretical physicists (Richman, 2001). Quantum theory is mind-bending, requiring a completely different way of thinking from that with which classical physics used to explain reality. For example, a quantum object (e.g. an electron) can exist in multiple states and places at the same time, can cease to exist in one place, but then simultaneously appear in existence in another place, while it is not possible to say that it went through the intervening space (the quantum leap). Quantum theory is full of uncertainties and paradoxes that cannot be explained using classical physics (Richman, 2001).

Over the past several years, there has been a slowly increasing tendency to bring scientific theories, including chaos theory, from new science into leadership studies. Blank (1995) and Wheatley (1999) are amongst those who have written at length on this subject. The theory of 'quantum leadership' stresses the need for leaders to be able to live with ambiguity, uncertainty, risk and change, to be aware that leadership is a 'field of interaction – a relationship between leaders and follower-allies', that leaders can exercise 'influence beyond formal authority' and that 'consciousness – information processing capability – creates leadership' (Blank, 1995: 10). The theory of quantum leadership emphasizes the need for leaders to live within natural laws, to enhance connectedness and relationships with follower-allies, and to increase control over the attention span of their consciousness (Blank, 1995). Further information on quantum leadership in relation to interviews with leaders in post-compulsory education is provided in Jameson (2006).

Staff perceptions of leadership: diversity and authenticity

Staff perceptions of diversity and authenticity in leadership within the FE system have particular resonance, given the relative lack of representation of diversity at senior levels of management in learning and skills. These issues are explored more fully in Chapter 9. Survey results from a leadership survey carried out on the sector including the views of staff on diversity issues are reported and analysed in Chapter 10, alongside other key statistics from the LSC and related agencies.

Summary

Chapter 2 examines leadership in terms of definitions and the elements making up good leadership. We reflect on a number of perspectives on outstanding leaders, together with the concept of 'just in time' learning. The concepts of paradox, trust and cynicism in relation to leadership are discussed, and the book looks at the definition of 'greatness and goodness' in a post-heroic age. Quantum versus 'classic' models of leadership are outlined, as is the way to deal with rapid change in further education. Staff perceptions of leadership in terms of diversity and authenticity are considered and reference is made to the views of staff on diversity issues reported later in the book.

3: Management in FE

Organization doesn't really accomplish anything. Plans don't accomplish anything, either. Theories of management don't much matter. Endeavours succeed or fail because of the people involved. Only by attracting the best people will you accomplish great deeds.

Colin Powell

This chapter will give an overview of some basic concepts in management in further education that will be expanded in Section 3 in a range of models of management. These will also be considered again in relation to the provision of some guidelines for practical action on good leadership and management in Section 4.

What is management?

Let's go back, first of all, to the 'official' definition of leadership and management we looked at in the previous chapter from the re-issued *National Occupational Standards for Leadership and Management in the Post-Compulsory Learning and Skills Sector* (Lifelong Learning UK, 2005). We consider this time the role of management. The cross-sector leadership and management board of the Sector Skills Development Agency (SSDA) defines management as being:

> concerned with planning, implementing, controlling and using resources, typically on a day-to-day basis. (Lifelong Learning UK, 2005: 6)

As the above definition indicates, management is essentially about planning, directing and supervising 'in the right way' the implementation of those priorities that the leadership teams or leader(s) have decided are 'the right things' for the organization to do. Management therefore includes the operations and maintenance of the systems, processes and resources of organizations to achieve institutional objectives effectively and efficiently in the best way.

Managers lead, direct, plan, organize, control, deploy, evaluate and monitor human, intellectual, financial, material and environmental resources to run organizational functions (Reh, 2006). Management is intrinsically linked with leadership in FE, as in FE organizations we need managers to be leaders and vice versa. With the exception of some informal and academic leaders who do not wish to or cannot occupy a formal management role, mostly we tend to associate leadership with some kind of managerial responsibility in education. So, the term 'leader-managers' usefully summarizes the conjunction of these functions when both aspects of this dual role are working well. We could envisage these as twin strands. They are different, but intrinsically linked together, to create a strong bond in the working practice of leader-managers.

Some theorists have regarded management and leadership as so intrinsically linked that they envisage management to be an 'umbrella' concept, of which 'leadership' is a sub-set. This may be true in terms of the academic discipline of business and management, within which we generally subsume leadership studies, though there is a growing leadership literature in subject-specific disciplines such as education, which has sometimes viewed these concepts differently. In terms of organizational operations in education, to subsume leadership within management is somewhat to underplay the growing importance of educational leadership as a concept, practice and area of disciplinary study. In fact, nowadays, leadership has arguably become so important in education and training that it could be seen the other way around – possibly educational management is now a sub-set of educational leadership. The role played by informal, distributed, team and collaborative leaders in education, including non-managerial leaders, is implicitly facilitated within definitions of leadership envisaging this function to be wider and more inclusive than management. 'Managers', by contrast, are assumed to be people appointed to a particular management job to operate in a specific way within hierarchies of authority within or closely related to educational institutions.

Visionary and facilitative aspects of 'leadership', in so far as they extend throughout, beyond, above and below hierarchies, can sometimes be more in tune with the global pedagogic, democratic and collaborative developments affecting new trends in education than the concept of 'management'. The practice of management is inherently tied into the specifics of implementation and delivery in structures and systems, operating in follow-up mechanisms that seem to hang onto the coat-tails of more trail-blazing leadership developments. This is particularly the case in inter-institutional partnerships in which recognition of and knowledge about the operation of managerial hierarchies and systems within other institutions is minimal. New trends, notably in global social software networking communications, e-learning pedagogy and collaborative partnership development, are of such profound importance that they may effect a re-shaping of the landscape of educational institutions and change the nature of leadership and management in the future. Instinctively, therefore, the concept of leadership has surged ahead in popularity and interest globally, while management has lagged behind as a necessary, essential and significant process, but perhaps one now seen as secondary. Good management is, however, essential to ensure tasks are done and the vision of leadership is implemented in reality, so the two concepts and practices are intertwined in the notion of 'leader-manager'.

In prior chapters, we considered the difference between leadership and management from the point of view of leadership. As part of this chapter on management, we now briefly return to that earlier consideration to flesh out 'what management is', citing interviewee and survey responses supplemented by evidence from CEL's Leadership Qualities Framework (LQF (LQF, see CEL, 2004)). Our first example here is from Professor Daniel Khan, Principal/CEO of Grimsby College, who discussed the difference between leadership and management in post-compulsory education in my interview with him:

I think the leadership role has to be one with a vision and a strategic overview, also one that sets an example, and very much is the driving force in terms of business development and taking the decisions as to the positioning of the institution. Management is very much in my mind more about managing the affairs of the institution. That is managing the resources, the courses; looking at the issues for the retention and achievement of students; managing the budgets and making sure that they are looking at quality. (Professor Daniel Khan, interview (Jameson, 2006))

To enrich this with a further example from the field on the difference between leadership and management, we note David Collins's observation:

Leadership for me is about creating a vision, and more than a vision, a set of underpinning values that can be understood and embraced by members of the organisation as they contribute to the achievement of that organisation's mission. It's about establishing clarity of purpose, and direction for the organisation and a culture, or *modus operandi*, within which individuals feel willing and able to make their own personal contribution to the greater whole. I think it's really a context for management. Although the two are linked, management, for me, is more concerned with efficiency and effectiveness, the operations of the structures, policies, procedures and actions that help deliver that vision. (Dr David Collins, interview (Jameson, 2006))

Andrew Morris provided further views on the difference between leadership and management as logically distinct, since in his view 'management' is a function whereas 'leadership' is an attribute:

I think [leadership and management] are categorically quite different ... 'management' is a function: it is a role, it is a function. Scientifically, I would call it a 'second order' function. The 'first order' function is teaching in the classrooms, maintaining the buildings, running the office. The second order functions are enabling the first order functions to be carried out: appointing the staff, setting out aims and objectives, agreed procedures and so on. I see a logically ... layered relationship. I am trying to avoid the word 'hierarchy' because that invokes a status hierarchy; I mean a logical layering. The first order activities can only happen properly, or to best effect, if you have got the second order activities working well. This is what you see in a well-functioning organisation. You see the first order activities and the second order activities all motoring. But if the second order activities are not motoring, then it is hit and miss. So if you have got badly organised management, procedures, processes, culture, then you might get the good art department, but you won't get a good functioning organisation, you know? . . . Leadership is categorically a completely different thing. Leadership is a personal quality that is exhibited in different ways by different kinds of people. You can have leadership in management. You can have leadership not in management. You can have leadership in a swimming pool. Leadership in a restaurant. It's just not the same kind of thing, it is more like . . . the way you use your voice, it's an attribute, really, not a function. (Dr Andrew Morris, interview (Jameson, 2006))

Giving guidance on leadership and management at a national level, the Centre for Excellence in Leadership published The Leadership Qualities Framework in 2004. This framework was designed to provide support for leadership development for staff in the LSC sector (CEL, 2004). The framework aims to give 'a perspective on the core characteristics of executive leadership that can be influential in successfully leading within organisations'. The framework differentiates between management and leadership, but also links then:

Leadership and management are interlinked. The ideal top leader is one who combines leadership with the skills and knowledge which a general manager requires. Not all managers are leaders. The key tasks in management may revolve around planning, organising and directing with the achievement of acceptable compromise. For leaders, the key tasks are defining purpose, creating shared vision and values and alignment with the organisation's purpose. (CEL, 2004)

So, how can a manager become a leader, using this framework? The framework specifies a number of key characteristics for leadership behaviours, designed to be 'a reference point for individuals and organisations'. The *descriptors* for developing successful leadership behaviour are that such a nascent or developing manager who wants to learn more leadership skills can, at ascending levels of competence:

- **Learn:** performs with leadership skills in basic key actions, has significant development needs in key areas;
- **Assist:** performs well in the core areas; needs some development in one or more areas or complex key actions;
- **Perform:** strong performer in many but not all key actions; emerging talent–enhanced performance capabilities;
- **Guide:** exceptional performer exhibiting core characteristics

(The Leadership Qualities Framework, CEL, 2004)

McTavish (2006), writing on *Further education management strategy and policy*, notes that there are two key areas in FE management we need to consider: the *internal* management of FE institutions, and the *external* public management dimensions. McTavish cites selected examples of studies on FE management that have analysed management in the post-1992 incorporation era (McTavish, 1998; Gleeson and Shane, 1999; Harper, 2000; Lumby, 2001; Leader, 2004) as well as studies on the external public management dimensions (Lumby, 2001, McTavish, 2003). McTavish puts forward new findings from his empirical study in five Scottish colleges. We discuss the findings of McTavish's research on management in FE in Chapter 8 in identifying the attributes of excellent management. For now, having noted the importance of both internal and external aspects of management, and considered the intertwined nature of leadership and management, we move on to discuss some key characteristics that have been identified as intrinsic to good management in FE.

What are the elements of good management?

Some people might say that the key elements of good management are everything that good managers do to achieve successful organizations, no more and no less. However, it is useful to consider a range of specific items managers should routinely consider in order to perform effectively. In the report, *Why Colleges Succeed* (2004b), Ofsted identified some key characteristics shared in common by 29 colleges which all had a Grade 1 'outstanding' for leadership and management and an average curriculum grade of at least 2.1. Ofsted's 2004 report was based on evidence from inspections of 309 FE colleges and 42 independent specialist colleges carried out in 2001–4. According to Ofsted's inspectorate judgements, these successful colleges shared in common 'a realisation by their leaders that an educational establishment's central purpose is to place the education and success of their learners at the heart of what they do' (Ofsted, 2004b: 20). They also shared in common the following features:

- very good retention and pass rates
- highly effective teaching
- extremely successful learning
- excellent support and guidance for students at all stages in their programme
- an exemplary response to educational and social inclusion
- outstanding strategic leadership and governance
- consistently good curriculum management
- rigorous quality assurance processes which include accurate self-assessment, a detailed and regular focus on class-room practice and effective performance management of staff
- excellent financial management ... providers gave excellent value for money
- there is a very 'hands-on' approach of senior managers to the college's core work, which they make it their business to understand fully
- the principal and senior management team are successful in creating a culture where students are at the heart of the college's work ... [t]here is an unrelenting focus on students and their achievements ...
- an open and consultative style ... staff are consulted regularly

- communication and consultation with staff help to create a culture in which staff morale is high, staff feel valued and share a common purpose with their managers ... [t]his shared vision is a critical prerequisite for success
- governors play a significant role in providing strategic direction and monitoring the academic and financial performance of the college
- governors share the vision for the college with senior managers and staff, and are active in pursuing the vision, being both supportive and acting as a 'critical friend'
- staff have access to reliable and accurate management information
- there is effective teamwork ... teaching staff meet regularly and good practice is disseminated
(Ofsted, 2004b)

In these successful colleges, a simple, coherent management structure enabled staff to know their purpose and function, and to have the autonomy to carry out their roles effectively. The Ofsted report is useful to assist us in identifying the practices that management need to carry out in order to be successful in the combined functions of leadership and management. These are the following:

Planning, consulting and communicating

Before undertaking management tasks, it is essential to plan the overview and details of the wider picture for the institution at a strategic level, so that there is a clear blueprint for both managers and their teams of staff to follow. This planning process needs to be communicated to and 'owned by' all staff in the college, who should regularly be consulted for their views as part of planning activities. In FE colleges, since 1993, a *strategic planning* process has been carried out by managers to assist staff across the institution achieve annual planning of work priorities for a number of years ahead, linked with the institutional mission and aims and the financial allocations granted by funding providers, in line with overall institutional targets for student recruitment, retention and achievement.

The strategic plan gives an overview of the current state of the institution's governance and management arrangements, curriculum and quality profile, student body, staff, staff development, finance, administration, resources, facilities and estates, as appropriate within the geographical area and student/client/ employer demographic profiles. Usually, the principal, vice principal and other executive management team members will be involved in preparing the overall detailed institutional strategic plan, often in a collaborative process lasting for some months, linked with the institution's *self-assessment report* (SAR).

Once agreed with the governing body (usually called the 'Corporation'), the strategic plan will be submitted to relevant funding providers (e.g. the LSC), normally as a plan for the institution with a longish timescale (e.g. three years). Once the plan is approved by the funding provider, a financial allocation is agreed and allocated for the year ahead. The process and remit of strategic planning is discussed in Chapter 8 in more detail and recommendations for follow-up further information on this are made. The strategic plan should be well publicized within the institution, with its key priorities known to and implemented by all managers.

Implementing the operational plan

The strategic plan outlined above needs to be underpinned at an operational level, with an *operational plan* outlining in detail the aims and objectives in the strategic plan in terms of specific tasks, timescales, priorities, people, departments and sections involved in making the strategic plan become a reality for the institution. Usually, there will be an annual operational plan to implement each year of the strategic plan. This annual plan will be followed up again and underpinned at lower levels of the institutional hierarchy with more detailed departmental and sectional operational plans, specifying who needs to do what and in what timescale in order to meet the institution's key targets.

Implementation of the detailed operations in accomplishing the strategic plan should take up far more time than the planning process itself – i.e. the focus should be on achievement and results, not on planning itself, which is only a means to achieve the aims, objectives and priorities in the plan. Some institutions get this balance wrong, and spend far too much time on planning rather than on the actions involved in implementing the plans. However, there is obviously no point in having wonderful plans that are not carried out. The balance needs to be right, as action without analysis is not advised.

Milestones and local action plans linked to the overall plans will identify a range of items to be monitored and evaluated for effectiveness in meeting predicted targets and outcomes, with associated outputs, such as reports, data collections, etc. If there are items in the strategic plan that are new or particularly difficult to achieve, e.g. a turnaround to improve retention of students, then special initiatives may be put in place to achieve these. Such initiatives could include the recruitment of new staff or the writing of more detailed strategic and operational plans for a new scheme, e.g. a retention strategy linked with tasks in an action plan with resources attached, linked, e.g., with staff development, to draw this to the attention of staff across the institution and ensure it is operationalized.

Organizing institutional operations
In order to carry out the actual work involved in implementing and managing actions in the institutional plans outlined above, managers at every level will need to engage in a wide range of organizing tasks, bringing together people, processes, resources and facilities to achieve this. Managers need to deploy and supervise staff with specific functions within the overall organization, having an overview of the range of tasks to be done and the goals that need to be achieved within the timescales in the plans. Organizing tasks for managers in FE can be demanding, involving bringing together teams of staff for particular initiatives throughout the academic year. Academic advance planners and openly shared diaries are useful to ensure that meetings, events, specific tasks and deskwork are all given adequate space and planning time in managers' diaries.

Line managing, supporting and appraising staff
As well as supervising staff with a wide range of functions across the institution, managers have specific duties for directly line managing some staff who report to them. This involves having

one-to-one meetings throughout the year to discuss annual goals for the staff member, their job description, changing priorities, work schedules, progress, professional development and personal well-being. An annual appraisal process will usually be conducted by the line manager and a report prepared which goes on file with the personnel department, following mutual agreement on its contents. Targets for staff members for the following year are prepared, as part of this process, on the basis of achievement/progress made in the current year. Line management is an important function which, if well-conducted in regular meetings, can be one of the most important processes in ensuring a good-quality institution achieves effective results for students through a fulfilled and successful workforce. However, if line management is carried out ineffectively or destructively, it is all to easy to create the opposite.

Coordinating college functions and responsibilities

As well as organizing, supervising and line managing staff, managers have a role coordinating a number of specific responsibilities for college functions. These could include, for example, maintaining an institutional strategic overview of the work of more than one department through cross-institutional functions. Managers will usually also have a staff coordination role, bringing staff together from different areas of the academic and administrative functions of the institution to achieve joint initiatives identified in the strategic plan. This could be done through chairing meetings and setting up working groups. For example, to implement a retention strategy, managers may bring together academic staff (e.g. tutors), administrative staff, technical staff (e.g. MIS staff) and service staff (e.g. catering, cleaning, security and estates staff) to put this in place and monitor achievement. Sometimes managers have unrealistically heavy responsibilities for coordinating a range of functions, leading to *rôle overload* – a concept explored by Ann Briggs in her book on middle management in FE (Briggs, 2006). Ann suggests ways in which managers can reconsider and re-negotiate unrealistically demanding tasks.

Monitoring and evaluating

Managers need to carry out monitoring and evaluation of the extent to which the planning, organization and implementation of the work being done under the strategic and operational plans is actually being achieved in the institution. Monitoring may take place on a daily, weekly and monthly basis of key targets identified in the plan – e.g. if one of the strategic aims of the institution is to improve student enrolment and retention, then close monitoring of these is likely to take place at points of recruitment during the summer (early applications and continuing students) and early autumn (new students, late applications), and at points at which retention is a key issue (e.g. monthly returns or key breaks in the academic year, like half terms and holidays, mid-year, end of year). Good monitoring and evaluation is essential to assess the extent to which targets in the strategic plan are being achieved.

Controlling, delegating, sharing ownership of tasks

Essentially, managers need to try to achieve an appropriate level of control regarding what happens in the institution to meet the targets objectified in the strategic and operational plans. The issue of 'controlling' staff, systems and processes is generally acknowledged to be one of the key tasks as well as potentially one of the key dilemmas of management, as managers need to balance 'control' with 'care' of staff. Challenges may arise from operational staff who do not agree with managers about areas that need to be 'controlled'. For example, academic and professional staff may feel they have a wider relationship with external professional, industrial, scholarly and research agencies outside and beyond the college, and may resist internal authorities in the college if they do not feel they are respected sufficiently and given sufficient autonomy. We have mentioned the potential of clashes between managers and professionals. These and other tensions between managers and professionals are explored throughout this book in a number of different chapters.

The question of delegation versus control is quite tricky. To what extent should managers delegate their work? Good managers tend to value the specialist knowledge, abilities and different strengths of their staff and are able to handle the tensions between controlling and delegating work, effectively managing teams of people and bringing together harmoniously different strengths within the institution. Talented managers often also give employees agreed areas of autonomy in which to work, thereby demonstrating trust and respect for the staff they supervise (as Ruth Silver and John Guy might say, they enable 'discretionary freedoms' in specific areas). Generating an atmosphere of trust and mutual respect is extremely important: coercive managers tend to create a negative atmosphere, as is demonstrated in Table 3.1, which illustrates Hay McBer's six different kind of leadership styles that managers can adopt. All styles except 'coercive' and 'pace-setting' leader-manager styles can generate positive results. Hence managers need to select and focus on a positive style that suits their situation, institutional environment and personal preferences. In practice, good results can be achieved from an effective balance of negotiated permissions, with good leader-managers often enabling professional staff to have some control over their work within an overall framework of agreed priorities for the institution to meet shared goals. This would be similar to the positive aspects of McGregor's Theory of management (McGregor, 1960). The *way* in which the balance of authority-delegation-autonomy is conducted is critical in achieving staff compliance, trust and mutual respect and 'buy-in' to college aims and objectives. Sometimes leadership attributes in managers can make or break this, e.g. if managers effectively use humour, empathetic understanding, inspirational example, demonstrate superior professional knowledge or simply show they are not afraid of hard grind.

Holistic practical management examples in FE

Having looked briefly at some elements of the different functions managers typically perform, how do these functions fit together within managers' jobs in the real-life situations of FE institutions? To give an example of the way in which these functions are brought together holistically in the day-to-day context of an FE college, I include here an excerpt from an interview on leadership with Ruth Silver about the way in which leadership and management at Lewisham College was operating when I saw her in her role as Principal/CEO in 2004.

Table 3.1: The six management or leadership styles (extract from the *The Reflective College Manager*, Association of College Management, 2001: 26)

Style	Way of Operating	In a Phrase	When the Style Works Best	Overall Impact on Climate
Coercive	Demands immediate compliance	'Do what I tell you'	In a crisis, to kick start a turnaround, or with problem employees	Negative
Authoritative	Mobilizes people	'Come with me'	When changes require a new vision, or when a clear direction is needed	Positive
Affiliative	Creates harmony and builds emotional bonds	'People come first'	To heal rifts in a team or to motivate people during stressful circumstances	Positive
Democratic	Forges consensus through participation	'What do you think?'	To build consensus or to get input from valuable employees	Positive
Pacesetting	Sets high standards towards a vision	'Do as I do now'	To get quick results for a highly motivated and competent team	Negative
Coaching	Develops people for the future	'Try this'	To help an employee improve performance or develop long-term strengths	Positive

'Another study by Hay McBer of 3,871 executives found 6 distinct management or leadership styles, each springing from different components of emotional intelligence. The most successful managers did not rely on only one leadership style, but used several depending on the demands and challenges of the situation.' (ACM, 2001: 26).

Ruth talks first of all about the general mission of the college and its key strategic decisions regarding overall direction about vocational work. She then focuses directly on the college's primary strategic priority (student success). Ruth describes the way in which the college fits in with and responds to its place in the community. She advises us on Lewisham's considered approach to the question of what is appropriate and what is not appropriate as educational provision for the local communities in Lewisham. Finally, she gives us a glimpse of the management and organizational processes taking place behind the scenes to ensure that college responsiveness and a lively vision of relevance for the community is maintained:

> Lewisham, for example, didn't abandon vocational areas of work 10 years ago when [these] were an expense and nobody else wanted them, because in this community getting a job was the first step to belonging. So for me to turn my back on plumbing and open up a few more '-ologies' would not have served the primary task of this organisation. Which is its students' success. Students' progression. I didn't want to become a 6th Form college you know – it's the same idea that the 'fit' for this community was the opportunity coming up in this community, it's what this organisation is about [and] is really what runs the curriculum. We have very strong management practices of reviewing, monitoring, allocating, inspecting. All of those go on apace here – I mean very excellent managers. (Dame Ruth Silver, interview (Jameson, 2006))

In another real example, Daniel Khan discusses the vision and strategic priorities of Grimsby College, the complexity of the management processes involved in achieving these, and the way in which management underpins and fulfils leadership:

> We all have a vision that means we help quality, but you have got to really manage that to make sure that the teaching quality is good; the resource quality for students is good. That is very much a management role, because leadership can, actually, look at the strategic issues, set mission statements or whatever, but the truth is the entire institution has

to deliver the management of it, because the management is so complex, it's not just about people in senior positions, it's about everybody, a lecturer in his class managing his lessons plans, his delivery, to make sure it meets that overall objective of being good quality and his good interface with his students. Because managing the learning process is crucial in an institution like this, and the people who do that are the lecturers. (Professor Daniel Khan interview (Jameson, 2006))

So here we have the concept of management operating genuinely at all levels, including at classroom management level by lecturers. Daniel reminds us that the core business of education is 'the learning process', but that this can also be approached in an efficient, high quality and financially effective way.

Business systems and solutions applied to education – lessons and dilemmas

As an expert financial manager himself, a principal/CEO like Daniel Khan is comfortable with business-led approaches, leading the college in applying advanced knowledge to these processes. Applying financially-driven business systems and solutions to education within the contexts of FE colleges does not always work so smoothly, however, if the principal/CEO does not have the advanced financial and systems management knowledge of an accountant or business expert. In such cases, it is important to have a vice principal or finance director with expertise in the area of financial, information and resources management. We noted earlier that excellent financial management and good knowledge of MIS data are two of the attributes of outstanding leadership and management that Ofsted had recorded during their inspections. It was also certainly an important part of the work of all of the successful post-compulsory education leaders interviewed in 2004–5 (Jameson, 2006).

In most FE institutions, either the principal/CEO or another executive leader will have expert knowledge of these important areas. Essential functions that need to be represented at the college executive level are wide-ranging, but notably include those of curriculum and quality assurance, financial and information management, communications, human resources, marketing and estates management systems. These need to be underpinned by more specialized processes for MIS data management of student recruitment, retention, achievement, qualifications outcomes and destinations monitoring. College ICT systems play a key role in maximizing income/funding, marketing and promoting the institution, recruiting new students, supporting quality management, and monitoring of learning programmes, student retention, achievement, management of daily administration and optimization of business processes. It really is worth spending extra time and money to make sure that college systems run effectively and that data management is well organized.

The lessons derived from a number of disastrous failures in FE in the early years of incorporation (e.g. financial and other irregularities reported by the National Audit Office at the fast-growing Halton College, Widnes, in 1993–98 and at Bilston Community College in the West Midlands in 1999) have been applied throughout the sector to such an extent that, in subsequent years, the audit function of external scrutineers is sometimes more rigorously and continuously applied than perhaps is strictly necessary, as discussed earlier in this book.

Given that an 'audit culture' therefore currently prevails, however, the extent to which data management processes are effectively administered and managed at local levels through the engagement and deployment of expert and committed staff is often the extent to which the principal/CEO and governors can sleep soundly at night without being unduly anxious about college performance. It is therefore well worth making special, sustained efforts to ensure that all staff who are employed to handle business and administration processes are effectively appointed, inducted, line managed, supported and assisted, especially at peak points of data collection during the academic year. The dilemmas that an institution can face when data management and business processes are not delivering accurate information and are not effectively handled are simply not worth risking.

Organizational learning – single and double loop learning

The idea of 'organizational learning' (OL) has been at the fore of business and management studies for some time (see, for example, Senge, Kleiner, Roberts, Ross, Roth and Smith, 1999, and, from the UK, Pedler, Boydell and Burgoyne (1988)) as a method of enabling managers to improve organizational performance. Senge (1990) and Senge *et al.* (1999) noted that there are five different disciplines in organizational learning: *personal mastery, mental models, shared vision, team learning* and *systems thinking*. Peter Senge's (1990) book *The Fifth Discipline* outlines these disciplines as practices for building capability in learning organizations, as follows:

Personal mastery
The discipline of *aspiration* can reduce the gap between the personal vision of managers and a realistic assessment of current realities. The tension between vision and reality can facilitate learning, as managers expand their capacity to make better choices and achieve more of the results they prioritize and envision.

Mental models
The discipline of *reflection* focuses on the development of inquiry skills to promote awareness of attitudes and perceptions affecting thought and interaction. If managers reflect on, discuss, consider and reconsider internal mental models, they can gain increased self-control over their actions and decisions, avoiding the 'ladder of inference' of counterproductive assumptions.

Shared vision
This discipline focuses on *mutual purpose*: managers collectively learn to build commitment in an organization by developing shared images of the future to be co-created and the principles and guiding practices to get there.

Team learning

The discipline of *group interaction* promotes dialogue and skillful discussion in which teams transform collective thinking through a synergistic learning process.

Systems thinking

A discipline that promotes *learning in systems thinking, interdependency and change*, this is based on theories regarding feedback and complexity, the innate tendencies of systems to lead to growth, decay or change. A circular 'feedback loop' underlies all natural growing and limiting processes: knowledge of this enables greater management skill and control.

Through these publications, Senge and his colleagues drew attention to the capacity of organizations to change by arguing that organizations are 'products of the ways that people in them think and interact' and that therefore you could give people opportunities to improve organizations, changing the ways people think and interact, and introducing practices to encourage organizational learning (Senge *et al.*, 1999: 33).

There are two different types of processes in organizational learning: *adaptive learning* and *proactive learning*. Adaptive learning, or 'single loop' lower-level tactical learning (Argyris and Schön, 1978), consists of fairly automatic changes in response to smaller incremental alterations in the environment. By contrast, proactive learning or higher-level strategic 'double loop learning' goes beyond reactions to environmental changes, and consist of learning from changes which were designed to question the system itself at a deeper conceptual level (Argyris and Schön, 1978; Fiol and Lyles, 1985; Dodgson, 1991; Senge, 1990). There are a vast number of publications in the field of organizational learning, which are well worth studying for their capacity to enable people to encompass significant benefits from changing their working practices to improve the capacity of organizations to improve. Further references are provided in the References and Appendices.

Mapping current achievements with target goals for institutions

The government's change programme for further education, Success for All, was launched in April 2002, aiming to improve quality, rationalize provision and generate improvements and opportunities nationally for lifelong learning in the FE sector (NAO, 2005). This was followed in 2005 by the Foster Review (2005) and the government White Paper on FE in 2006. The range of major policy initiatives and changes recorded by the National Audit Office are shown in Figure 3.1.

In the Introduction to Yvonne Hillier's book in the *Essential FE Toolkit Series, Everything You Need To Know about FE Policy*, I wrote about John Brennan's speech to the AOC Annual Conference in November 2005, in which John observed that there had during 1995–2005 been 36 different government or government-funded reports/White Papers or other policy initiatives on post-16 education. Since then there have been (at least) the above two major policy papers, making 38 at a minimum. The number of top-down targets flooding down on the FE sector in terms of expectations for the measurement of its performance are legion. How can people cope in this situation? Well, it calls for excellent leadership and management on a daily, continuous basis, to meet the multiplicity of targets set for the sector in the best way, mapping achievements of colleges and students closely against target goals in ways that are locally empowering, not disengaging. To promote the ability of leader-managers in FE to achieve this holistically is the aim both of this book and of a number of current initiatives in the sector, including the work of the Centre for Excellence in Leadership. In Chapters 8, 10 and 11, we consider a range of strategies for the development of excellent management skills in FE, and also suggest a range of follow-up materials and initiatives that managers in the learning and skills sector can engage with to improve management skills and to meet the plethora of targets that are thrust upon managers in the FE system.

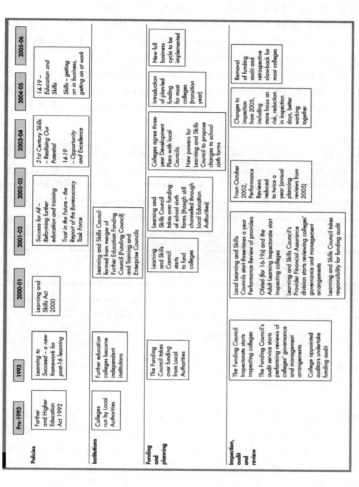

Figure 3.1: Selected extract from National Audit Office, Report on major organizational and policy changes affecting the FE sector, 1993–05 (NAO, 2005:7)

Staff perceptions of management

A survey carried out on leadership and management in the LSC sector in 2006–7 as part of the leadership and management work linked to the *Essential FE Toolkit Series* has collected 79 responses from FE college participants, of whom 71 answered question 7. This question asks respondents to state if they agree with the phrase, *Overall, upper management in the organization I work for do a good job and treat me with respect* (see Figure 3.2). The interim results indicate that 76.1 per cent of respondents feel that this is the case (either 'somewhat agree' or 'strongly agree'), while 14 per cent disagree (9.9 per cent 'somewhat disagree' and 4.2 per cent 'strongly disagree').

7. Overall, upper management (Heads of Dept and above) in the organisation I work for do a good job and treat me with respect.		Response Percent	Response Total
Strongly disagree		4.2%	3
Somewhat disagree		9.9%	7
Neutral		7%	5
Somewhat agree		32.4%	23
Strongly agree		**43.7%**	**31**
Not applicable to my situation		2.8%	2
Other (please elaborate on any of the above)		0%	0
	Total Respondents		71
	(skipped this question)		8

Figure 3.2: Question 7 – Respondent views on management in the learning and skills sector

Caution needs to be applied to the validity of the numerical indicators in these results, as the numbers involved so far are small in representing such a large sector, and contain also a fair number of senior management responses, which may mean the operation of some bias (or not) weighted towards upper management in relation to such a question. However, the findings are of interest in relation to the detailed qualitative textual comments provided below and also to the results for question 9, which is, *Most leaders at senior and middle levels in my organization visibly demonstrate a commitment to high quality provision for learners* (see Figure 3.3).

9. Most leaders at senior and middle levels in my organisation visibly demonstrate a commitment to high quality provision for learners.			
		Response Percent	Response Total
Strongly disagree	▮	2.9%	2
Somewhat disagree		0%	0
Neither agree nor disagree	▬	4.3%	3
Somewhat agree	▬▬▬▬▬▬▬	28.6%	20
Strongly agree	▬▬▬▬▬▬▬▬▬▬▬▬	65.7%	46
Not applicable to my situation		0%	0
		Total Respondents	70
		(skipped this question)	9

Figure 3.3: Question 9 – Respondent views on management in the learning and skills sector

In this result, there is a clear picture emerging that 94 per cent of respondents (68 individuals) feel that leader-managers are committed to quality provision for students, with only 2.9 per cent of respondents (2 people) disagreeing with this. From this small snapshot, indicating a range of staff perceptions about management in FE, we can see that, even with a weighting attached to upper management responses, there is a greater level of ambivalence about the performance of managers as a whole than there is about managers' commitment to learners. The core indicator of 'passion to achieve' in the CEL framework for leadership is therefore arguably already in strongly place in the sector. This is interesting also in relation to the qualitative open-ended text responses to question 11, *I would describe the leadership and management of the organisation I work for in the following way* (see Figure 3.4).

These open-ended text responses give a very useful and diverse picture of leadership and management, from first-class outstanding work going in some organizations (three of the responses indicate 'outstanding' performance) right through the spectrum of good and fair performance (most responses indicate what appears to be a reasonable level of leadership and management effectiveness) to a bullying and very difficult

	I would describe the leadership and management of the organization I work for in the following way:
1.	Constrained dedicated committed but not visionary and often not strategic
2.	Open, progressive but sometimes reactive rather than proactive. Honest and consultative as far as is reasonably practicable. Extremely supportive, willing to try out new ideas and take calculated risks. Definitely 'can do' and business focussed at the top and in some middle management positions however responsiveness to business requirements etc needs to be more flexible
3.	Very business and target focused sometimes forgetting the barriers that exist that hinder achievement
4.	Not always willing to make tough strategic decisions
5.	Open and consultative, firm but fair and resolute when necessary
6.	Thoroughly committed to excellence and to ensuring students get the greatest opportunity to succeed. The College is extremely efficiently managed and effectively led.
7.	Effective, open and transparent
8.	Outstanding – that's what Ofsted said and that is also the perception from, for example, the (former) LSDA staff opinion survey where we are above sector benchmarks on 38 out of 38 issues
9.	Open progressive strategic as opposed to operational
10.	Passionate and committed but lacking in part the necessary acumen to bring about change sufficiently quickly in a few key areas. I include myself in this!
11.	Intentions are good, communicating those intentions can be difficult
12.	Very supportive with a clear vision
13.	Competent but not inspiring
14.	Having authentic strategic vision for the whole college but as with all large organisations it is communicating that and enabling it further down. We are definitely working towards this aim

15.	There are four members of the SLT, of these only one has had any experience in other colleges. This means that there is a lack of broad experience within the team which has manifested itself as naivety at times and has sometimes impacted upon their decision making. There is a lack of middle management consultation regarding strategic planning and insufficient cascading of information regarding strategic planning and three year development planning. The lack of consultation and information cascading has been recognised (by the member of SLT that has had wider college experiences) and is action planned. The team is improving from a didactic management approach to a more integrated leadership and management approach and is committed to continuous improvement
16.	Autocratic
17.	Visonary, committed to the delivery of high quality education and training, experienced and expert in their areas. Areas of emotional intelligence probably need developing as little attention to management and leadership development had taken place prior to my appointment
18.	Transitional and working in the right direction
19.	Well focused for the most part but works best when sufficient head room is given at an operational level
20.	Strong, organized, effective, supportive
21.	Committed to moving the institution forward with the learner at the centre
22.	Sensitive to the needs of all staff at all levels with a view to place the needs of students at the heart of all that we do. Our leadership support staff to work as a team with all being valued in the contribution they make. We also are aware that such trust and motivation is only sustainable within limited means which will impact upon the needs of the individual and those of the College as a whole. Our cry is for all things teaching and learning, all else must be viewed in the context of such a vision
23.	Honest open leadership, I am not afraid to confront underperformance in senior and middle managers. I set a good example of how managers should perform their roles, we have a number of policies and processes that are monitored regularly to ensure managers are effective in carrying out their roles and responsibilities

24.	Proactive and effective
25.	Learner centred and focused on improving the quality of the learner experience whilst maintaining the financial health of the College
26.	Good at processes, efficiencies etc, less good at people. But willing to learn!
27.	Clear vision for themselves, however, more work needs to be completed to motivate and empower all staff in the organization. The SMT has recently showed commitment in changing the way they lead and it is clear that they hope to empower staff and have started to listen!
28.	This is a double Beacon College and I am the principal so the views expressed need to be seen from that perspective. Here Leadership is defined as 'having the capacity to win hearts' for the primary purpose and spirit of the college. It is high profile, visible, public and passionate about success. The leadership of thinking is key, we see ourselves in the Future business and we steer our course to that end. Management has 2 domains – the general management tasks of our role and the professional management of our specialisms. We work through, with and by others to deliver the organisation's mission and targets
29.	The College has a didactic, transactional approach to l&m – i.e. do as I say without question
30.	Slightly mercurial. Things are not always followed through and macho management styles still prevail
31.	Benevolent, authoritative
32.	Very focused individuals who want the best outcomes for all students. Not concerned with how it's done so long as it is done – could therefore be more supportive/coaching
33.	Bullying style of management who say there is no blame culture! If somethings goes wrong they are very quick to blame. Staff are frightened to contradict SMT even if they know what is being done/said is wrong. So long as we know that whatever we do will not be good enough we will never be disappointed. Sorry to be so negative but that's what it's like
34.	Highly committed to the College vision and values. Highly committed to securing the best possible success for our students
35.	Purposeful and consultative

36.	Very committed but still needing better 'team' focus
37.	Poor people skills, unable to motivate staff and very poor recognition of the skills of the staff. This seems to reflect an insecurity and fear of competent staff rather than celebration of effective staff
38.	Remote, not enough communication or team–work
39.	Open, honest, very busy
40.	Middle managers seem strongly committed to high quality provision for learners, while maintaining a working understanding of the pressures on staff at lower levels. This fosters good relations and morale among employees. Senior managers seem, on the whole, to be much more interested in their own and the college's image, as well as speaking and acting as if they were Whitehall politicians. Along the way they appear to have lost touch with the reality of life at the point of education delivery and, in most cases, seem not to care at all about teachers or learners – just so long as government targets are met, we keep within budget and all the right boxes are ticked
41.	Clear, committed to quality throughout the college
42.	Senior management is very effective and commited to providing a high quality service. Middle management are interested in being noticed and furthering their own careers
43.	Strong and proactive most of the time
44.	Very disappointing
45.	Too focused on the organization direction from top down without giving opportunities for a range of staff views to be fed back up through the system. Lack of staff membership in decision-making, that is, all decision-making and associated consultation involves managers, with no 'academic board' style opportunities for constructive and open debate
46.	No focus, no direction, reactionaries
47.	There is a commitment by the Principal and SMT to leadership and management for all staff, both teaching and support
48.	Remote, detached, out of touch, unaware of the reality of F/HE of the past 5 years, focused on money, short-sighted, short term obsessed, Teflon people
49.	They keep abreast of developments, plan and prioritize accordingly and communicate well. They are approachable

50.	Participative
51.	Driven by administration, frightened of delegation and consequently stifling innovation and creativity in the workforce
52.	Although a strong vision and direction are set from the top the approach is broad brush. Implementation and follow through, monitoring and evaluation are weak. There is a predominance of shapers and plants at senior level which means that we suffer initiative overload which is then handed on to middle managers half thought through and poorly set up
53.	There is good strategic leadership, but the Senior Team members are not equally capable
54.	Rather remote from middle management
55.	High profile leadership. Management presently going through restructuring exercise that should get rid of dead wood

Figure 3.4: Question 11 – Respondent views on management in the learning and skills sector

environment in others (four responses indicate poor leadership and management, with one that seems to be at 'unacceptable' levels). From this small snapshot of staff perceptions about management in FE, we can see that there appears to be a great deal of need for staff development work, confidence-building and sharing of best practice to take place right across the learning and skills sector, including in FE colleges, so that the lessons from those operating at 'Beacon college' levels of performance are genuinely learnt in other parts of the system. With this in mind, we include a summary overview of the earlier FENTO Management Standards (2001) at the end of this chapter, mindful that the FE Bill (2006) has proposed that all FE Principals will shortly need to possess a qualification in leadership and management. We return to the question of leadership and management standards later in the book.

Summary

Chapter 3 provides an overview of management in FE, including definitions of management and the elements of good management. Business systems and solutions applied to

ANNEX 4 SUMMARY OVERVIEW OF FENTO MANAGEMENT STANDARDS

A. DEVELOP STRATEGIC PRACTICE
To analyse, plan, develop and implement a shared vision
A1. Develop a vision
A2. Plan to achieve the vision
A3. Manage change and continuous improvement

B. DEVELOP AND SUSTAIN LEARNING AND THE LEARNING ENVIRONMENT
To plan, implement and review the quality and range of services to promote positive outcomes and success
B1. Develop and sustain services for learners
B2. Manage quality in the delivery of services
B3. Manage human resources to support the provision of services

C. LEAD TEAMS AND INDIVIDUALS
To teams and individuals to enable them to achieve objectives and lead continually improve performance
C1. Manage and develop self and own performance
C2. Maintain and develop team and individual performance
C3. Build and maintain productive working relationships

D. MANAGE RESOURCES
To manage the acquisition, deployment and development of resources to facilitate and promote learning
D1. Plan resource requirements
D2. Manage finance
D3. Manage physical resources

Figure 3.5: Summary overview of FENTO Management Standards (from: The Reflective College Manager, *Association of College Management*, 2001: 86, Annex 4).

educational management, lessons and dilemmas for management are considered. The concept of 'organizational learning' in terms of single and double loop learning is outlined. Mapping current achievements with target goals for institutions is considered, as are staff perceptions of management in FE. Some results from a leadership survey carried out in the sector in 2006 are reported and analysed in the context of views about leadership and management.

4: 'Senior' and 'middle' management roles

Great spirits have always found violent opposition from mediocrities. The latter cannot understand it when a man does not thoughtlessly submit to hereditary prejudices but honestly and courageously uses his intelligence.

Albert Einstein

Hierarchical models of leadership and management in FE

Most models of leadership and management in educational institutions are hierarchical in terms of the formal structures of management, and further education is no exception to this general rule. The organogram for most colleges of further education, for example, would probably look something like the simplified institutional hierarchy depicted in Figure 4.1, with the Principal/CEO post at the top of the hierarchical structure, assisted at executive level by a Vice Principal and a series of Executive Directors reporting to the Principal. The Directors line manage Heads of Department or Area, who in turn line manage Programme Leaders or other Supervisory staff

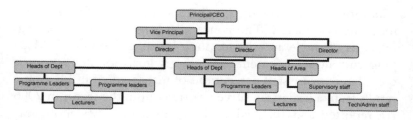

Figure 4.1: Simplified organogram to demonstrate key hierarchical relationships in FE

who have first-line responsibility for the lecturing, administrative and/or technical staffing of the institution. These hierarchical models are explored in more detail in Chapter 6, in which we discuss a range of different kinds of leadership models.

Bush (2006) writes on the limitations of hierarchical models of leadership and management in education, while still reminding us of the necessity of these for everyday operations in colleges and schools. Bush notes that conceptions of leadership and management too closely allied to the upper end of formal hierarchies of educational organizations may alienate professional staff. This may occur particularly at lower levels of the formal hierarchy, if the imposition of 'top-down' command-driven leadership and management ignores the importance both of professionalism and of the role played by individuals working in teaching, administrative, technical or other roles at relatively subordinate levels. The traditional hierarchical structure implies that, for example, the duty of teachers is to obey the commands and implement the orders of senior managers, a militaristic style of operations that does not sit well with educational professionals whose primary concern is for learners in the classroom. This kind of structure feeds off the Weber/Taylor conceptualization of management from industrial production.

Executive and senior management roles

The roles of executive managers in further education normally include the following:

- Principal or CEO (Chief Executive Officer) or Head of Institution
- Vice Principal, Deputy/Assistant Principal(s), Executive Directors

There may, however, be a cross-over between some of these levels, depending on the hierarchical model adopted by the institution. For example, some institutions call the head of the institution a 'Chief Executive Officer' (CEO), while others have agreed to use the title 'Principal' or 'Head'. Some institutions have Assistant Principals who are equivalent in status to Vice Principals, while others have Deputy Principals, and yet others do not have a Vice Principal post, but only Executive Directors. In some institutions, Deans of Faculty or Heads of School or Departments are at executive level, while in others they are not. There is a mixed bag of titles, levels, pay scales and duties to be found in institutions across the learning and skills sector, partly resulting from the accidents of history and partly from the collective and individual preferences of governing bodies, senior management staff and local stakeholders.

The roles of senior managers normally include the following:

- Directors at senior but not executive level
- Heads, Deans of Faculties, Departments, etc., at senior but not executive level
- Heads of Centres, Administrative and Financial Services, etc.

As above, there may be a cross-over between some of these levels. Mostly, Directors will be at executive level, but there may be some for smaller areas of work not carrying out executive functions. In some institutions, Deans of Faculty or Heads of School or Departments are at executive or senior level, while in others they are not. In some institutions, there is a Finance Director at Executive or Vice Principal (Resources) level who works directly on financial matters, but in other institutions the specialist day-to-day responsibility for finance may be at the senior management level reporting up to a Vice Principal with an overall responsibility for the institution. An analysis of and guidebook for the roles of senior college managers and leaders in FE has been carried out by David Collins in the *Essential FE Toolkit* book *A Survival Guide for College Leaders and Managers*.

The role of the Principal/CEO in FE

The role of the Principal/CEO in FE has gained in stature, difficulty and importance during the past two decades. Michael Austin observed in 2006 in an article in *FE Focus* in the *Times Educational Supplement* (Austen, 2006) that applicant numbers for FE principal posts have declined dramatically in the past few years. Austin's explanation for this is that the job of principal, previously characterized by a kind of excitement at being on the metaphorical 'big dipper' of this demanding top role, is now increasingly mundane, requiring compliant, conformist attitudes to fit in with pre-given centrally controlled LSC and other government agency targets. Austin observes that challenging, innovative leadership is no longer necessary or useful in the FE principal's job. However, Austin's explanation for this decline in applicant interest in FE principal posts has been strongly countered by David Collinson (2006), who argues that, far from being mundane, the role of principal is, in fact, still like a 'roller coaster' ride – far too challenging and demanding for most applicants:

> Our research suggests that many incumbents and potential candidates considered the job of principal as having too many challenges rather than too few. An important effect of excessive auditing, inconsistent funding and multiple community engagements is a growing disinclination for qualified applicants to apply for principal vacancies. In contrast with Mike Austin's contention that 'the white knuckle excitement of the big dipper' has been replaced by 'the certainties of a comfortable ride on a roundabout', our research suggests that the roller-coaster metaphor continues to be a fairly accurate description for the work of FE principals. (Collinson, 2006)

If the job of principals in leading and managing FE institutions is in fact distinguished by significant difficulties generated by different sources, many of which do not focus on key academic and development challenges but on audit, finance and compliance-to-target, how does this manifest itself in the day-to-day roles of senior leaders in colleges, and how can we collectively alleviate the stressful burdens on top managers? In an earlier exploration of leadership in the sector, Ferreday, Hodgson and Jones (2005) noted that principals had regularly reported that, 'It's a fairly lonely job'. Ferreday *et al.* draw on their research to propose that a 'networked management learning' (NML) approach is of value in supporting principals and other leader-managers in FE to gain confidence and support for leadership development. These researchers note that in recent years there has been a culture of individualistic leadership responsibility in FE generally.

We explore these issues relating to the overload on principals and other staff in FE in a number of chapters in this book and also in the *Essential FE Toolkit Series* in other books. In Chapter 10 we look at specific evidence from and views about leader-managers in the sector deriving from a survey carried out in 2006. We draw on this to develop, in Chapter 11, a practical guide to bring out the leader-manager within you. An extended analysis of the role and duties of principals and college leaders is explored by David Collins in the *Essential FE Toolkit* book *A Survival Guide for College Leaders and Managers* (2006). We give an overview of issues affecting senior and middle management here, but also refer readers to other volumes for further information and analysis.

Middle management roles

The roles of middle managers in further education normally include the following:

- Heads of Faculties, Schools or Academic Departments
- Heads of Administrative and Service Areas
- Senior teachers with coordinating cross-institutional roles

As above, however, there may be a cross-over between some of these levels, depending on the hierarchical model adopted by the institution. For example, some Heads of Faculties, Schools or Departments may be middle managers at upper tiers of middle management or even sometimes senior managers, while others might have a lower level of status and salary. Most heads of academic and administrative or servicing department will normally be at middle management levels in FE, however, reporting to an executive director or other senior post at executive level. An analysis of middle management roles in FE is given by Professor Ann Briggs in her book, *Middle Management in FE* (2006), which looks at the duties, responsibilities, benefits, conflicts, issues and contradictions middle managers cope with on a daily basis in colleges.

Line management roles and duties

Line managers in further education normally include the following:

- All of the above roles at executive and senior levels
- Programme leaders
- Other academic and administrative staff with line management responsibilities

The traditional hierarchical model of management in FE has been somewhat business or armed-forces-like in its adoption of the language and culture of 'line management' since incorporation in 1992. Lumby (1997) carried out research on management development during the post-incorporation period, using Pedler's (1988) framework for analysing organizational maturity. She found that colleges were relatively underdeveloped at first-line management levels. The study also found that staff development was under-resourced at this level, at which there was an under-recognition of the role carried out by management, in comparison with senior and middle managers (Lumby, 1997). Since then, the situation has improved somewhat, particularly since the establishment and growth of the Centre for Excellence in Leadership, but this area is still underdeveloped and needs further consideration.

Functional management

Functional managers in further education normally include the following:

- All of the above roles at executive and senior levels
- Programme leaders
- Specific appointees to a particular function on top of another role
- Other academic and administrative staff with line management responsibilities

Functional managers will normally carry out a range of cross-college responsibilities for particular areas, which overlap and extend between hierarchical departmental layers and, for example, for ILT (information and learning technologies), college working groups on retention, specialist projects, events coordination, etc. Functional managers may often have a 'loose' non-line management supervisory responsibility for people in other line management chains of command for duties to be carried out within the specialist function. Some of these tasks can be challenging if they compete with the routine work of staff for time, resources and energy, as the functional manager may have only loose control over the performance of staff and may sometimes be in tension with line managers and line management duties.

'Governance' versus 'leadership and management'

College governors are volunteers comprised of people from the college's community. They include business, local authority and community governors, staff governors, parent governors, student governors, associate and co-opted governors. Governors have an important role to play in ensuring the accountability, effective leadership, management, operations and evaluation of FE institutions, including sixth forms, adult education institutions, work-based learning and training providers, youth and community institutions and related organizations. (NB: note that sometimes the constitution of charitable or voluntary organizations requires them to have trustees, not governors.)

The motivation for governors to give of their own free time to carry out this important role usually arises because these volunteers want to make a positive contribution to the education of learners, genuinely have an interest in the welfare of their local college and its students, or want to make links with FE for business and work-related reasons. Sometimes key representatives from local businesses or universities will be invited to be governors in order to represent 'the voice of the community'. The presence of student governors is particularly important as they have a unique role to play in representing the 'voices of the learners', so that the governors know what is really going on in the institution from the student point of view.

Meeting several times a year, usually at least once a term and sometimes more, governors set the strategic direction of the further education institution, ensure accountability, monitor and evaluate overall college performance, and provide advanced voluntary senior services to the institution within their roles by, for example, attending student disciplinary panels or carrying out monitoring visits to particular curriculum areas in which they are interested. Governors are usually careful not to step on the toes of senior management: the role of governance is one stage removed from the college and, in a 'critical friend' type of way, governors need to monitor, evaluate, guide and advise managers objectively, fairly, sensitively, openly and selflessly, rather than interfere with management roles. They need to be fully appraised, informed about and involved in strategic decision-making, but are rarely if ever involved in operational tasks in the college (see Figure 4.2). Governorship is a guardianship type of role, in which elders (the governors) do not get in the way of those with more direct responsibilities for the institution such as the senior management, but at the same time watch carefully over the whole operation and ensure it is headed in the right direction and performing effectively. The 'critical support' role played by governors is of crucial importance in assisting a college to achieve its objectives fully, as Ofsted reports in its overview of the reasons why outstanding colleges tend to succeed (Ofsted, 2004b). Hence governors need to make 'declarations of interest' to let the organization know of any conflicts of interest they may have in performing the role of governor: for example, if any of their relatives are college staff or they have financial dealings with matters which may affect the institution. Governors are required to abide by the *Nolan Principles*, the seven principles for holders of public office: *Integrity, Objectivity, Accountability, Openness, Honesty, Selflessness* and *Leadership* (Nolan Committee, 1995).

Links with national, regional and local leaders and managers

All further education institutions need to be rooted into and responsive to their local LSC, local communities and regional areas, in terms of relationships with employers, local education (children's services) authorities, other post–16 providers, universities and regional development agencies. Strong links with

Thinking of becoming a Governor?

College Governors are people from the college's community who wish to make a positive contribution to the education of learners of all ages. Governors are a volunteer force who have an important part to play in raising standards through their three key roles of setting strategic direction, ensuring accountability and monitoring and evaluating college performance.

The Selection and Appointment of Governors in the FE Sector

Governance Model:

The current governance model is a representative one, comprising a number of categories to which members are selected and appointed. For example, General FE colleges are required to have 'no more than seven' members from the business community and 'at least one and no more than three' members from the college staff.

Selecting and Appointing Governors to newly incorporated FE Colleges:

The Secretary of State is the appointing authority, under the Instrument and Articles of Government (FE college regulations), for providing the initial members of a college governing body when a new college is created. In practice, the Governance and Organisation Team carry out this role under delegated authority. The Governance and Organisation Team liaise with the LSC and the project steering group which is tasked with setting up the new college, who identify potential candidates for nomination.

Selecting and Appointing Governors to existing FE Colleges:

The college is itself responsible for selecting and appointing new governors to existing governing bodies, providing the number of members doesn't fall below quorum. If so, the responsibility reverts to the Secretary of State. The selection process for members varies according to which category of governor is required. Staff members, student members and parent members are nominated, elected by their number and then appointed by the governing body; Community members are nominated by a voluntary body and then appointed by the governing body; Local authority members are nominated by local authorities proposed by the Corporation; Business members and co-opted members are identified by means of a statutory 'Search Committee' which then recommends candidates to the governing body for appointment.

Scrutiny of the selection and appointment process:

At the time of the FE inspection carried out under the Common Inspection Framework, the LSC scrutinise the governance practice of colleges, including a number of areas relating to the selection and recruitment of governors. The LSC looks at whether appointments have been made to the appropriate categories of membership, how the governing body ensures eligibility for membership, how long positions have been vacant, how recently a skills audit of members was undertaken and whether there is an induction programme for new members.

Governors are responsible to ensure that:

- they are fully informed of and involved in the strategic decision making in the College. This is to enable them to contribute effectively to the creation of the College's vision and the development of clear and comprehensive strategic plans which achieve that vision,
- they are provided with financial information and Performance Indicators (PIs) on all aspects of the Colleges activities and they should check this information with periodic reviews by the College's internal auditors,
- the College has the capability to produce clear and reliable financial forecasts,
- they receive a report on the College's financial position at least once a term but more frequently if the College's financial health is in question or looks likely to become so, and that
- their Governing Body meets the Learning and Skills Council requirements in approving financial forecasts and budgets and monitoring of financial performance throughout the year.

Figure 4.2: Thinking of becoming a governor? Governor selection and appointment (DfES, 2006)

national, regional and local leaders and managers at a range of levels are crucial in assisting the FE institution to engage proactively in partnership activities, employment, training and skills initiatives, fundraising, the generation of sponsorships, business and community contacts and new programmes of activities. A college that is well connected with the local and regional environment tends to be valued by the community and achieves greater success in generating income, students, sponsorship, business clients and viable training programmes for local industry. The role played by the principal, vice principal and other executive and senior managers is of vital importance in this area: successful senior staff in further education will tend to be recognized, well connected and valued in local and regional areas.

It's all change!

The FE system is changing again following the Foster Review (2005) and Government White Paper on FE (2006), and some of the areas covered in this book will undergo radical change during the next two years. Some of the recommendations arising from these policy changes may result in substantial improvements (e.g. enhancing the reputation of FE and reducing auditing requirements), but other recommendations (narrowing the focus of FE to vocational skills) may be negative and/or the results to come from their future implementation remain unpredictable and still to be determined in the process of implementation itself. We include in Table 4.1 some selected recommendations from the Annex to the White Paper: *Further Education: Raising skills and improving life chances* (DfES, 2005), a response to *Realising the Potential: A review of the future role of FE colleges* (2005) that demonstrates the way in which the DfES and LSC are addressing Sir Andrew Foster's recommendations in the context of the White Paper and Further Education Bill in autumn 2006.

It's all change again! As we watch this space, there will be yet further changes to come. We urge leaders and managers in FE to stay positive in the face of these massive changes to the system yet again.

No	Foster Recommendation	Response	White Paper Reference
	The Achievement Imperatives (pages 13-40)		
R1	**The Purpose Imperative** The Government articulates a core role for FE colleges, in particular GFECs, in supplying economically valuable skills. General FE, tertiary and specialist colleges should adopt as their primary purpose improving employability and supplying economically valuable skills.	**Accept.** We propose a refocused primary mission for the sector on employability and economically valuable skills embedded through new funding and performance incentives. We will ensure that this skills focus is clear in individual providers' missions. Sixth Form Colleges will retain their distinctive form of specialism, academic achievement and progression for 16-19 year olds.	Chapter 2 Para 2.4 – 2.9 Para 2.25 – 2.32
R2	The Government recognises that a primary focus on skills does not exclude other significant purposes in promoting social inclusion and facilitating progression.	**Accept.** Social inclusion and community purpose are still important roles for colleges and training providers. The sector will continue to offer opportunities for second-chance learning and personal development and to play an important role in ensuring learners progress as appropriate into further learning or work.	Chapter 2 Para 2.35 – 2.36
R5	An independent organisation should review the recruitment processes for Chairs of FE colleges to assess their effectiveness and make recommendations to the Government.	**Accepted and developed.** We propose to develop, in consultation with the sector, a revised governance framework. The consultation will include questions about how governors, including chairs, are appointed.	Chapter 7 Para 7.42
R7	The Centre for Excellence in Leadership (CEL) and other partners should expedite and augment the Black Leadership Initiative and the outstanding recommendations of the Commission for Black Staff in FE.	**Accept.** We will extend, from 2006, the eligibility criteria for subsidies for CEL programmes and services to include groups currently under-represented in leadership positions.	Chapter 4 Para 4.34
R9	**The Quality Imperative** The LSC should, working with FE colleges, develop an intensive one year development programme for the under-performing colleges who are in the failing category. The QIA and CEL should give major support to these institutions during this period. Those colleges or departments that do not pass a re-inspection should be made the subject of a contestability review, organised by the LSC, which could result in the removal of services, changes in management or the closure of the college.	**Accept.** We will intervene rapidly and decisively to tackle failure and underperformance. The LSC will give notice to improve (usually 1 year) to underperforming providers or source alternative provision. Such providers will be expected to work with a QIA improvement advisor and CEL (where appropriate) and to produce an improvement plan. Where sufficient improvement is not achieved, the LSC will take appropriate action which could include securing alternative provision or new management from another (public or private) provider which could be via contest/competition.	Chapter 5 Para 5.2 – 5.8
R32	**The Reputation Imperative** The Government and the LSC should promote widely the clear purpose and strong brand for FE linked to the skills mission and there needs to be a long term consistency in this promotion.	**Accept.** Focussing the sector on employability and economic impact as its primary mission will strengthen its image and reputation. We will address Government and LSC promotion of this purpose as part of the reputation management review – see R34 below.	Chapter 8 Para 8.8 – 8.10
R33	All college principals should be active locally in promoting their services and the college brand and vision to local stakeholders. Principals of the larger FE colleges, in particular, should take on	**Accept.** We welcome steps colleges are already taking to raise their own profile, including through the 157 group of large urban colleges.	Chapter 8 Para 8.10

	a promotional role at regional and national level.		
R34	The DfES, LSC and AoC should be invited to bring forward proposals for reputation management.	**Accept.** We have commissioned a review of reputation management to look at how Government, LSC and colleges could improve the way colleges, providers and the system are promoted. The review will include developing proposals for a communication strategy for the FE system.	Chapter 8 Para 8.9
	Improving Management and Funding (pages 41-55)		
R44	College governance arrangements should not be changed, but the Government, with FE colleges, should take steps to improve the diversity of governing bodies. The Government should also develop a guide to good governance to underpin the new purpose and clarity roles and responsibilities.	**Accept.** We will consult on a new governance framework which clearly articulates the roles and responsibilities of governing bodies and includes consideration of its composition.	Chapter 7 Para 7.39 – 7.42
	The Strategic Architect		
R45	The Government gives a stronger focus and interest in FE colleges, and what they can offer.	**Accept.** Our proposals for a clear mission and action to drive up quality and responsiveness will strengthen the position of colleges and place them at the centre of our agenda for skills. We will work with the sector to promote that purpose widely and to raise the profile of colleges and providers.	Chapter 2 Para 2.4 – 2.9 Chapter 8 Para 8.8 – 8.10
	The Learning and Skills Council		
R47	The LSC should develop its operational leadership role of the system, including a key regional role between the national body and localities.	**Accept.** The LSC are implementing this as part of their *agenda for change.*	Chapter 7 Para 7.33 - 7.38
	Improving Infrastructure (pages 63-68)		
R70	The Government introduces clearer 'standards' and 'measures' for effective leadership that incentivise and reward outstanding work.	**Accept.** As part of the workforce strategy, LLUK will be producing nationally recognised standards and consulting on the mandatory qualifications for leaders in colleges.	Chapter 4 Para 4.28
R71	The Government introduces new, radical approaches to bring in effective leaders from outside and ensure their success and impact. In the first instance it would be prudent to devise a programme to recruit and train 50 new senior middle managers a year from other sectors.	**Accept.** We propose to introduce a flexible support package for institutions seeking to recruit managers from outside the sector.	Chapter 4 Para 4.30
R72	The Government should consider how the synergies between National College for School Leadership, HE Leadership Foundation and CEL could be developed to simplify the leadership landscape, make best use of resources. And the Government should consider whether amalgamation is the best way of doing this.	**Accept.** We expect the CEL Board to work closely with both the National College of School Leadership and the Leadership Foundation for HE to secure alignment of missions. Looking ahead, we will explore whether there is scope or need for closer integration.	Chapter 7 Para 7.32
R73	Government and colleges find a solution to make leadership development more affordable so more colleges engage.	**Accept.** CEL will continue to offer a wide range of support for leaders, managers and aspiring managers. We expect individuals and organisations to invest in development for their own benefit but we have asked CEL to review and extend their subsidies for particular groups. We have also asked them to explore the use of technologies to make learning more efficient and accessible.	Chapter 4 Para 4.34

Table 4.1: Selected recommendations from: *Realising the Potential: A review of the future role of FE Colleges: How DfES and LSC are addressing Sir Andrew Foster's recommendations*

Note: this is a selected list of some recommendations mainly affecting leadership and management. For the full list, see the government White Paper on FE.

Summary

Chapter 4 outlines 'senior' versus 'middle' management and 'executive' roles in the context of senior management, and line management roles and duties in further education, depicting these in a simplified example of a hierarchical organogram. The concept of functional management is described and briefly discussed. The role of 'governance' versus 'leadership and management' is outlined, as are links with national, regional and local leaders and managers, and the importance of these is noted. A DfES notice outlining the role of governors is included for reference. Selected recommendations from the Annex to the White Paper are included in Table 4.1: the full list of recommendations is available online.

5: Problems with rotten managers and leaky leaders

When evil men plot, good men must plan ... Where evil men would seek to perpetuate an unjust status quo, good men must seek to bring into being a real order of justice.

Martin Luther King Jr

Problems with leadership and management

In 1887, British historian Lord Acton, later Regius Professor of Modern History at Cambridge University, wrote in a letter to Bishop Mandell Creighton:

> Liberty is not a means to a higher political end. It is itself the highest political end ... liberty is the only object which benefits all alike, and provokes no sincere opposition ... The danger is not that a particular class is unfit to to govern. Every class is unfit to govern ... Power tends to corrupt, and absolute power corrupts absolutely. (Acton, 1887)

Lord Acton was an insightful and knowledgeable historian, whose words, '*Power tends to corrupt, and absolute power corrupts absolutely*' have lived on, echoing a stringent awareness of principles about human nature regarding the use of power that have rung true for more than a hundred years.

Admit it or not, we humans tend to enjoy having power. When we get too much of it, which we are able too easily to weald over other people in leadership and management situations, there can be problems if we let this go to our heads. If this characteristic is additionally combined, in leaders, with ambition for more power and/or with naive and weak judgement, we can be in for real trouble – and sometimes, as in many political stories about rotten managers and leaky leaders, in serious trouble that will badly affect many professional and personal lives.

Problems with leadership and management are often about the misuse of power by those who have grabbed it more or less ruthlessly for themselves. As Stephen Covey observes, '90 per cent of all leadership failures are character failures' (Covey, 2004: 147). What is puzzling is the reason why so many otherwise intelligent people are taken in, even sometimes cleverly beguiled and charmed, by manipulative managers and problematic leaders. And why so many otherwise intelligent and pleasant people can become somewhat monster-like when they realize they have enough authority and Teflon-like cunning to begin doing more or less as they like if the few people who might challenge them can easily be bought off, hoodwinked or got rid of. Hence the profound importance of the work done by the Nolan Committee on Standards in Public Life (1995), which monitors and reminds us of these all too human tendencies.

There are destructive educational leader-managers who, regrettably, demonstrate what Bob Challis referred to as 'bad faith' to students and, furthermore, shrug this off as unimportant. When I interviewed him in 2004 just prior to his retirement from a long and successful career as a Principal in Abingdon College, Bob observed:

> . . . what I have always tried to assert . . . is . . . quality and student success, particularly student success. I feel very strongly that when students come here they are entering into an understanding with the college and there is a strong moral dimension to this . . . It's the moral issue that if a student for any particular purpose joins the college to achieve some particular goal, then, if the college doesn't believe sincerely that they can achieve that goal and that they, the college, can help them and make sure it happens, then there is serious bad faith in there somewhere. So I think any areas where students tend not to succeed need very, very close looking at . . . the first priority has to be the proper growth and success of the students who join us . . . (Bob Challis, interview 2004 (Jameson, 2006))

Values-based leadership and management is necessary to achieve good faith in college provision and among staff and students at all levels. At the opposite end of the spectrum, when managers start to display a lack of ethical awareness, a dearth of humanity, an overweening competitiveness and insensitive levels of arrogance towards their staff, it is time to try to change this or else begin to show such managers the door. Sometimes people grow to develop undesirable characteristics as a direct result of holding privileged positions. In other cases, individuals will do anything to be promoted, demonstrating unhealthy levels of competitive greed in lying, cheating, stealing other people's work, bullying subordinates away and pushing themselves forward aggressively, showing, in all, such undesirable characteristics that you wonder how interviewing panels can be so blind when such individuals are appointed to higher levels. 'Toxic' leaders are, however, notoriously obsequious to their superiors and so may not be spotted by managers above them. A typology for spotting rotten managers, leaky leaders and toxic bosses is provided in Figure 5.1, adapted for FE from a *Personnel Today* article. Regrettably, it is not entirely a work of fiction.

Ethical fading
Mistakes in appointment in senior, middle and first-line leadership and management still happen, all the time. Interviewing panels are sometimes poor at separating out the wheat from the chaff. Alvesson and Sveningsson (2003) begin to provide some answer to the reasons why this happens, describing three moral aspects of leadership: the 'good, bad and ugly'. These researchers indicate that leaders and managers can move between these states when facing the ambiguous and difficult challenges of the many demands of tricky situations requiring leadership. In other words, some leader–managers become tainted by the very situation of being in possession of power ('power corrupts'), gradually declining in performance and in their sense of ethical duty of staff, students and the institution, on the slippery slope towards the creation of unhealthy institutions. The question is, to what extent can this process be turned around? Sometimes, it is possible for leader–managers who have become too controlling to effect a turn-around if circumstance or individual warning propels them towards a change of practice.

Failures of leadership: How to identify bad managers and toxic bosses in FE

In *Personnel Today*, Angela O'Connor (O'Connor, 2006) listed her selection of the top ten mistakes made by leaders, as cited below, based on the book, *Bad Leadership* by Barbara Kellerman. We have adapted and added to these specifically for further education.

1. *The 'I'm invisible' leader*: if things are going pear-shaped, you won't find me around. I won't be out in the institution, either. I'm much more likely to be doing important stuff, like emails, or pursuing my own interests to further my career in sunnier places or at important meetings with the LSC.
2. *The 'I'm ready for my close up' leader*: I'll take the credit without acknowledging the contribution of the team. I like to talk about valuing people, but I don't want them to make me look bad. There's only room for one ego around here and that's mine. When I am up for promotion, I will mercilessly take your work, claim it as my own, and be photographed for the press in front of your work without acknowledging you.
3. *Mr or Ms Teflon*: it won't go wrong on my watch, and if it does it'll be your fault. I'll make sure my back is covered by always asking for advice to be confirmed in writing. After all, I have to put myself first. When the heat is on for an inspection or audit, I will make sure I am out on an important mission so that you have to do the work in my place. On my return, if you were successful, it will be my success and my promotion, and if you failed, it will be your failure and your departure.
4. *The coward*: I talk tough, but when there's bad news, I think you might be the right person to give the message rather than me. I also run away from the key tasks in inspections and audits, like Mr/Ms Teflon.
5. *The corporate hypocrite*: there is one rule for me and another for everyone else. Not practising what I preach means I pretend to adhere to corporate values in public, but behind closed doors do the opposite. I also tend to cheat on my family, partner, friends and sometimes my bank, if I can get away with it.
6. *The 'couldn't manage my way out of a paper bag' leader*: I talk about performance management, then set people off without giving clear direction. When my expectations are not met I know who to blame: you. I may have to yell at you in public – no harm in showing my authority.
7. *The incompetent*: I am incompetent, condescending, patronizing, paternalistic and somewhat reminiscent of a bad day in *The Office*. I say all the right words but you still want to punch me because, fundamentally, I can't do my job. What's worse, I really don't know this, and I think I'm great. Always.
8. *The micro-manager*: I love getting involved in your work. I need to know every detail of what you are doing and why. It may mess up your deadlines a bit, but that's your problem. No, I am *not* a bully!
9. *The emotionally obtuse*: I always listen to the 'yes' people rather than the 'what if' people because I'm afraid of challenge and see it as disrespectful. I like the 'three wise monkeys' way of management: I neither see, hear, nor speak evil (it has kept me in this job). I like to run a safe, very tidy ship.
10. *The rude, bullying and/or unreconstructed leader*: I use football and cricket analogies, littered with funny references to staff, when I am not swearing wittily or telling my clever jokes. I don't know why you find my jokes offensive: my pub friends always laugh at them. I have not yet understood the college's *Diversity Policy*, because I didn't read it: it's all overblown nonsense, anyway: I don't see what the fuss is all about with this political correctness. Of course I never say this, though, because the governors might not like it. I am always charming to people in power. I enjoy looking at the office secretaries, using my whistling skills. Someone once tried to complain that I was harassing them, but they didn't get very far: I have lots of friends in high places. So I just rang them to say the person had a mental problem and they should ignore the story. If you ever *really* try to get at me, I will make your life an endless misery.

Figure 5.1: Analysis of leadership failures from article in *Personnel Today* by Angela O'Connor

'Ethical fading', identified by researchers Tenbrunsel and Messick (2004), comments on the important role played by self-deception in unethical decision-making. These writers analyse the progressively deteriorating shifts in moral standards that can occur in unethical leadership and management situations. It can be difficult to explain, otherwise, how intelligent people who regard themselves as conscientious and worthwhile leaders can succumb to unethical practices. A self-interested slippage in moral standards can occur in leader-managers who believe that they are upholding moral principles while simultaneously sanctioning unethical or shady 'deals' on the other (Tenbrunsel and Messick, 2004: 223–36). This useful identification – that leaders can deceive themselves through the 'fading' morality of ethical slippages that rationalize their own poor behaviour, greed and immoral actions, with arguments of economic necessity or the need for change, for example – is helpful in explaining how corrupt practices can occur in otherwise seemingly well-ordered institutions. It also helps to explain why many in power usually vigorously deny any such thing. There are complex psychological mechanisms by which those who engage in problematic professional practices protect themselves by progressively avoiding self-blame.

Cultivating inner freedoms

Lord Acton also believed that 'Liberty is the prevention of control by others'. He observed that achieving freedom from control by other people 'requires self-control and, therefore, religious and spiritual influences; education, knowledge, well-being'. Whatever our personal value system or religious persuasion, in order to be truly free, we need to evolve to the point at which we are capable of acting as self-actualizing, authentic, values-based human beings in the work situations in which we find ourselves, at whatever place in the hierarchy we happen to be. The concept of 'distributed leadership' envisages that leadership roles are distributed throughout management hierarchies, and that individuals have the power to participate fully in the shaping of an institution, at whatever level they find themselves. This idea of fully functioning democratic distributed leadership is rare to find in practice, however, and may only be cultivated through the good offices of genuinely collaborative upper-level managers promoting values-based collective understanding. It is also essential, within that, to ensure there is a recognition of diversity and pluralism in the agreement of a common values system for the institution. Unfortunately, some organizations are not capable of recognizing diversity, pluralism or employee autonomy and freedom.

Failing colleges – scandals, messes and scapegoats

The Foster Review (2005) on further education, making recommendations on England's 389 FE colleges (NA, 2005) in November 2005, warned that 'one in 10 further education colleges is failing to give students a decent education and should be subjected to tougher sanctions including outright closure'. In calling overall for a more distinct focus on skills and employability, more coherent education policies and better leadership for the FE sector, Foster recommended punitive actions against what the review team described as 'a significant minority' of colleges (around 10 per cent) which, for FE, were 'a millstone around its neck' in failing to provide a good education for students (Foster, 2005; Smithers, 2005). The Government White Paper *Further Education: Raising Skills, Improving Life Chances* (DfES, 2006) has indicated that part of the drive to improve standards in teaching and learning nationally in FE will result in the 'elimination' of failing colleges, following improvement orders which will allow changes to be made within one year.

Foster and his review team (2005) labelled further education as 'the neglected "middle child"' between universities and schools, saying that the UK was 'in danger of being complacent about skills . . . By all league tables I can think of we are falling behind. We will not have the current powerful economy we have in this country if we do not invest much more seriously in skills' (*ibid.*). The Foster Review ruled out a 'big bang reconfiguration of FE', in terms of large-scale restructurings, but called for the 'residual rump' of the 10 per cent or so underperforming colleges to be 'given notice to improve which will last for one year', following which continued failure would lead to take-over by another institution or closure (Foster, 2005). John Brennan, Chief Executive of the AoC (Association of Colleges), commenting on the Foster Review in November 2005, broadly welcomed its recommendations, including the need to be tough with failing colleges, stating that colleges would 'welcome an even sharper focus on skills and a closer relationship with employers' (Smithers, 2005).

We have therefore moved from the position in the 1990s, in when colleges such as Halton and Bilston Community College were able to perform in ways which were deeply problematic but which remained undetected for some time. Although there may have been elements of scapegoating in the Bilston Community College affair, researchers Goddard-Patel and Whitehead (2001) point out the serious concerns about management in FE which affected the sector in the 1990s and at the beginning of the new century:

> One important and very visible consequence of the plight of FE has been a series of college 'failures'. The colleges of Bilston, Halton and Wirral were particularly prominent in this regard, but the litany stretches back through the 1990s ... At a Public Accounts Committee hearing ... [in] ... 2000, the Chief Executive of the FEFC admitted that the number of colleges described as 'financially weak' had risen from 56 to 72, 17 per cent of the sector. He also accepted that despite substantial additional funding, student numbers had dropped from a peak of 3.543 million in 1997/98 to 3.417 million in 1999/2000 (House of Commons, 2001). The growing list of 'failing colleges' merely serves to confirm the fragile state of FE, a point not lost on the current government when it ushered in yet another major shift in ... policy via the 'Learning to Succeed' White Paper (DfEE, 1999a). (Goddard-Patel and Whitehead, 2001:181–2)

Goddard-Patel and Whitehead explored the problem of 'failing colleges' in this era in detail, noting a number of factors which contributed to 'failure', including the lack of staff training in management techniques in the early 1990s post-incorporation period and the problematic sudden introduction of a quasi-market economy to FE. They examined the counter-productive effect of market-driven policies on further educational institutions, analysing in particular the case of Bilston Community College, which was closed in 1999. These authors (*ibid.* 2001) note that the 'naming and shaming' policy adopted by the government at this time in respect of 'failing colleges' was destructive in its effect. These lessons are instructive as a warning to those involved in FE in the future. Nevertheless, the disastrous messes and scandals of that era have now been resolved, hopefully never to be repeated. We are now into a new era in which the numbers of low performing providers have radically been reduced to 10 per cent or below, and those that still remain will be 'weeded out' even further in coming years. The problem with the language used for 'eliminating' failure tends to open up, however, a micro-management type of coercive approach which does not necessarily directly result in improvement.

Loss of staff in constant restructurings – amnesiac organizations

Constant institutional restructurings in response to external demands, centrally-imposed government, LSC/FEFC targets and regional imperatives for mergers have occurred in the further education system for some decades. An incessant drive to 'restructure' can lead to loss of important organizational memory. Sometimes staff with the most valuable skills, knowledge and qualifications leave the institution quickly when they realize potentially negative changes may be on the way. In Jameson and Hillier (2003: 31–52) we discussed the issue of organizational change in post-compulsory education and proposed that organizational changes should be planned and researched in advance effectively using a 'Reflect' model which encourages leader-managers in institutions to take control of changes proactively. Good planning, consultation with and recognition of staff can facilitate minimal negative results from ill-thought through top-down imposed changes. If good planning and consultation does not take place, there may be increasing alienation and loss of staff. This includes the loss of rich, locally-situated institutional memories of departing staff and tends to erode the kinds of collegial culture that may be an important feature of organisations in which people know each other well and have built up both friendliness and trust (McNay, 2002).

Organizational amnesia and anorexia

Organizational amnesia is discussed in Jameson, 2006, in which we note that radical thinning out of the institutional workforce can lead to *'anorexic'* organisations (Bedeian and Armenakis, 1998). These kinds of negative changes can occur as a result of staff loss following top-down management imperatives to perform in heavily audited institutions. McNay observed in 2006 that the supposed benefits of 'new managerialism' can be described in the following way:

> The new order is variously described as being characterized by rampant entrepreneurialism; regulation and surveillance; corporatism; complicity and collusion; a burgeoning audit culture; increased 'instumentalism'; and massification, marketization and managerialism. New Managerialism's benefits are celebrated as producing enhanced levels of the three Es – Economy, Efficiency and Effectiveness – in tandem with accountability. Noticeably – a fourth E – for Equity – is absent . . .' McNay, 2006: 186

McNay writes here about university cultures, but the description is also, to an extent, applicable within FE. A managerialist culture which values efficiency over values-based leadership and collegiality in both FE and HE can arise in which leaders engage in restructuring without effective planning and consultation. Leaders are sometimes impelled by pressing needs to meet the instrumentalist demands of government and the market-place, becoming increasingly task-focused, sometimes at the expense of the well-being of staff. The most talented, valuable staff may become disillusioned by a 'managerialist' environment in which they lack creative freedom and autonomy. Well-qualified able staff may apply for posts elsewhere, leaving those who cannot be appointed to other institutions to fill up the ranks of the hierarchy in an increasingly 'amnesiac', 'anorexic' failing institution, which then tends to fulfil the famous *'Peter Principle'* ('In a hierarchy every employee tends to rise to his level of incompetence', Peters and Hull, 1969). Bedeian and Armenakis note of this kind of 'vicious circle':

> In contrast to successful organisations in which cream rises to the top, organisations falling victim to decline often suffer from the 'cesspool syndrome', wherein, figuratively speaking, dreck floats to the top. In declining organisations, the early departure of qualified employees will inhibit recovery and, if unchecked, can accelerate decline. Bedeian and Armenakis (1998)

Numerous examples of leadership and management failures occurred during the 1990s in further education, notably in the post-incorporation era in which colleges also faced significant new corporate demands, funding cuts and incentives for quick entrepreneurial growth. Many of these could perhaps have been avoided with greater levels of support and structured staff development to leader-managers in the FE system, of the kind that is now being ably provided by the Centre for Excellence in Leadership through its training and research programmes. Leader-managers and staff in FE also often tended to have high levels of occupational stress in previous eras, as noted by Shain and Gleeson (1999). McNay also described much earlier research findings on the difficult realities of college management in terms of stress, financial cutbacks, work overloads and problems with restructuring, based on the experiences of around 200 staff in the late 1980s (McNay, 1988). McNay's executive summary from nearly twenty years ago could in fact still apply to many areas of FE today:

> This report paints a vivid picture of aspects of day-to-day life in colleges, and of the range of problems which managers face at all levels. Many of these managers feel that they are under-resourced and under-prepared; that they are over-restricted in the exercise of their professional judgements and skills by factors and agencies beyond their control; and that

when they struggle to perform to their best within the limits which exist, they are under-recognised. (McNay, 1988, vii)

Things that block achievement in further education

In 2004–05 I interviewed a range of successful leaders in the learning and skills sector about the problems in leadership and management that FE leader-managers can experience. They all replied with useful examples of things that blocked achievement and prevented progress in organizational effectiveness. Selected quotations on this from Sedgmore, Khan, Challis and Moss are provided in Jameson, 2006. We provide here further responses from Andrew Morris and Ruth Silver on 'things that block achievement in post-compulsory education':

> What is clear to me is that people in positions in the top layer have to know what their scope for intervention, or action, is, and what their scope for knowing about things is. And it is nothing like the scope that people in the middle layers or lower layers have: it is completely different. It is very difficult, this, because you have to re-learn everything as you move from one layer to another. You have to abandon your previous command knowledge and action, and the rules at the next layer may be actually the reverse of the rules at the lower layer. So, for instance, if I want to be a good physics teacher, it is crucial that I have a good command of the factual details of physics and of the students I am teaching, and I absolutely cut myself off from French teaching, or history or anything, so focus is important. Whereas at the higher levels, you must not do things that the person on the level below you should be doing. This is what is very common ... people carrying out these crazy roles, where they are trying to attend to every detail and trying to keep command: a) they do it badly, because they can't fit it in, and b) they disempower the people underneath them.. So you get dysfunctional organisations all the way through. Andrew Morris, interview, 2005 (Jameson, 2006)

Ruth Silver observed of things that block achievement that:

I think the hardest one is when you lose wonderful key members of staff – that's a mixed feeling, because you're so pleased that they are going on to greater things, but they leave a hole in your plans and in your desires and so on. And that loss of memory is also a loss of desire in the organisation, because they were the ones pushing things forward and my experience has taught me it takes two years to catch up again. ... I've also learned that new people bring new things so I've learned to let go of it, but it does stunt achievement for a while. I think the bidding processes of the government because sometimes you've no idea why you've been successful and the money is never enough: in a community like this we don't get lots of money from student fees: they are poor students. So we depend on bidding successfully for projects to expand the learning offer and if that doesn't happen, then again achievement is stunted until we find another way of doing that. Systems changes: you know 'we're not funding this anymore' or 'we're funding that instead'. Quite often, colleges are kind of in a hiatus in the pursuit of achievement for the organisation and students. And some of the measures used by the measuring bodies I think are inappropriate. So the achievement measures that are flaunted don't begin to reflect how much work it took for my students and staff to get there. You know, the fact that getting these achievements in this college is not the same as getting them in a sixth form college so some of the measures themselves, are blocks to achievement ... Ruth Silver, Interview, 2005 (Jameson, 2006)

Support for failing colleges and leaders in trouble

A useful feature of the growing interest in supporting and raising the status of the FE sector demonstrated by the recent Foster Review (2005) and Government White Paper on Further Education (2006) is the recognition that failing colleges at least need some support and time to recover as well as scrutiny. Failing colleges get that way through a combination of problematic institutional histories, the legacy of others' many failures, personal problems with leaders, difficult staff, over-demanding targets, family or health problems, and difficulties specific to the local area. Leaders in trouble should seek help. Support can be provided by mentors, coaches, supervisors, peer group 'buddies' in management roles themselves, friends and family members. Sometimes just sharing the burden of difficulties can help to turn the corner towards solving the problem.

The first, crucial step for leaders challenged with significant difficulties in 'failing' institutions is to be honest about the real problems the institution faces, and to address these directly with a realistic series of action plans to overcome difficulties, in a progressive sequence of ongoing improvements. Resources and support from external partners may be available if leaders acknowledge problems and ask for help. Truthful self-analysis on the part of leaders to determine whether they are in fact in the right job is important. Not everyone is suited to management roles, especially the demanding role of principal, and it is good to acknowledge this.

Spotting rotten managers and leaky leaders

It is quite difficult to identify destructive trends in leadership and management, particularly if leader-managers are pseudo-charming and pull the wool over people's eyes with skill and charm. Remember the story of the development of Nazi Germany? Chater (2005) outlines the problems caused by archetypes of destructive leadership in education, saying that although management, as a discipline, has become well defined and respected as a science and philosophy, it still lacks a strong ethical values base, and hence it urgently needs to address this 'theoretical poverty':

> ...The evidence of these undeclared values is also in literature and in the traumatised imagination and memory of the previous century. That century's greatest crime was also among its most organised, managed operations; it is with a dreadful chill that we read the personal accounts of survivors, and try to see into their experiences, for instance through this memory by Victoria Ancona-Vincent:
>
> > After climbing out of the wagon on to the ramp, we were separated.... all I could see was a mass of people in front

and behind me.... slowly the column moved forward until I found myself standing in front of a small wooden desk. (Ancona–Vincent 1995: 332–3)

In this and other Holocaust accounts of meeting a desk, it seems sometimes that the desk has become the symbol of implacability, of the means whereby people are dominated or manipulated into acquiescence in their own destruction. If the practice of management can lend itself to such ends, as easily and well as to those which promote life, there are questions to be asked about its ethical roots and its sometimes implied claim to higher rationality than other disciplines. (Chater, 2005)

Management as a discipline needs to come to terms with these potentially devastating consequences of the unethical and problematic sides to managerialism when the corrupting potential of power is allowed to take root and replace the more beneficient good values of managers. Let's look at some of these problems in a bit more detail.

Defeating bullies, outlasting 'mobbing' and blame cultures

There are many ways in which leadership and management staff can defeat bullies and outlast a 'mobbing' and blame culture. The first step, however, is to be aware that this is what is affecting your institution or yourself, so that from this awareness, action can be taken. We provide, in the leadership and management guidelines in Section 4, some recommended strategies for organizational development to address these problems. Anti-bullying strategies and tactics can be employed non-violently and straightforwardly to address these problems. The psychology of workplace bullying and 'mobbing' is quite complex, but is well worth investigating if you think that your institution is affected by problems of harassment, bullying or victimization of staff. The website Bully on Line, part of The Field Foundation (www.bullyonline.org/), has a wealth of free resources and recommendations of publications available on anti-bullying strategies and techniques, including guidance on the identification of bullying, the problem of blame cultures at work, and mobbing by gangs of people in the workplace (Field, 1996).

Healing anorexic and paranoiac institutions

Action to improve emotional intelligence in the workplace can be of beneficial use in healing the kind of anorexic and paranoiac institutions we have outlined above. Other strategies to improve organizational learning include the following:

- Continuous improvement and quality improvement cycles
- Cultural change through communities of practice
- Knowledge management theory and practice
- Learning organizations theory and practice
- Programme and course evaluation techniques
- Strategic planning and self-evaluation
- Total quality management (TQM)

We provide references and further details on these and other organizational improvement techniques in Section Four and in the Appendices.

Creating holistic transformation through good leadership

In Section Four we also recommend ways to create holistic transformation through good leadership at a range of levels, distributed throughout the organization. If leaders can employ change strategies to enable their staff to face up to, acknowledge and address deep problems within the institution, by, for example, techniques for knowledge management and the recognition of under-examined assumptions, wholesale beneficial change can be achieved.

Summary

In this chapter we reflect on leadership in the context of problems and failures. We note the requirement of leaders to maintain a sense of personal ethics and integrity without succumbing to temptations of power. We consider 'good, bad and ugly' leaders, noting the key issue of 'ethical fading' that can occur when leaders explain away poor behaviour by deceiving themselves. We provide an adapted article from *Personnel Today* developed for the book in Figure 5.1: 'How to identify bad managers and toxic bosses in FE'. We discuss institutions in trouble in the context of 'organizational anorexia' and 'the cesspool syndrome' (Bedeian and Armenakis, 1998) and then look at things that block achievement in FE, citing extracts from interviews with leaders on this question. We round up the chapter with a recommendation that leaders in trouble should seek help, as significant support may be available to them if they have the conscientiousness and courage to ask. Finally, we suggest some ways to spot and deal with rotten managers, leaky leaders and 'toxic' bosses, bullying and mobbing cultures. We advise on some strategies for the creation of holistic organizational transformation, recognizing that the discipline of management itself needs to incorporate a higher prioritization of values-based ethical standards and emotional intelligence.

Section Two: Models of Leadership in FE Institutions

6: Formal and informal models of leadership

In organizations, real power and energy is generated through relationships. The patterns of relationships and the capacities to form them are more important than tasks, functions, roles, and positions.
Margaret Wheatly, Leadership and the New Science

Positional authority and formal hierarchical models

As we discussed in Chapter 4, traditional models of leadership are based on positional authority linked to formal hierarchical institutional models and a range of different levels of authority and power in further education. A typical model of college leadership envisages the institutional hierarchy as a pyramid, with the Principal/CEO at the top, reporting to governors, the LSC (mainly) and/or DfES overall for specific purposes.

The Principal/CEO is supported usually by a Vice Principal or Assistant Principals and by a small team of senior managers (including Directors). Managers in and above this layer tend to form the Executive. Senior managers, typically everyone including directors and above, tend to line manage a number of middle managers, such as heads of departments or administrative services. These people in turn line manage progressive levels of staff within the overall teaching and administrative staff workforce.

To simplify, the model depicted here does not have all the multiple varieties of management possibilities in further education, e.g. deans and heads of faculty, subject coordinators, programme leaders, librarians, MIS staff, ILT/ICT officers, learning resources staff and cross-institutional functional coordinators. There are many different interpretations of hierarchical modelling of basic power structures in further education. Different models will depend on the individual history of the institution, the regional priorities from past history, the type of institution and the results of organizational restructurings or initiatives carried out in the past by a range of senior staff and agencies.

Sixth form colleges, for example, typically have a more teaching-centred workforce. A sixth form college principal and senior managers may perceive themselves to be senior teachers, carrying a partial teaching load in addition to management duties. By contrast, in a general FE college offering vocational training, managers are more likely to have adopted businesslike management models, with senior leaders who regard themselves primarily as full-time managers without teaching duties. The college executive, governing body and local and regional LSC management will invariably influence the structures in particular institutions.

Positional authority

Positional authority is critically important in shaping institutional hierarchies in further education, in which a more 'managerial' culture has been prevalent than in some other sectors of education since the Further and Higher Education Act of 1992 and the resultant incorporation of colleges in 1993. During 1993, the Further Education Funding Council was set up, managed the strategic operations of colleges, and was disbanded, to be replaced by the Learning and Skills Council, with its 47 local arms, in 2001. Many challenges were placed on leaders and managers in the sector during this period by the numerous demands placed on colleges to manage their own budgets in the same way as corporate businesses operating competitively. As we explored in the Introduction and Chapter 1, and as many researchers and academic writers have noted (see Avis, 2003; Frearson, 2002; Leader, 2004; Lumby and Tomlinson, 2000; and Randle and Brady, 1997a, 1997b) a culture of 'managerialism' and 'performativity' developed to meet FEFC and LSC market-led funding systems, in which the concept of 'bums on seats' (i.e. numbers of students enrolled) was critical to meet funding targets.

In this era, significant emphasis was placed on institutional strategic planning processes and on meeting external target-driven funding requirements. Mission statements, institutional strategies and operational plans, performance indicators, performance targets, quality assurance systems, business-led processes, appraisal systems and a range of financial control and monitoring systems became the norm for learning and skills institutions.

'Boys' own' culture

To meet these demands, specialist FE management posts were created to take over certain functions formerly alien to many colleges. Facilities management, marketing, MIS, ICT and enterprise initiatives of colleges created a business-driven approach uncomfortably different from the professional ethos of staff previously more used to public service traditions of teaching, student support and administration. The values of principals and senior management teams were shaped increasingly by the demand for a 'tough' style of operating which distanced management from teaching and support staff (Lumby, 2003). Shain (1999) and Lumby (2003) also noted that the prevailing style of management in this era tended to be one described by critics as 'boys' own' or 'real men', while other researchers described this kind of domineering style as 'chauvinistic', 'cowboy' or 'bullish'. The implication in all such descriptions is that the leadership and management styles adopted during the post-incorporation era were primarily dominated by values labelled more 'masculine' than 'feminine', such as autocratic, aggressive, controlling and directing behaviours. By contrast, more 'feminine' types of behaviours might be labelled in this kind of definition as more democratic, yielding, negotiating and 'softer' in style.

This kind of division is, however, somewhat superficial, providing only a rough hypothesis. It is evident that there are many women who operate with predominantly or exclusively 'masculine' styles of leadership. In addition, many men often operate with 'democratic', 'negotiating' and 'softer' elements of leadership, which are sometimes superficially labelled 'feminine'. The picture is therefore generally much more complex than any single definition could capture: the concept of gender-specific styles is problematic. Nevertheless, whether 'male' or 'female', there is evidence that a bullying culture emerged during this period, which has not entirely disappeared, as the results of the leadership survey reported earlier indicate.

The gap between senior and middle managers in FE

The gap between senior and middle managers has been described by Lumby and Briggs (Lumby, 2003: 286) as 'the well-documented difference in perception of the middle manager role from the perspective of senior and middle managers' (Briggs, 2001). As discussed earlier, in general FE colleges in particular, a form of 'new managerialism' developed in the post-1992 incorporation era, which was distinguished from other levels of leadership in colleges. Lumby noted that the 'stretching of tasks over senior and middle management' seemed to have resulted in leadership situations in which 'neither middle managers nor senior managers appear to be focused on learning' (ibid.: 288).

Lumby reported from the results of her research that this situation observed in general FE colleges seemed to be very different from the more pedagogically focused distributed leadership culture found more often in sixth form colleges. In sixth-form institutions, possibly because they tended to be smaller, with a more focused mission and client group, the whole of the leadership team tended to be focused on learning. Working in FE colleges and adult education institutions myself during the era 1984–2000, I certainly noticed this tendency for sixth form institutions to be focused on teaching and learning activities at senior levels, as, for example, most principals of sixth form colleges had a small teaching timetable, whereas the CEOs of colleges seldom, if ever, did, as we noted earlier in this chapter. This difference in focus between FE and sixth form leadership was also noted by one of the interviewees in research on leadership and management during 2004–6:

> ... I worked in an organization that comprised FE staff and school staff, a sixth form centre. Essentially, the key role for leaders in schools was based on the 'leading teacher' concept

that you lead the core business, that you lead the teaching, whereas in further education, the leaders didn't necessarily see themselves as championing learning or teaching, they saw themselves as essentially business managers of an operation, or business entrepreneurs of growth strategy for a department, or something like that. (Interviewee for leadership research study, 2005)

Current changing conditions are affecting models of leadership, including changes and updates to governance and to conditions of service for staff, changing roles and responsibilities (with the introduction of new standards for teachers and managers), new legislation, and the changes in profiles of principals and other key leaders in PCET, including demographic shifts, with the inclusion of more female and black leaders. Leaders have a constant need to keep up to date with new developments, and so we include a range of links to further information in the Appendices and References.

Models of leadership: conceptual pluralism

Bush (2006) is among those who has noted that theories of leadership tend to be 'normative' in that they suggest to us how things should be done, rather than just describe them. Simkins (1999) observes the difference between descriptive models of leadership and normative models, noting that descriptive models attempt to describe what is happening in leadership situations, whereas normative models outline what should happen in FE. All theories are only attempts to either explain or prescribe what actually does or should happen through the actual practice of leadership, so all are somewhat partial, and therefore Bush (2006) notes that the most useful leadership model may be the recognition that a 'conceptual pluralism' (Griffiths, 1987) is best suited to deal with the multiplicity of real-life situations that we encounter in educational institutions, since some theories are suited to some situations, and others are relevant in other contexts.

Within the debate on leadership, it is important that both practice and theory have an ongoing role in shaping our concepts and practices. Bush observes that 'theory is an unfashionable notion in education, particularly in England and Wales', since theory and practice in education are often regarded as separate (Bush and Bell, 2002: 15), but that the '... ultimate test of theory is whether it improves practice' (*ibid.*: 29). We point out here some major leadership theories (see Figure 6.1) and provide further information on follow-up sources in the References and Appendices. We provide 48 of some of the basic models of leadership in Figure 6.1, in recognition that, internationally, there are many different leadership theories.

Formal models – structural, systems, bureaucratic, rational models

Formal models of leadership are based on positional hierarchy and are generally described as *managerial leadership*, in which leader-managers are mainly concerned with the existing duties, functions

• Authentic leadership	• Great Man theory	• Synergistic leadership
• Authoritative leadership	• Group leadership	• Super-leadership
• Autocratic leadership	• Heroic leadership	• Self-managed leadership
• Behavioural leadership	• Instructional leadership	• Servant leadership
• Charismatic leadership	• Intellectual leadership	• Shared leadership
• Coercive leadership	• Invisible leadership	• Situational leadership
• Cognitive resource theory	• Leader-member LMX)	• Spiritual leadership
• Collective leadership	• Living leadership	• Strategic leadership
• Community leadership	• Managerial leadership	• Systemic leadership
• Conscious leadership	• Moral leadership	• Theory X/Theory Y model
• Contingency theory	• Organisational leadership	• Toxic leadership
• Creative leadership	• Participative leadership	• Transactional leadership
• Democratic leadership	• Path-goal theory	• Trait leadership theory
• Distributed leadership	• Pedagogic leadership	• Transformational ldrship
• Fiedler's LPC Theory	• Person-centred leadership	• Visionary leadership
• Four framework model	• Post-herioc leadership	• Vroom-Jago-Yetton Model

Figure 6.1: Models of leadership – 48 theories (updated version of earlier model in Jameson, 2006).

and tasks to be done by employees within the organization in order that the jobs of work to be done as outlined in the strategic and operational plans can be carried out effectively. Managerial leadership tends to be task-focused and concerned more with the effective achievement of existing activities rather than envisioning a new future for the institution. In that sense, managerial leadership can sometimes be narrow-minded, bureaucratic and overly rational, assuming that employees are like cogs in a machine who just need to be set working and then maintained for everything planned to be achieved. Managerial leadership has great similarity with transactional theories and the two may be strongly aligned in organizations, stressing the task-based performance aspects of leadership at the expense of other aspects.

This can ignore the irrational, affective dimension of more people-centred dimensions of leadership, and also the importance of the larger environmental systemic aspects of leadership, which can be beyond the influence of rational individual control without systemic changes. Bush (2006) points out that:

> Most approaches to managerial leadership also assume that the behaviour of organisational members is largely rational. Authority and influence are allocated to formal positions in proportion to the status of those positions in the organisational hierarchy. (Bush, (2006)

Early leadership models – trait, behavioural, situational theories

Early *trait theories* of leadership assumed that you can distinguish leaders from followers on the basis of certain characteristics or 'traits', as observed by Stogdill (1948) and Mann (1959), for example. Popularly held assumptions that specific characteristics were necessarily attributable to leaders led to a range of early leadership studies which tried to identify what is exceptional about leaders, including a notable study by Gardner (1989).

To some extent, humans beings readily and easily tend to fall into unreflective assumptions that leadership is marked out by particular characteristics. However, further thought on this subject begins to reveal the deeper awareness that in fact leaders everywhere are differentiated by so many competing kinds of characteristics that there is no one 'dictionary of leadership attributes' which would be large enough and adaptably flexible enough to contain them all. In educational settings facing challenges in terms of diversity and inclusiveness, such as further education, it is important that 'trait' theories are not implicitly or overtly utilized to exclude certain kinds of people from leadership positions on the basis of secondary assumed factors, such as whether people who are leaders are necessarily tall, healthy, cheerful, or possess particular physical or other cultural attributes. The concept that leaders are distinguished by 'this' or 'that' characteristic in physical or personality terms is nonsense: the dangers of 'trait' theories are that these can lead to unthinkingly discriminatory appointments practices. Wright (1996) is amongst those who found that no particular characteristics differentiated leaders from followers in respect of secondary characteristics.

Behavioural leadership theories

When early researchers on 'trait theories' of leadership realized that there was no list of reliable characteristics that could always differentiate leadership, interest in behavioural leadership theory grew during the 1950s and 1960s. The managerial 'grid' of Blake and Mouton was devised (1964) to diagnose leadership behaviours and to develop these. Behavioural leadership is based on the concept of four main distinguishing elements, including concern for 'task' versus concern for 'people' (Blake and Mouton, 1964), and directive versus participative leadership, as in McGregor's (1960) 'Theory X' (directive, controlling) versus 'Theory Y' (participative, empowering) versions of leadership theory, with McGregor placing a preference on the more participative 'Theory Y' management style. Further analysis of these behavioural theories revealed, however, that they were inconsistent and also neither all-inclusive nor infallible in determining or describing what happens in effective leadership situations (Doyle and Smith, 2001; Sadler, 1997). When leadership theorists began to recognize that neither 'trait' nor 'behavioural' models really stood up in terms of the rigour of research evidence, the hunt was on yet again for an all-embracing theory of leadership. Hence researchers turned to examine contextual and situational factors in contingency models of leadership based on the specific times, places, cultures and contexts in which leadership operates.

Situational or 'contingency' leadership theories

The idea of situational leadership is that the demands of specific situations require different kinds of leadership skills. For example, it was popularly assumed that Winston Churchill was an effective wartime leader, but was not particularly suited to leadership in peacetime, when the 1939–45 Second World War was over. The adaptability of leaders to change their style to the demands of different kinds of situations was therefore regarded as the new 'holy grail' of effective leadership in the 1960s and 1970s, i.e. the idea that effective leadership was 'contingent' on the interactions between different factors, including the models of positional power accorded by the institution to the leader, the nature of the tasks and duties involved in leadership, the relationships between leaders and followers, and a range of other local variable factors.

Hence leadership and management 'gurus' Hersey and Blanchard (1977) identified that there were four different leadership 'styles' appropriate to different situations and people: (1) the *telling* style in which people need a high level of task and low level of relationship behaviour from the leader; (2) the *selling* style in which 'coaching' is necessary and a high level of task behaviour is also combined with a high level of relationship behaviour; (3) the *participating* style in which followers have a high degree of self-direction combined with low task behaviour from the leader but high relationship behaviour; (4) the *delegating* style in which followers have the greatest degree of unsupervised freedom to carry out the work, as the leader has both a low task and low relationship behaviour towards the follower (*ibid.*, 1977).

Newer models – transformational, distributed, team, ambiguity theories

In an era which is to an extent obsessed with self-improvement (see, for example, the multiplicity of 'how to' reality television programmes offering the latest fix for our various multiple faults), and in which increasingly democratic perceptions of leadership have emerged, newer models of leadership have tended to concentrate on 'transformational' and 'distributed' concepts of leadership during the past decade. Within this, 'team' or collaborative models of leadership have also increasingly emerged in education with an emphasis on practitioner professionalism and agency, while ambiguity models have developed in response to post-modernist conceptions following Foucauldian analysis of the histories of power and discourses of authority.

Examining more closely the popular idea of 'transforming' ourselves and our institutions, we need to caution that the concept of 'organizational transformation' is not necessarily tied to the question of leadership, though the 'transformational' model is sometimes understood to imply a direct link with successful change programmes. Lumby notes that there is little if any empirical evidence that either leadership itself or leadership development is directly linked to organizational performance in PCET (Lumby et al., 2004: 7). Nevertheless, there tends to be a strongly held popular assumption that there is a relationship between the leadership of an organization, the operations and outcomes achieved within it, and the programme of leadership development available to the leaders within that organization.

Transactional and transformational models of leadership
Since 'transactional leadership' essentially involves carrying out tasks in 'transactions' or exchanges between leaders and 'followers' for rewards linked with the achievement of targets and completion of work, this form of leadership can, in theory, be linked with any kind of organizational culture. McNay (1995) identified four types of institutional culture, including 'collegium', 'bureaucracy', 'corporation' and 'enterprise' cultures: each of these can coexist with transactional leadership in different ways. Transactional leaders set tasks for followers, outlining the employers' expectations and 'contingent rewards' (gains) for complying with work demands. The potentially negative outfall of non-compliance or failure involves critical feedback ('management by exception') and is discussed by Northouse (2004:178–9), Bass and Avolio (1990) and Jameson

(2006). Since transactional leadership is a rational, task-focused model of leadership which involves a theoretically straightforward exchange of work for rewards, it is situated towards the 'management' end of the leadership-management spectrum. The achievement of employment duties are linked to the 'payoff' for successful completion of tasks: transactional leadership tends to be conventional and unemotional, fitting into the existing structure, culture and expectations of the organization.

Transactional leadership appeals to the intrinsic motivations of employees for task-payment exchanges and is founded on behaviourist principles of reward for effort: a basic expectation of most management-employee salary-based employment situations. Some form of transactional leadership therefore is a useful part of most working arrangements and the model can be combined with many other types of leadership, including 'transformational' models. However, since transactional leadership is focused somewhat unemotionally on performance against tasks and goals, it is not capable within itself of extending the performance of employees beyond the norm of task completion. To that extent it is a limited model, as discussed by Northouse (2004: 179), comprised of exchanges, rewards and 'passive' or 'active' negative reinforcements. Transactional leadership does not tend to inspire vision, nor additional efforts to go beyond achieving minimum expectations. Leaders using only transactional methods may assume they are achieving all that is necessary for an organization's success, but may have difficulties raising levels of improvement in institutions when innovation, exceptional effort and new developments are required. (see also Jameson, 2006)

Transformational leadership

Transformational leadership aims to enable individuals to change and improve educational provision, and is sometimes linked to charismatic leadership models and organizational change theories. Transformational leadership is differentiated from transactional, task-focused leadership (Downton, 1973; Northouse, 2004), forming part of the 'New Leadership' concept advocated by Brymann (1992), which involves affective and charismatic aspects of leadership (Northouse, 2004:169). The process of 'transforming' organizations raises followers' hopes to achieve beneficial change in people and organizations, involving the 'whole' person, including emotions, thoughts, motives, values and longer-term ideals and plans. Similar to visionary and charismatic leadership, transformational leadership influences followers to achieve more than is ordinarily possible, by invoking distinctive moral values and ideals appropriate to the mission of the organization. Although popular, the model has also been criticized for ambiguity, vagueness and a lack of precise measurement (Northouse, 2004: 185), since proof of its success is debatable.

Transformational leadership tends to seek collaboratively to establish an idealistic 'transforming' vision, with goals and values for the institution to change the consciousness of followers in an attempt to move the organization forward in achieving the vision and values. The transformational approach can create a productive organizational culture. Bush (2003: 76–7) notes that: 'Transformational leaders succeed in gaining the commitment of followers to such a degree that ... higher levels of accomplishment become virtually a moral imperative.' However, Bush cautions that transformational leadership can become despotic respect (1992: 77–8) if the leader's values are imposed on followers inappropriately. Bass and Steidlmeier (1999) distinguish between *authentic* transformational leadership and *inauthentic* or *pseudo-transformational* leadership.

Lumby *et al.* (2004) summarize models of leadership development in post-compulsory education, including prior research findings on the positive aspects of transformational leadership from Crowther and Olsen (1997) and Leonard and Leonard (1999). Lumby *et al.* report that transformational leadership is potentially capable of achieving greater success than 'more formal' approaches, notably within education. These researchers cite evidence collected in the LSRC project *Leading Learning* (2002–04) case studies of ten 'effective organisations' in the learning and skills sector that:

A mix of transactional, transformational and distributed styles are in operation [in these successful learning and skills sector case study organizations]. Though a transformational style is seen as most effective to improve organisational performance, line managers are more often seen as employing transactional approaches ... Transformational leadership is seen as likely to be most effective in leading for and with diversity. (Lumby 2004: 8–9)

Transformational leadership is, potentially, one of the more useful adaptable new models for the learning and skills sector to achieve widespread change to implement the goals in the White Paper on FE (2006). Lumby *et al.*, (2004) observe, based on Bush and Glover (2003), that 'transformational approaches are not easily implemented' (Lumby *et al.*, 2004: 37). These researchers ask, 'If transformational approaches are indicated as highly effective and an ideal for many, why then is transactional leadership so common?' (Ibid: 149). Leaders may default to transactional models in the absence of sufficient training, mentoring, confidence and external support from, e.g. coaches and mentors.

Since transactional models of leadership are based on hierarchical or positional power, the model is often contrasted with transformational leadership. However, transactional leadership can also adopt transformational characteristics (see Figure 6.2). In this diagram, we can see transactional leadership leaning towards being transformational. Transformational leaders can also adopt transactional characteristics, for example, in order to get tasks done.

Ambiguous leadership, laissez-faire and non-leadership

In terms of ambiguous leadership situations, the absence of leadership, or 'non-leadership', is somewhat similar in its results to a *laissez-faire*, completely 'hands-off' model of leadership. 'Absent' leaders are simply not there physically and/or mentally: they do not do anything at all to intervene in concern themselves with the processes of running their organization (Northouse, 2004:179). In this kind of loose leadership situation, leaders may go away for lengthy periods of time, e.g. to conferences. They may delay making decisions, fail to make any

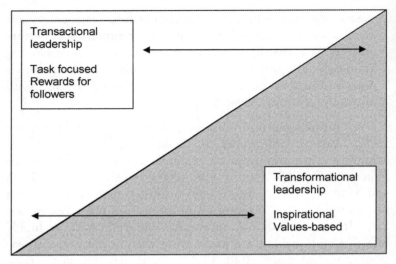

Figure 6.2: Interaction between transactional and transformational theories of leadership

plans for the organization, neglect to talk to staff, leave jobs undone, and fail to set any goals for staff they line manage. There may be one positive aspect to a *laissez-faire* model – notably, in the fact that the leader tends not to be around to mess up anything that followers are doing. Otherwise, this is a highly negligent, unsatisfactory model of leadership, and the results gained under such a style by institutions would be dependent on how well the different parts of the organization can operate, in despite of and without the leader.

Emerging models – pedagogic, servant leadership and quantum leadership

Pedagogic leadership is perhaps one of the most important and appropriate forms of leadership in education, linked to the development of the kind of 'practical wisdom' which we discussed earlier in linking practice with theory. McNay (2002) reported from an earlier study on the governance of small colleges that:

> The small, monotechnic colleges were managed as a unity; in the diversified general colleges there was another layer of

management. In colleges with under 100 academic staff and a similar number of support staff, the Principal can know everybody. There was a commitment to collegiality and 'management by walking about'. Again, events provide opportunities for informal contact. The grapevine operates, too – 'the grapevine spreads information quicker than formal processes' said one Clerk [College 6]. Issues can then be identified before they become problems and problems tackled before they become critical. It works in other ways: 'if I do something silly, everybody will know by morning' [sub-dean, College 2]. McNay, 2002

This kind of collegial atmosphere is reminiscent of Ofsted's (2004b) findings on the reasons why colleges succeed, amongst which are high visibility levels of senior managers, good communication and positive staff consultation. Sometimes characteristic of smaller educational institutions, as reported above by McNay, a collegial atmosphere is often pedagogically focused, developed in a spirit of friendly, relatively informal self-critical professional development activities through shared reflective practice. Teacher-leaders within a collegial culture in schools are described by Lingard, Hayes, Mills and Christie (2003) as 'pedagogic leaders' who, since they regard themselves as learners, tend to have a greater understanding of students' needs than more distant leader-managers in a corporate culture. Critical pedagogic leadership which is both democratic and participative is also promoted by Avis and Bathmaker (2004) as a useful, positive approach in post-compulsory education, since the collaborative engaging dialogue of 'critical friendship' through pedagogic approaches fosters mutual respect in a professionally supportive people-focused atmosphere. Creative interaction and trust can be developed through 'high LMX', or high levels of engagement in leader-member exchanges in a productively developmental pedagogic culture (Briggs, 2005: 224; Howell and Hall-Meranda, 1999). This kind of meaningful regular interactional dialogue between reflective professionals in a learning culture tends to create what Paulo Friere (1972) termed a 'point of encounter' between people engaged positively together in authentic dialogue and learning: (Freire, 1972: 63; Jameson, 2006).

Quantum leadership and servant leadership
The emerging theory of quantum leadership envisages that individuals can change and improve educational provision in ways responsive to a rapidly changing post-modernist world. Often linked with servant leadership, transformational leadership and the field of knowledge of quantum mechanics, quantum leadership tends to be strongly differentiated from reactive, mechanistic management styles and from transactional leadership, a task-focused style some find more appropriate to management than leadership (Downton, 1973; Northouse, 2004; Frearson (2003).

In the *servant leadership* model, leaders avoid hierarchical top-down styles typical of managerial leaders, but envisage their role and themselves as serving others, focusing strongly on the achievement of results to fulfil the values and mission of the organization. Servant leadership aims to be collaborative, trusting and empathetic towards 'followers', setting up team-working structures and using power in an ethical way. A number of key personal characteristics are noted in the literature as appropriate for servant leadership. Larry Spears, Chief Executive of the Greenleaf Center for Servant-Leadership, observes that he 'particularly like[s] Warren Bennis's short list as contained in his book, *On Becoming a Leader*, in which he identifies, "vision, inspiration, empathy and trustworthiness" as key characteristics of effective leaders (p. 140)' (Spears, 2005). We provide further information on the above models in the References and Appendix.

Informal models – collegial, shared, everyday leadership

Positional leaders are always potentially at risk from those with informal respect and authority in the form of everyday acknowledgement of their leadership skills, specialist attributes, behaviours or leading responses to particular demands and situations in educational institutions. Sometimes, this is linked with a specific role – for example, a role as a sports leader, social organizer, or staff newspaper editor in colleges. Leader-managers in formal authority over such staff can treat such staff in a range of ways, winning them to their cause, alienating or ignoring them. Sometimes, positional leaders are worried or fearful that informal leaders may step up to take on a role in the formal hierarchy which challenges them. This can be a particular problem for leader–managers in situations of rapid change, such as restructuring or the introduction of new initiatives, when the role of informal leaders with strong collegiate relationships with other staff can threaten or resist change.

Collegial and collaborative/team leadership

The interdependency of leaders and followers is best acknowledged and cultivated by people in formal authority. This can be done, to some extent, through *collegial models of leadership*, in which leader–managers draw on common points of interest with followers – for example, in professional communities of practice or in staff development sessions. *Shared* and *everyday models* of leadership, often particular to community, voluntary or more informal settings in the learning and skills sector, can be particularly beneficial, with good relationships being established to take forward the aims of the organization. However, the danger in all types of informal leadership – and notably in everyday leadership, in which local or community members predominate – is that there can be insufficient regularization and accountability for the standards of the practices adopted in the name of the organization. Such models are also notoriously subject to the formation of unhealthy cliques and power groups.

Summary

In Chapter 6 we discuss a range of leadership models, beginning with an overview of leadership models and the role of theory. We then put forward some formal and informal models of leadership, tracing these historically in terms of the development of leadership. Positional authority and formal hierarchical models are briefly explained. A range of specific formal models including managerial, bureaucratic, rational concepts in leadership are outlined. Early leadership models, including trait, behavioural, situational theories are noted for their historical contributions and briefly evaluated. Newer models of leadership are briefly discussed, including transformational, distributed, team, ambiguity theories. Emerging models such as pedagogic, servant leadership and quantum leadership are examined for their relevance to FE. Informal models such as collegial, shared and everyday leadership are then discussed and analysed, and it is noted that sources of further information are provided in the References and Appendices.

7: Links between theory and practice

It is a paradox that every dictator has climbed to power on the ladder of free speech. Immediately on attaining power, each dictator has suppressed all free speech except his own.

Herbert Clark Hoover

Pointing out the naked emperor: 'transformational' theories of leadership

We noted earlier in this book that 'transformational' theories of leadership tend to be popular in education and may be particularly relevant to FE institutions, given the government's drive to engage in major improvement programmes, as announced in 2002 in the *Success for All* initiative and subsequent developments in policy and strategy. Bass (1998) reported that, going by the available evidence at the time, transformational leadership is likely to be more effective, productive, visionary and satisfying for 'followers' than transactional leadership.

The concept of 'transformation' is, as the name suggests, linked both to inspirational, innovative leadership and to change management, as well as the agenda for self-improvement which is a current feature of UK popular culture as well as of government programmes for reform across the public sector, as we noted briefly in Chapter 6. Visionary leaders, goes the theory, can transform organizations through the sheer power of their personality, passion and enthusiasm for a particular field of work, and their ability to motivate and inspire others. In Bass's theory of transformational leadership (1990, 1998), authentic transformational leadership is linked directly to moral foundations, including four main aspects (idealized influence, inspirational motivation, intellectual stimulation, and individualized consideration) plus three moral aspects that distinguish the more genuine form of 'transformational leadership' from 'pseudotransformational leadership': (1) the moral character of the leader and their concern for self and others; (2) the ethical values embedded in the leader's vision, articulation, and programme, which followers can embrace or reject; and (3) the morality of the processes of social ethical choices and action in which leaders and followers engage and collectively pursue (Bass, 1998).

The 'transformational' leadership method can be helpful when allied also with expertise, a high level of energy, a strong sense of communal purpose, sound ethical and quality standards, as well as managerial skill in 'turning around' organizations to achieve rapid improvements. There are a number of current examples of highly successful leadership situations in which all of these characteristics have been demonstrated in the learning and skills sector. We could regard the teams who have achieved such change, and the leader(s) who inspired them to do so, as genuinely effective examples of 'transformational leadership'. There are, no doubt, also some new leaders currently in development who may one day be regarded as visionary and enthusiastic transforming leader-managers. This is good news for the FE system, and we have included in this book a number of examples of such leadership situations, mainly but not exclusively focused around particular leaders who have inspired teams of others to achieve excellent results.

However, sadly, the story here is not all good, as there are also those who may have some of the passion and energy, but do not have the other required elements of effective transformational leadership. As we have noted above, these are termed 'pseudotransformational leaders' by Bass (1998), who alerts us to the need to differentiate between pseudotransformational and authentically transformational leadership in practice:

> Self-aggrandizing pseudotransformational leaders can be branded as immoral. But truly transformational leaders, who engage in the moral uplifting of their followers, who move them to share in the mutually rewarding visions of success, who enable and empower them to convert the visions into realities, should be applauded, not chastised. (Bass, 1998)

The problem with pseudotransformational leaders is that it can be hard to distinguish them from more genuine leaders. Transformational leadership programmes also tend to sound good on paper or in theory, but may have a somewhat chequered history in terms of actual achievements. Practical outcomes can be in contrast with the theory and planning of transformational change programmes, which are often expressed in visionary and fine-sounding inspirational rhetoric.

In further education, in which managers tend to have a large number of bureaucratic, administrative tasks to do to meet external performance indicators (following the incorporation of colleges in 1992), the 'audit culture' that has tended to prevail has also sometimes made genuinely student–centred transformation difficult both to conceptualize and to achieve. As Iszatt White, Kelly and Rouncefield (2005) have commented, the work of leader-managers in the learning and skills sector tends to be 'routine, meticulous and unglamorous – mundane in every sense of the word', in order to achieve the large number of external demands for outcomes to targets; yet at the same time the meeting of these targets is vital for institutional survival:

> ... Our findings show that leadership in the learning and skills sector is less about the work of a few talented individuals and more about the successful organization of a complex network of distributed leadership practices involving staff from across the organization. Our research clearly shows that leadership is neither mystical nor heroic, but consists of relentless attention to relatively mundane tasks, and much of leadership is management. Leadership depends on doing the 'grunt work' before any form of vision kicks in. In turn, improving the experience and culture of a college comes through attention to everyday mundane details. Our research evidence also shows the importance of technology (including management information systems and email) in their work, for example, in providing new ways of presenting data about colleges. The importance of the 'audit culture' on everyday leadership work is also evident in our research. (Iszatt White, Kelly and Rouncefield, 2005)

These researchers noted from their interviews with staff in colleges that staff were telling them 'what interviewees thought we wanted to hear, that is, that leadership is both real and that it has had an important role to play in the success of the college' (*ibid.*). However, White *et al.* (2005) become aware during the course of their research that interviewees were using language that tended to reify and create the concept of 'leadership' in ways they thought would be acceptable to and expected by the research team, rather than reporting, necessarily, on something that was actually taking place. They were participating in creating an illusion, as if pretending that the emperor was wearing new clothes. They recorded:

> Yet having spent time in several colleges, we quickly become aware of how important the language of 'leadership' and particularly *being seen to be doing leadership* has become in the learning and skills sector. As such there is some evidence to support Calder's claim that leadership in FE is produced through perceptions and attributions, and that the skill of leadership is to be sensitive to the perceptions of audiences inside and outside of the college. As we discuss elsewhere (Atkinson *et al.*, forthcoming) the work involved in being a good leader may therefore depend to a certain extent on how well your organization 'plays the leadership game.' (Kelly, Iszatt White, Rooksby and Rouncefield, 2005)

Is it the case that perceptions of transformational leadership are sometimes so much of a chimera, when actually what is taking place is a complicated game, in which people are too compliant to point out that the emperor is actually naked? Fox *et al.* (2005) also suggested that the popular idea that only one person or a small team was responsible for leadership success in the learning and skills sector was a myth, and that the collaborative nature of effective leadership needs to be given a higher profile in the sector:

> In contrast to much leadership literature that suggests leadership is about the embodied talents of one or two extraordinary individuals, our research suggests that in practice much leadership work involves ordinary skills that are

recognisable to anyone working in a college, but which are rarely discussed or analysed in mainstream leadership literatures (Alvesson and Sveningsson, 2003c; Bresnen, 1995). As such, our research suggests that leadership work in FE may be more usefully characterised as a collaborative activity. One that involves the successful co-ordination and organization of people, technology and systems (Kelly *et al.*, in press). It is recommended that any attempt to address the effectiveness of leadership in the sector must also recognise the collaborative nature of leadership work and its reliance on complex internal systems and information and communications technology (Collinson and Collinson, 2005a:9–11). (Fox *et al.*, 2005: section 2.2)

If collaboration is vitally important for effective achievement in successful leadership situations, as all of our interviewees have suggested that it is, then we do also need to acknowledge that particular leaders are adept at bringing together teams and enabling such collaboration to take place. The examples of some of the outstanding leaders mentioned in this book are therefore perhaps of key importance in terms of their facilitatory and inspirational role in enabling people to work together effectively and creatively for shared institutional goals. We could therefore redefine the concept of the 'transformational' leader to include the idea that, in such an 'audited' sector, this could be regarded as one who induces collaborative activity successfully.

The role of reflective practice – why intermittent navel-gazing can help

Reflecting critically on received ideas about leadership and examining these in challenging ways is helpful to test the reality of leadership concepts that appear to be useful 'soundbites', but are actually untested. Ruth Silver's thoughts on the balance between 'distributed leadership' and the final accountability of principals are of interest here (see Figure 7.1). Ruth challenges the received notion of 'distributed leadership' and urges us to look at this critically, recognizing that, while you can and

In answer to the question from Jill Jameson – *Do you think leadership roles and duties should really only reside at the top of an institution or should these be distributed throughout the organization in different people and systems that flow through the institution?*

Ruth: I believe in leadership and leading and I think that's a dimension of absolutely everybody's role. But ... I'm slightly sceptical about this notion of 'distributed leadership' because I think there is only one person held accountable for this organization, by way of law, you know: it's: 'I'm the one who is answerable to the Public Accounts Committee in the House of Commons', for example. 'I am the one who is the named person under Health and Safety.' So there is something about 'Yes, you can distribute it, but you actually can't distribute blame'. So I think it's a neat and easy and somewhat trite concept, but I know it's very popular. So I'm into 'everybody taking up that leadership dimension on their role', but think that in the end it's one person whose head will roll. And there's no place to go with that: you just live with it. But that notion of leadership as *winning hearts*, that notion of leadership as *the animation of ideas*, that notion of leadership as *ethical and giving a value system,* and that notion of *creativity*. All of that, I think, are dimensions of everybody's role in college. What varies, and what's not distributed across the college, is *discretion.* And I think that's what – maybe what people are getting at – when they talk about distributed leadership: you can certainly distribute discretions.

JJ: Could you just explain what you mean here by 'discretion' a little more?

Ruth: Yes, people's taking up the authority. You know, so not having to ask to do things, but being clear about the edges of themselves, the edges of themselves in their roles. And I think *the deployment of discretion* is, really, what makes creativity thrive. Following rules, on the whole, though I insist on it, quite often it is a counterpoint to that, so that kind of dialectic, you know ... sort of Leninist saying, that the socialist worker has to be the best worker, well actually that's true of everybody. In order to mobilise the creativity, you have to make sure that the basics are done. I also am clear in the organization for our purposes that you cannot be a good leader without being a good manager.

JJ: So you develop 'leader-managers'?

Ruth: Yes. And teacher-managers and teacher-leaders, you know, we really [do]: it is a dimension of another role.

JJ: So essentially, I think, that's very clear: which is that you see leadership throughout the organization, but there is one place where the buck stops.

Ruth: Yes, absolutely.

Interview with Ruth Silver, 2005 (Silver, 2004; Jameson, 2006)

Figure 7.1: Viewpoint on distributed leadership: Ruth Silver

should support leadership and management as existing proactively throughout an FE organization, essentially, there is still one place 'where the buck stops'. Within that perception that leadership can effectively be distributed as 'the deployment of discretion' throughout an institution, the role of emotional intelligence and effective collaboration with staff is of crucial importance.

Elements of effective leadership situations in practice – enigmas and answers

Given these priorities, who should and can carry out leadership and management work in colleges effectively in practice? What is the actual difference between leaders and managers in operation in FE institutions? Let's examine these somewhat complex and enigmatic questions a bit more and try to find some answers that really apply to local situations in colleges, adult and community education and work-based learning institutions. For this, we return to the question of differentiating between leadership and management discussed earlier in the book, and provide some examples from leaders in the field, in order to arrive at 'teachable moments' about what actually constitutes effective leadership in practice in the learning and skills sector.

'Leadership' versus 'management' – differences in practice

We need to consider briefly the differences and overlapping areas between 'leadership' and 'management' as this relates specifically to further education in practice, in order to arrive at effective solutions. There are many thousands of books outlining the differences between leadership and management. To summarize, we can say that, in further education as well as more generally in the public sector, leadership tends to be concerned with vision, strategy, values, the enthusiastic communication of ideas, 'the big picture', and with stimulating inspiration, trust, commitment and motivation through wide-ranging relationships with people in institutions (as we noted earlier in this book). The inspiration of commitment, motivation and trust by leadership is needed to 'win hearts and minds' to implement policies which are often imposed 'top-down' or 'outside-in' from the government, central learning and skills council or regional LSC agents. Management in further education, by contrast, as we noted earlier, tends to be concerned more with the operations, authoritative control and maintenance of processes in FE institutions. Managers tend to concentrate on determining the way that organizations and their functions can run effectively and smoothly, implementing also controls to monitor effective operations.

One of the most famously succinct definitions of the differences between leadership and management, which we have mentioned briefly earlier in this book, is the idea that 'managers are people who do things right, while leaders are people who do the right thing' (Drucker, cited by Pascale, 1990; Bennis, 1994). This applies as much in further education as it does in a client-focused business environment, except that this distinction is usually mediated by and differentiated from the professional values and interests that are particular to further education. Leaders need to be authentic to the further education system, influential about it and within it, and regarded as legitimate within it, if they are to have a truly beneficial effect on institutions.

During interviews with ten successful leader-managers in the learning and skills sector during 2004–5, all interviewees cited the above definition by Peter Drucker, demonstrating clearly that this distinction, despite its business world connotations, is nevertheless still highly appropriate within college contexts. People readily tend to distinguish between leadership and management, but they also tend to see these as complementary aspects of the senior roles college managers have. The boxed examples of verbatim quotations from leaders I interviewed in 2004–5 on the question of leadership and management in the FE system (Figures 7.1–7.3) are included to clearly outline the way in which leader-managers see these differences operating in FE, and the ways in which they can work effectively together to achieve real change and improved educational provision.

In response to the question from Jill Jameson: *'What in your experience is the distinction if any between leadership and management in post-compulsory education?'*

Lynne: I believe there are generic attributes, qualities, and skills for both leadership and management, generally. So, wherever you are, there are *generic* attributes, qualities and skills, for both leadership and management, as well as specific contextual ones for post compulsory education. So, in a nutshell, on a generic front, for me leadership and management is a spectrum or a continuum, with a leader more able, skilled, 'natural', even, perhaps, at visioning, engaging in the commitment of others, co-creating and bringing about empowering environments. Fundamentally, for me, a leader thinks, acts and impacts more in the 'meaning and purpose' realms. If you like, they win hearts and minds: they generate followers, they're highly relational. They live 'distributed leadership', they live 'learning', actually, they are in a constant inquiry, they believe in leadership at all levels, they ensure that the community, whatever it is, or that group that they work with, is doing the right things.

Whereas I believe that managers are more focused on 'doing things right': systems, monitoring, operational realities, and that more kind of 'control' and 'environment'. Now I think outstanding effective leaders also need to be good managers or to have the ability to have good management around them. I don't believe it's an 'either/or'. And not all managers can or choose to be leaders, so it's a *spectrum* for me. So, where the overlap begins between management and leadership is in the strategic realm. Managers can generate strategy, but it's more of a kind of a 'head' thing or a 'product' thing, whereas leaders live, generate and live strategy. I think you have to have managerial operational excellence, strategic excellence, relational excellence, learning excellence, personal mastery: learning as a way of being and that's your outstanding leader, who's able to go across all of those. And they might be a very ordinary leader but at the same time they're skilled across that function. Now, for me, *educational* leadership and management, I think the essence of that requires a focus on *student outcomes and student learning*. And it's about bringing all that generic into the specific context of bringing everything to bear on the *success of students*. And then it's harnessing all the resources and the capacity, the people capacity, of the organization to put students at the heart of everything and to ensure their success.

Interview with Lynne Sedgmore, February 2005

Figure 7.2: Viewpoint on the distinction between leadership and management: Lynne Sedgmore, CBE, CEO of the Centre for Excellence in Leadership

To the question from Jill Jameson: *'What in your experience is the distinction if any between leadership and management in post-compulsory education?'*

Talmud: ... What leadership *isn't*, is this kind of *lone commander* striving forward with people following behind. To truly lead or inspire leadership is to have an overview of the needs of the whole, so you look at what the needs of the young people are, what the needs of the organization are and then you make your judgments based on that and that alone. You also need to be aware of what your personal needs are in a professional context, so what you need to most be effective in your role. On a personal level, what you need personally is to prepare yourself to be in a position where you are not only going to be offering support to young people but also to members of staff and providing them with trust for members of staff and young people to work effectively.

You have to be aware of that which we call 'ego' in order to put it to one side in a sense. It's not being a hollow shell, it's more about being clear about what the focus is ... You really need to kind of think, *'It's not about [being] singular.'* I may have a role and responsibility, but my role and responsibility is to take things forward and offer encouragement and inspiration ... if that isn't clear, then for me personally that which I do would become corrupt. Because even if you haven't acquired all the necessary skills – which I think none of us ever do in ... entirety – if we have the feeling that we've arrived, we stop growing. Even if you haven't got the necessary skills, you need to have the right intention and that always comes through if what you are trying to do is true.

... in terms of management, it's about keeping context and creating such an atmosphere ... facilitating and providing structures which ... enable people to manage themselves and ... offering ... support and guidance for when they need a sounding board or need advice ... to encourage self direction and offer support and provide structures to work within as well. [Leadership and management] kind of end up mixing, because at the end of the day you may initiate something but then it becomes no longer yours, so you need to be able to say, 'This is what our focus is and what do you think about it?' and then let the idea flourish.

Interview with Talmud Bah, 2005

Figure 7.3: Viewpoint on the distinction between leadership and management: Talmud Bah, Assistant Director, Second Wave Youth Arts, Deptford

Identifying good leaders – assessment techniques for learning leadership

How then can we identify good leaders and good leadership? There are many methods of assessing and measuring both leadership and management, notably using such tools as customized personality tests, quizzes, Myers–Briggs psychological self-assessment tests, observational tests and even handwriting tests. The field of leadership and management assessment is an enormous, swift-moving, vital global industry. Many specialist providers charge considerable sums of money for engagement in and staff development programmes connected with the assessment of skills and knowledge in leadership. Some of these are linked with coaching and mentoring programmes for leader-managers, sometimes bought in by companies to train up an entire workforce of leaders simultaneously. Many of these assessment tests are available online in free versions or demonstration packages, or can be accessed via specialist publications.

A range of recommended resources is outlined in the References and the Appendices to this book, but for now, Figure 7.4 is a summary of some of the more popular leadership assessment techniques. We note that the success of these in terms of accurately capturing the ability of leaders and managers is still in dispute. This is particularly the case for those assessment tools that have no scientifically validated procedures connected with their design, and are based on no empirical findings. Hence such tests are perhaps best taken undertaken with an inquiring and critical mind, in terms of their potential leadership development value, but with a great deal of caution attached regarding the accuracy of any profile generated by them.

Well, having looked with caution at the idea that candidates for leadership and management can be, and are, often 'measured' for their ability and effectiveness, sometimes with relative scientific validity and sometimes not, we return to the long-suffering idea that, 'by their fruits you shall know them'. In the longer term, we suggest that good leadership in the very practical situations of educational institutions tends to emerge from the actual results leaders achieve with their staff. We suggest that this is neither a particularly new idea nor a revolutionary one, but it is a sensible and enduring method that has stood the test of many years and is likely to survive well beyond current generations of leader-managers and their followers.

This proposal – that we should measure leadership by what it actually achieves long term in practical situations over many years through the operation of grounded wisdom – may not be

Leader values self-assessment
A five-minute anonymous test based on the 4 Es (Envision, Enable, Empower and Energize) with some directional action steps for self-improvement.

An assessment of leadership qualities and skills
A ten-minute assessment which can be done alone or with input from colleagues, prompting an introspective look at leadership qualities and skills.

Leadership quiz
A two-minute leadership quiz about knowledge management.

Leadership skills questionnaire
A ten-minute leadership skills questionnaire with brief analysis.

Leadership development methods quiz
A five-minute quiz about the most effective leadership development methods with feedback on proven effective methods.

Innovative leadership assessment
A self-assessment or company-wide assessment for leaders or their peers on leadership competencies.

The leadership difference snapshot
A ten-minute leadership quiz with feedback.

IT leader quiz
Two minutes to test IT leaders, but applicable to any field.

Leadership self-assessment
Thought-provoking questions for many aspects of leadership.

Are you ready to manage in the 21st century?
Five minutes to test eleven important skills for contemporary managers by assessing the degree to which you practice these skills.

Myers–Briggs type self-assessment
A longer (10–15 minute) Myers-Briggs-type personality test.

Figure 7.4: Leadership assessment tools provided by Robert Gordon University (www.rgu.ac.uk/hr/leadership)

radically exciting, but it is, we suggest, probably more reliable and fairer as a judge of the success and effectiveness of leader-managers than the many fads and fashions of new assessment methods for leadership. In other words, we would suggest that, to match the 'mundane work' of ordinary leadership in colleges, there is a process of 'mundane assessment' attached. Within this, it is important that leader-managers are given time and space to succeed, as sometimes an improvement process in institutions can take at least two to three years to achieve real, lasting and measurable results.

Summary

In Chapter 7 links between theory and practice are demonstrated in terms of leadership duties and the practical situations of leaders and managers on the ground in further education. The concept of 'pointing out the naked emperor' is discussed in terms of 'transformational' theories of leadership. The role of reflective practice is considered. We briefly examine whether intermittent navel-gazing can help leaders to develop their skills. Elements of effective leadership situations in practice are outlined in terms of their enigmas and some possible answers to these. The differentiation between leadership and management in terms of the reality of work in practical situations is discussed. Some methods for identifying good leaders, with assessment techniques for learning leadership, are put forward, and we return to suggest that 'by their fruits you shall know them' is in the end the most reliable way of judging the effectiveness of leaders.

Section Three: Models of Management in FE Institutions

8: Managing for excellent high-quality provision

The conventional definition of management is getting work done through people, but real management is developing people through work.

Agha Hasan Abedi

Attributes of excellent management

As we noted earlier in this book, the cross-sector leadership and management board of the Sector Skills Development Agency (SSDA) defines management as broadly being: *'concerned with planning, implementing, controlling and using resources, typically on a day-to-day basis'*. Good practice in carrying out strategic planning, finance, audit, quality assurance, effective curriculum delivery, systems and people management and governance are essential attributes of excellent management. Leader-managers in further education need to address all of these effectively if they are to achieve their tasks well and manage FE institutions in such a way that excellent, high-quality provision results. This has sometimes been extremely difficult in FE.

McTavish's research in five Scottish further education colleges revealed that:

> It was ... felt that the essentially local nature of FE made it difficult for senior college staff to think and act strategically and that there was a 'strategic capacity gap' within the sector not addressed by any of the support or representative bodies. (McTavish, 2006: 425)

Research by Watson and Crossley (2001) also critiques the management, marketization and strategic management process (SMP) of further education colleges. Watson and Crossley comment that these processes do not just satisfy the demands of external auditors: such management processes also contribute to change in the socio-cultural contexts of colleges, and can be used as a vehicle for learning in organizations and for increasing professional participation in institutions. These researchers note that such management tools are under-recognized and under-theorized in terms of organizational learning potential, and that they can enable a greater degree of ownership and socio-cultural sense of 'belonging' among staff in further education, if used to good effect.

Building on the ideas of Watson and Crossley, we note that it is not only the formal processes of strategic management that can enable and empower staff in FE institutions. A range of other useful leadership and management development techniques can also be used to develop good management in colleges. One such tool that was used to good effect in the research on which this book is based is described below in terms of emotional intelligence (EI/EQ) and its effect on a sixth form college and its value-added achievement, as recorded in the college data monitoring.

Values-based ethical management and emotional intelligence

When interviewed, Dr John Guy, OBE, Principal of Farnborough Sixth Form College recalled the training for principals organized by the Hay Group he had attended earlier in his career. This was focused around emotional intelligence (EI). John perceived that the training had had a remarkably beneficial effect, not only on himself as principal, but in wider ways, on the whole institution, as first he and then the college senior management had incorporated this into their developmental thinking and then the mission of Farnborough Sixth Form College. The college now has:

> ... a shared mission, we wrote it ... together, back in 1992. It's in two parts.... the first part is about excellence, the mission is: *to develop as a distinguished major provider of the*

highest quality academic and vocational education. . . . There was a lot of discussion about the word 'distinguished' . . . What it means is that people will recognize [the college] for its excellence . . . It will be distinguished for [that] . . . The second part is *to develop the caring ethos of the college. Equipping young people with the qualifications and skills to meet the demands of a changing world with confidence and assurance.* (John Guy, interview 2005 (Jameson, 2006))

The incorporation of emotional intelligence (EI) into the college mission to be implemented at every level, including for both students and staff, has been exceptionally effective at Farnborough. John discussed in detail with me the results of the longer-term benefits of explicitly working to improve EI in terms of measurable improvements in value-added ALIS data (see Jameson, 2006). This has resulted in outstanding success for the college.

Tools and techniques: 360°, 3 Cs, SWOT, time managment, 7 Ps, CEL Framework

360° feedback

The theory behind 360° feedback is that it can be used to provide information to staff to improve their performance and increase job satisfaction, by using a customized designed survey completed by each staff member's manager and peers, as well as by the staff who report to that employee. The aim of a 360° survey is to help all staff see themselves as others do. The risk involved in this form of feedback is that it may be biased, inaccurate, insensitive and actually harmful if improperly used, for example by those who have a 'grudge' against other employees or who have inadequate evaluative skills to be able to determine what the actual performance is of their colleagues. It may also be extremely negative if employees who have a low self-image or who are particularly sensitive to criticism are given thoughtlessly negative feedback with little follow-up support.

Such a tool may, in addition, inadvertently be used as part of a culture which is subtly 'mobbing' or manipulative in effects if not intention, if managers try to control members of staff to fit in with a predetermined plan and existing culture. The survey tool therefore has to be accurately and sensitively designed and analysed, and the feedback very carefully reported within a clear, compassionate and supportive framework, linked to staff development for those giving and receiving feedback, and follow-up coaching to encourage improvement. What is very important in the 360° feedback process is that no one is harmed by it. There have been cases in which organizational performance has declined following its use, so caution is suggested if adopting this model.

The 3 Cs of knowledge sharing

The 3 Cs of knowledge sharing are defined as 'culture', 'co-opetition' and 'commitment' (Skyrme, 2002). It is necessary to build a knowledge-sharing organization if people are to trust each other, collaborate together in team working and develop organizational learning in beneficial ways for leadership and management really to operate effectively at all levels of the institution. Some form of collaborative or at at least cooperative culture is required if an FE institution is going to develop high-quality provision across all areas and disciplines, or else excellence will be confined to specific pockets of good quality. Developing a new or renewed culture of trust is a difficult and challenging process, particularly if there are scores to settle amongst staff as a result of a past history of conflict. We provide information to follow up on techniques to develop management skills such as the 3 Cs of knowledge sharing in the Appendices, including techniques to encourage people to share knowledge, rewards and incentives schemes, and recruitment programme ideas for generating income for new staff.

SWOT analysis

Most people in further education will be very familiar with carrying out a SWOT (Strengths, Weaknesses, Opportunities, Threats) analysis as part of the self-assessment process that is routinely developed and cascaded throughout colleges every year. The concept of SWOT is that you begin to identify, understand and analyse your Strengths, Weaknesses, Opportunities and Threats (Manktelow, 2005). See Figure 8.1.

Strengths	Weaknesses
Opportunities	Threats

Figure 8.1: The SWOT model is used to identify self-assessment tasks for improvement

The SWOT tool can be used to do an analysis of the areas of operation you are currently focusing on and critique these, so that you can adjust and improve your perspective and knowledge about the organization and your place in the further education landscape. In a SWOT analysis, you categorize all of the things that represent strengths, weaknesses, opportunities and threats, and then take remedial action to address areas in which you need to take action. SWOT analysis can be helpful in collectively agreeing areas of strengths and weaknesses, and the opportunities and threats you face, for example, as part of a staff development session or strategic planning day. This will help you to focus on your strengths as an institution, minimize weaknesses, and take the greatest possible advantage of the opportunities available − for example, for new funding opportunities, new programmes and students in the local or regional environment. SWOT analysis is just one of many good techniques that can help you build a strong, excellent provision and a competitive position for the FE institution. It is a highly effective tool when used appropriately in institutional staff development sessions.

The time management matrix

The time management matrix is another familiar technique for effecting powerful change for the better in your workload and in organizations as a whole. An example of one of these is provided in Figure 8.2.

CLASSIFY TASKS	Urgent	Not Urgent
Important	**Urgent/Important** Crisis situations Immediate problems Upcoming deadlines Timed meetings Booked appointments	**Non-urgent/Important** Preparatory tasks Preventative measures Values clarification Planning Networking Envisioning
Not important	**Urgent/Not important** Interruptions and visits Selected phone calls Selected email and mail Selected meetings Many urgent demands Some social activities	**Not urgent/Not important** People wasting your time Escapist activities Trivial time-waster tasks Some recreation Spam emails Unwanted post Unnecessary surveys

Figure 8.2: A time management matrix to assist in scheduling and sifting work

To use the matrix, you need to draw up a list of tasks you routinely do, and classify these according to the matrix of 'urgent', 'non-urgent', 'important', 'not important', being disciplined and honest with yourself about the kinds of tasks you actually carry out every day. If you do this rigorously, and begin to discern patterns in your working life, you may find that you can save yourself a lot of time by quickly learning to jettison those things that are 'time wasters' and that get in the way of your fulfilling the most important and urgent tasks. Often those that are in the 'non-urgent but important' category such as planning, responding to new opportunities and values clarification are the tasks that have long-term benefit if you are able to find time to carry these out effectively and diligently. Some things that are notorious time-wasters are the following, including both the symptoms and some of the causes of the distractions:

- Not being strict about the end-time for meetings
- Ringing or visiting people unnecessarily to chat
- Doing things yourself that can be delegated to others
- Carrying out tasks that are not part of your job, but which you like
- Allowing anyone to walk into your office anytime
- Keeping unnecessary paperwork or records
- Having too many competing jobs without weeding these out
- Doing unnecessary 'non-urgent/not important' work first
- Failing to say 'no' to trivial or unnecessary requests
- Not working towards a given deadline in good time

The 7 Ps of marketing adapted for FE provision

The idea of the 7 Ps management model is based on marketing. It is used by marketing executives to evaluate and constantly re-evaluate activities in business. Although this is not directly relevant to further education, as it is drawn from business and marketing practice, to achieve excellence in provision it is nevertheless worth considering the competitive market facing you in further education in terms of the following 7 Ps of marketing: *product, price, promotion, place, packaging, positioning* and *people*. In the case of further education these would be interpreted as:

Product
What is the curriculum, learning resources provision or other education and training activity that you offer? Is it as good as it could be? Could you change it or improve it? What is distinctive about the provision you run? Why would people want to come and study here? If you can't answer this positively, how can you change this situation? Have you achieved any CoVE or other funding for Centres of Excellence? Can you develop this further?

Price
What are the fees you charge students – should they be higher or lower, should there be more subsidies, scholarships and

grants, benefits or other attractors for students? What do other providers in the neighbourhood charge?

Promotion

How are you attracting students and business clients to the college – can you change your methods, have you considered new methods like mobile phone messaging? How many times a year does your prospectus come out? Do you use radio or TV advertising? Are there regular newspaper articles locally talking about the successes of the institution? Have you put forward any of your staff for STAR awards or other honours?

Place

Are the places in which you are offering your courses suitable for the courses and the students? Is there anything that can be done to change the accommodation, improve facilities, offer provision in different premises, consider distance learning?

Packaging

How does your provision appear to the students and clients who come to your institution? Are you scheduling and running your programmes and courses effectively? Are these positioned at a good time in relation to each other? Are the brochures/ prospectuses/ leaflets or other advertising and course materials attractive and informative? Are the reception staff helpful and do they look welcoming and attractive? How do your security present themselves? Are they off-putting for students? What does the outside of the institution look like? Is it neat and pleasant, or is there a lot of litter and are there weeds instead of flowers? How can you change these things? Are there simple things you can do to improve the look and 'feel' of the institution? Are you responsive to diverse, multicultural student needs?

Positioning

Is the local and regional 'positioning' of the college's provision among its neighbouring institutions, students and client groups the correct one for its image, profile, curriculum, mission, staff and strategic aims? How have you 'positioned' the institution effectively in relation to the local, regional and national political, academic and economic landscape? Is the college meeting local demands effectively? Should you consider repositioning the college or any of its key constituent structures such as departments, subject groups and centres?

People

Are the staff who teach, organize and administer the courses friendly and helpful to students? How do they present themselves? What does the college/other institution look like from the point of view of visitors? Take a walk around your sites and really look at them. Would you want to study here yourself? Would you let your children study here? If the answer is 'no', how can you improve this situation for your students and trainees?

In order to implement all of the above, you need to constantly assess and re-assess these attributes using the methods of continuous improvement – i.e. you can never be complacent that all of the above will be satisfied in the way that you want them to be to achieve excellent provision. Think about the institution as you would if you were a visitor seeing it fresh for the first time. What do you want to change? How can this be achieved? Are there staff in place to help you do that? It is important to gather together appropriate people in your team who will carry forward your vision for an excellent institution and implement this fearlessly and energetically every single day.

Inspections – measuring the difference between good and poor management

Having considered some tools for the achievement of excellent provision, we need to consider the inspection process by which this is judged. The Centre for Excellence in Leadership (CEL) developed the *Leadership Qualities Framework* (LQF) in 2004. The framework identified the four following key areas for the development and practice of leadership:

- Focus to achieve
- Mobilize to impact

- Sustain momentum
- Passion for excellence

Within these, the following items are summarized in CEL's diagram for the LQF (CEL, 2004):

- **Focus to achieve** – Shaping the future, business acumen, action orientation, cultural sensitivity
- **Mobilize to impact** – Organizational expertise, influential relationships, distributed leadership, performance accountability

---

The Centre for Excellence in Leadership (CEL) attributes for the Leadership Qualities Framework (LQF) can be considered against the following duties for leader-managers, with the CEL areas above summarized against them as **F2A, M2I, SM, P4E** (*Focus to achieve, Mobilize to impact, Sustain momentum and Passion for excellence*):

- to communicate a clear vision, strategic direction, identity and focus for the institution and its governors, staff, students, business clients and partners, demonstrating influential strategic and communicative leadership (F2A, M2I);
- to supply effective, good-quality further education provision for learners (F2A, M2I, SM, P4E);
- to successfully meet key external requirements of the LSC, inspectorate, auditors, students, business clients, employers, politicians, parents and partner organizations, demonstrating high levels of accountability (F2A, M2I, SM, P4E);
- to provide an appropriate, safe, healthy, well-balanced, successfully functioning educational and training environment for learners and staff (F2A, M2I SM, P4E);
- to meet internal demands from students and staff for good management, administrative and financial systems, quality educational provision, appropriate resources, effective teaching and good student achievements (M2I, SM, P4E);
- to fulfil the college's social justice and inclusion agenda in proactively addressing the need for equality, diversity, inclusive provision and sustainable development priorities across all of the institution's activities (F2A, M2I, SM, P4E);
- to address the complex, diverse needs of learners and staff effectively in flexible, sustainable, responsive ways in senior roles, including those of principal, senior and middle managers, responding appropriately to ongoing changing conditions and new priorities for national and global leaders (F2A, M2I, SM, P4E).

Leadership Qualities Framework (LQF) from CEL (2004).

Figure 8.3: The CEL Leadership Qualities Framework (LQF): mapping against tasks

- **Sustain momentum** – change management, building organizational capability, growing future talent, driving for results
- **Passion for excellence** – Self-awareness and growth, learning orientation, common purpose, drive and direction

These attributes are mapped against a range of duties for senior managers in FE in Figure 8.3 in order to consider the measurement of different attributes for excellent leadership in the sector.

Summary

Chapter 8 considers the importance of management techniques in achieving excellent high-quality provision. Attributes of excellent management are discussed: the role of strategic planning, finance, audit, quality assurance and governance are very briefly outlined. The key importance of values-based ethical management is proposed drawing on an example from Farnborough Sixth Form College. Tools and techniques for managers, including 360° feedback, 3 Cs and 7 Ps, time management matrix and elements of change management models are referenced for further reading. The question of whether inspections measure the difference between good and poor management is discussed in relation to the Centre for Excellence in Leadership Leadership Qualities Framework. The LQF is briefly mapped against leadership tasks to be done to achieve excellent provision in FE.

9: Diversity and authenticity in management

Some leaders are born women.

Anonymous

The diversity of leaders and managers in the learning and skills sector

In a notable report on leadership and diversity in the learning and skills sector, Lumby, Harris, Morrison, Muijs, Sood, with Glover, Wilson, Briggs and Middlewood (2004, 2005) observed during 2004–5 that sustained action was needed to address the promotion of equality and diversity. These researchers commented on the unequal representation of women and black and minority ethnic leaders at all levels of the learning and skills sector, particularly at top levels of senior management. They also noted that 'effective leadership for diversity requires commitment at all levels' (Lumby, 2004: 99). The problems of unequal representation are historic and long-standing in the sector. They cannot easily be solved without sustained, long-term work to address the key issues underlying what we could call 'the diversity problem'.

More recent work by Lumby and colleagues (Lumby, 2006) problematizes the notion of 'diversity', taking it beyond the issue of representation alone to conceptualise greater depth in understanding. For many years, diversity issues within a target-focused FE system have been problematic, as identified earlier by McNay, who reported on FE as 'a disturbing picture of a system in stress' (McNay, 1998).

Fox *et al.* echoed the concerns of Lumby *et al.*, reporting in 2005 that:

We ... know that women are under-represented at senior
levels, with 26% of college principals being women, which is
a worse position than two years ago before CEL's contract
commenced, when DfES informed us that 40% of FEC
principals were female. There are also significant equality
issues in terms of socio-economic background, age, disability
and working patterns. Fox et al. (2005)

In 2006, there were only 7 black principals of colleges, just
1.8% of total numbers, with c.50 black and minority ethnic
(BME) senior managers in c.400 colleges. Yet more than 18%
of FE students are from BME backgrounds (Persaud, 2006;
eTeach, 2005; NBM, 2002). This is a parlous situation for a
sector ostensibly committed to equality and diversity. Lumby et
al (2005) advised that the lack of leadership diversity should be
tackled through 'a national framework' for inclusive leadership,
noting that that diversity issues are as yet both inadequately
addressed in the sector (ibid).

Bearing in mind these figures, we need to query whether
women have a significant enough role in FE leadership. Global
evidence suggests women now occupy more important leadership roles, but this is not the case yet in FE, nor, as McNay
reports, in HE (2006). National evidence suggests career progression is still difficult for women in FE, especially for older
women, BME women and candidates for top roles. A 'glass' or
'concrete ceiling' is still evident in predominantly male managerial environments (see also Jameson, 2006, McNay, 2006).
Overt commitments to diversity have been made to get to grips
with these long-standing, difficult issues.

Morrison, M. (2006) explored the 'rhetoric of engagement
with diversity' in post-compulsory education and discovered a
relative paucity of actual engagement. Her findings suggested
that issues of diversity and diversity management were not of
great interest to participants in her study. Definitions of
diversity were both mixed and problematic, and organizational
action to promote diversity was patchy and located predominantly in conceptions of 'representativeness' from earlier
eras. Morrison called for a more vigorous and vital theory and

practice of engagement with diversity, reporting the following findings, among others (Morrison, 2006: 174):

- Leadership development in diversity and diversity management was largely unrecognized or peripheral.
- Perceived pressure to consider staff diversity and inclusion issues varied widely from provider to provider.
- Interest in and engagement with diversity at all levels was weak, being resisted by a substantial proportion of respondents.
- The understanding/definition of diversity was not always clearly articulated on an agreed basis, even within the same organization.
- 'Representativeness' in relation to the local or national profile of the community in which the institution/service was located was the most common aim, sometimes leading to a focus upon equal opportunities rather than diversity, and upon students rather than staff.
- Examples of committed providers whose actions were moving towards diversity and the empowerment of staff were evident, but in the minority.

Representation of women, black and minority ethnic and disabled staff

The Learning and Skills Development Agency (LSDA, 2003) survey on *Tomorrow's Learning Leaders: Developing Leadership and Management for Post-compulsory Learning* analysed data from 2,000 questionnaires from leaders and managers in the LSC sector, reporting that senior management was still mainly 'white, middle-aged and male' in 2002 (p.15). Over 50% of respondents were female, yet women managers were much more likely to be supervisors or middle managers than executive or senior managers (p. 2). During 1997–2002, numbers of women in learning and skills sector management remained more or less constant, with only marginal increases in supervisors and middle managers.

The analysis of data from a Further Education Development Agency (FEDA) 1997 survey of 3,000 managers in over 250 of the then 452 FE colleges in England and Wales (Stott and Lawson 1997) reported that more women than men (554: 410) were recruited into management positions during 1993–7. By the end of 1997, 17% of principals were women in comparison with just 3% in 1990 (Jameson, 2006, Pritchard et al., 1998, yet in a sector with a predominantly female workforce, this was a disappointment, since women were then (and still are) more heavily represented in lower levels of middle management, where they comprised 50–60% of the workforce compared with under 20% at the very top (FEDA 1997). Though this has now increased slightly, as noted above, progression has again slowed and declined. Similarly, disabled staff were and still are seriously under-represented in the sector: for every step forward there seems to be some backward movement as well.

In Jameson, 2006, we discussed studies by Deem, Ozga and Pritchard (2000) who analysed data on women managers in FE, finding 'some social and cultural as well as demographic feminization of FE management' appeared to be occurring at middle management levels, although more masculinist styles still prevailed in senior management(Deem et al., p. 233). At the time of writing, women, black and minority ethnic (BME) and disabled principals, chief executives and governors remain still vastly in the minority in FE, despite this evidence of some earlier progress in diversity and inclusion. A 'masculinist' culture remains, linked to the performativity of transactional management which pervades senior management teams, while there is less evidence of transformational, collaborative and democratic styles more suited to women and men with egalitarian tendencies. In an audit culture with constant stringent task-focused demands for which senior managers are perpetually accountable to many local and regional bodies, it is difficult to effect culture changes.

Clancy reported in 2005 that the Commission for Racial Equality had called for greater attention to be paid to the lack of BME staff in senior management in FE. As we noted in Jameson, 2006, this call has been strongly reinforced by the work of the Commission for Black Staff in Further Education, which is working long-term to facilitate equity in the representation of people from black and minority ethnic groups in senior posts, including that of Principal, in which BME representation remains at around 2% across the UK. Beulah Ainley's book in the *Essential FE Toolkit* series on *Race Equality* for leaders and managers follows up on this important subject in making recommendations on race equality to be implemented at every level of institutions in the FE system (see also section below).

Is there a 'feminine advantage' in leadership?

As we discussed earlier (Jameson, 2006) a debate about *feminine advantage'* in leadership has been the subject of analysis in recent years (Yukl, 2002, Vecchio, 2002, Eagly and Carli, 2003). Eagly and Carli (2003: 808) wrote in a *Business Week* article, 'New Gender Gap', that 'Men could become losers in a global economy that values mental power over might' We note here again that stereotypical gender effects attributed to females may suit popular modernist *'transformational'* leadership styles which, have tendencies to be androgynous and are therefore arguably more easily taken up by women in comparison with the 'transactional' styles some argue are more likely to be assumed by men (ibid., p.816). Eagly *et al.* (2003) report a relatively recent international trend for more women leaders to be represented at very senior levels. These researchers comment that '43 of the 59 women who have ever served as presidents or prime ministers of nations came into office since 1990' (p.809). Vecchio (2002) echoes this, observing that there has been an 'exponential' increase in the numbers of women in very senior political leadership roles. Leadership styles that focus more on collaborative working, democratic consultation, empathetic understanding and people-focused leadership than on formal hierarchical control, tend to be those associated with 'feminine' leadership. However, sometimes these styles are also possessed by men, so the picture is complex.

The question of whether it is a myth or fact that there is a 'female' advantage in leadership is therefore up for discussion. There may now be a leadership advantage in some occupations for certain *kinds* of leadership sometimes labelled as 'more feminine', rather than an advantage for one gender over another in appointments procedures. In addition, in some more 'exclusive' professions, such as the law, medicine and in higher education professorial roles, women are so far behind in equity terms that recent analysis indicates it will take 50 years for them to catch up . At the time of writing, 84 per cent (11,620) of the UK's HE professors are men: the representation of women is so low that, if current trends continue, it will take half a century to change this (Tysome, 2007).

Challenging racism, encouraging equal representation

As noted above, there still exist a range of prejudices against the appointment of black and ethnic minority staff at Principal and senior management levels in the learning and skills sector, as Professor Daniel Khan noted in his interview (Jameson, 2006). Racism in appointments procedures for FE needs to be challenged through ongoing programmes of race equality and diversity training. The Commission for Black Staff in Further Education has on numerous occasions, notably in the report, *Challenging racism* (2002a) urged FE institutions to take responsibility to eliminate both racism and the lack of equal representation of BME staff at senior and governing body levels in FE (Commission for Black Staff in Further Education (2002a). The Centre for Excellence in Leadership has also committed itself to address this under-representation by declaring that its second key priority is: 'Improving the diversity profile of leaders at all levels' in the sector (CEL, 2004:1). The lack of diversity and inclusion in FE management is the subject of a range of research and development programmes (ibid), which are of much importance in addressing this important issue.

Synergistic leadership theory

Irby, Brown, Duffy and Trautman (2002) put forward a new 'synergistic leadership theory' (SLT) to include feminine and post-modernist leadership perspectives and principles of geo-metry-based synergistic thinking from R. Buckminster Fuller

(Fuller, 1979). Irby et al. challenge the predominance of masculine leadership styles, which saturated leadership theories during 1950–2000, rendering the role of women virtually invisible and ignored. They analysed 24 major leadership theories from this period, finding that leadership theory development had been almost exclusively limited to male-dominated perspectives (ibid., 2002). SLT is the first key leadership theory to combine principles from feminism and post-modernism in a tetrahedron model (Irby et al, 2002: 313) comprised of four different factors, rather than concentrating in a more limited ways solely on leadership behaviours and/or organizational structures: (1) attitudes, beliefs and values; (2) leadership behaviour; (3) external forces, and (4) organizational structure (Irby et al., 2001). SLT outlines new aspects of leadership emphasizing a complex interaction between individuals and integrated institutions. It can be implemented using feminist principles also relevant to wider diversity and inclusion issues. The 'fit' between a leader and an institution can be examined using SLT, to diagnose, understand and remedy difficult leadership situations, and to analyse other diversity and ethnicity-related tensions and organizational differences. There can be a cognitive dissonance between norms and operational realities in the management of organizations (Becher and Kogan, 1992).

Developing authentic situation-specific management

What is 'authenticity' in leadership in situation-specific contexts? We suggest that it may be characterized by *other-connectedness* in observable behaviours. Michie and Gooty (2005) observe that some researchers have previously regarded 'authentic leaders' as those who are 'guided by a set of values . . . oriented toward doing what's right and fair for all stakeholders' (Bass and Steidlmeier, 1999; Luthans and Avolio, 2003; May, Chan, Hodges and Avolio, 2003). Michie and Gooty (*ibid.*) also note that authentic leaders try to achieve correct actions and fair outcomes for everyone and 'may willingly sacrifice self-interests for the collective good of their work unit, organization, community, or entire society'. Therefore, authentic leaders can be

identified through their adherence to 'self-transcending beha-
viors ... they are intrinsically motivated to be consistent with
high-end, other-regarding values ... shaped and developed
throughout the leaders' life experiences' (Bass and Steidlmeier,
1999; Luthans and Avolio, 2003).

Recognizing diversity, implementing policies for inclusion

In relation to FE and diversity, therefore, we can observe that
authenticity indicates a quality of genuineness or truthfulness
linked to self-transcendent actions in which leaders put the
interests of those they serve above their own ego-serving
interests. There is a widescale need to recognize diversity and
implement policies for inclusion based on beneficial understandings of the need for authentic and values-driven leadership, which recognizes the intrinsic value of all staff working in
the learning and skills sector and enables everyone to have the
opportunity to achieve leadership posts and promotion, without prejudice against them for secondary reasons to do with
class, gender, race, religion, creed, sexuality or any other irre-
levant factor. The diversity research and policy initiatives currently being undertaken by CEL should go some way towards
addressing this problem, but there is still much work to be
done.

The authentic manager – how to crack this nutty problem

In interviews with ten highly successful leaders in 2004–5, I
observed that the concept of *values-driven leadership* was a key
factor that interviewees cited as one that constantly drove
forward their actions. Such self-transcendent values included an
overriding interest in student success and staff welfare as being
the most important motivating factors for leaders' actions.

Describing 'self-transcendence' as a classifying feature of
authenticity in leadership, Michie and Gooty note the work of
Schwartz (1994), who categorized a 'self-transcendent' value
system into 'a higher-order bipolar dimension' of 'self-

enhancement versus self-transcendence'. Whereas 'self-enhancement' comprises actions adding to the leaders' own sense of self achievement through the pursuit of ego-gratifying success and dominance over others, 'self-transcendence' is aligned in Schwartz's (1994) model with benevolent values in which leaders are concerned with the welfare of others, and are truthful, responsible and loyal in serving the interests of social justice, inclusion and tolerance of other people's views (see Figure 9.1).

Inauthentic leadership	Authentic leadership
Self-enhancement	Self-transcendence
Power-driven	Values-driven
Pursuit of personal power	Concern for others
Self-achievement	Success for welfare of all
Achievement of self status	Achievement of group
Dominance over others	Cooperative relations with others
Self-centredness	Centred on common good
Cynical manipulation of others	Benevolence towards others
Personal justice	Social justice
Relative intolerance of other views	Relative tolerance of other views

Figure 9.1: Authentic and inauthentic leadership bipolarity, building on Michie and Gooty (2005)

Using this model, we therefore observe that one way to distinguish 'inauthentic' from 'authentic' leadership is to note the extent to which the language and actions that leaders use are characterized by an explicit interest in the welfare of others. In theory, actions that result from this may be more or less effective in serving the interests of common welfare in institutions, and in benefiting 'followers'. Another potential way to judge authentic leadership actions, therefore, is to observe the responses of staff and students to the perceived ethos of institutions, and the extent to which transformational effects result in improved performance. Leadership which is more or less honest and genuine, in this theory, will tend to be leadership that is observably 'other-directed', more or less transformative, and appreciably effective in resulting in improved welfare and performance, for the common good of all (see Lumby *et al.* 2005 research results cited earlier, on the relative effectiveness of transformational leadership in the FE sector).

Summary

In Chapter 9, diversity and authenticity in management are considered, together with intrinsic solutions which map skills to local goals and demands, including considerations of prior research on leadership and diversity in the learning and skills sector. We outline the development of authentic situation-specific management. Recognizing the need for diversity and the relative lack of this at senior management level in FE, we recommend the implementation of policies for inclusion. Facts on the representation of women, black and minority ethnic groups and disabled staff in leadership and management are considered. The question of authenticity in management and leadership is discussed in relation to local potential solutions for cracking this nutty problem.

Section Four: How To Be a Good Leader-manager in FE

Chapter 10: Lessons from leader-managers

The best leaders are those the people hardly know exist.
The next best is a leader who is loved and praised.
Next comes the one who is feared.
The worst one is the leader that is despised.
If you don't trust the people,
they will become untrustworthy.
The best leaders value their words, and use them sparingly.
When she has accomplished her task,
the people say, 'Amazing:
we did it, all by ourselves!'
Lao-Tzu, Tao Te Ching, *Ch. 17 (trans. McDonald)*

By their fruits you shall know them.
Matthew 7: 15–16.

Results from the Leadership and Management Survey 2006

Stringent requirements for auditing, and the multiple challenges of complex demands on staff at principal level as well as lower down the hierarchies in FE institutions were among the views echoed in staff opinions emerging from the FE sector in an online survey conducted on leadership for this book in 2006–7. I consulted staff working in FE and in areas relating to leadership and management in the learning and skills sector in a research survey on leadership carried out nationally. The survey asks a wide range of staff the following question: *In your view, what are the most important qualities needed, now, to develop good leadership in the learning and skills sector?* (see Appendix, question 14).

Details about the survey were distributed to a range of groups across FE, including senior managers, principals, teaching and research staff. There have been 79 respondents so far overall, of whom 52 gave responses to question 14 (including one nil response). The replies are reproduced in detail in the Appendices. Selected responses from question 14 are outlined below in Figure 10.1 (note – minor spelling mistakes in the originals were amended for easy reading, but the original verbatim responses are reproduced in full in the Appendices for reference purposes).

It is important to note that, in the overall survey, at least 14 respondents were at principal level, 2 were vice principals, 2 were directors, and at least 13 were at head of department level. This indicates a potential for bias in favour of senior and middle management perspectives which cannot be discounted without further data collection and investigation. However, what it also provides is an important insight into the views of staff operating mainly with responsibilities for leadership and management. I am indebted to the Principals' FE online private group and Learning and Skills Research Networks in particular for their willingness to contribute to and inform this survey. More than 80 per cent of respondents declaring their place of work came from the FE sector, including general FE colleges, adult education, sixth form colleges and FE/ACL/HE mixed economy institutions.

As part of the same survey, I also asked staff about the confidence they had in leadership in general across a range of specific areas within the learning and skills sector, including national and local LSC leadership, institutional, business, union and local informal leadership (see Appendix, question 12).

The 65 respondents who replied to this question gave answers which were of much interest. Overall, responses indicated fair confidence in leadership throughout the sector, as demonstrated in Figure 10.2, with the highest number of all responses being for the reply 'somewhat agree' regarding strength of confidence across all areas of sectoral leadership (238). Among the many positive leadership characteristics identified in the sector were: vision, willingness to be innovative, flexibility, empathy, commitment, a balance of strategic

Question 14
In your view, what are the most important qualities needed, now, to develop good leadership in the learning and skills sector?

Innovative leaders who understand the needs and demands of customers, and the sector who serve them, 20 year vision, ability to inspire and motivate; business sense, not ideology.

Sharing of peer practice but also recognition that there are good lessons to learn from outside the sector. Stability at national LSC level would be very helpful.

Stamina, vision and drive and a belief in social justice, a head for data and networking skills.

Commitment, stamina and drive, commitment to excellence and continual improvement, passion for education and students.

People-centredness. Consensus management techniques. Organic, inclusive, collegial, empowering leadership models.

Identification with the effects of decisions at the 'chalkface'. It is not effective to put in new initiatives without the gift of time or some other reward to enable them at lecturer and curriculum management level. The standard of many of our practitioner level people far exceeds that of industry in my experience, but we do not get the best out of them because they are often exhausted.

Thorough understanding of the national and local political demands that impact upon FE. Excellent interpersonal skills, a high standard of leadership and management skills, the ability to manage a team but also to be a team player. Effective analytical skills, good communication skills.

Clear vision, good communicator, listening skills, decision-maker, able to prioritize, able to empathize with those on the ground and willing to roll up sleeves and lead by example at appropriate times.

Empathy with followers. Clarity of what needs to be done. Humility. Willingness to do what needs to be done and having the 'bottle' to see it through.

Vision, creative ability, problem solving, good communication, empathy and tolerance. Leading by example and being willing to demonstrate what needs to be done then roll up our sleeves and get on with it.

Experience gained within the education sector, a focus on learner success and financial acumen.

The capacity to relate to the external world and to continually connect to the fact that we are public servants, not neo-business folks. Good communication skills, a sense of adventure, to talk as educational leaders not as management moaners caught continually in power struggles. To be well educated themselves, with a cultural hinterland of their own which contributes to them making meaning to others of the world we find ourselves in as it relates to our task and values. To be an example.

Emotionally intelligent and transformational approach allied to decisive and rational planning.

Clarity of vision and values. An uncompromising commitment to excellence. A real focus on the success of students. The guts to drive through change in every college by tackling the 'difficult bits'. A willingness to really engage with the staff in following this through so that it impacts on every teaching and learning session, every hour, every day!

The ability to motivate diverse groups of staff, to provide vision, strategy and, above all, optimism and energy.

Knowledge and understanding of the sector in balancing the needs of both customers (employers) and clients (students/trainees). Clarity of direction. Determination and strength of leadership. Recognition of teamwork.

Vision, flexibility, empathy, commitment to learners and to excellent teaching.

A balance of a strategic and hands-on approach. It seems to be either leaders who are too concerned with policy/strategy, are too remote and non-involved, or those who are very hands-on and involved locally but do not invest enough time in keeping abreast of changes/new directions.

Innovation and standardization which leads to raising quality – it seems that many services have been left to their own devices, and quality is too varied.

Target setting should be a working tool, rather than a 'benchmark' plucked at random out of thin air. Leaders who maintain regular contact with learners and staff are in a better position both to decide on priorities and to set targets accordingly. Good leaders are trusted by – and put their trust in – the staff under them. This usually holds true for middle management, but not for senior management, where distrust on both sides appears the norm. This must change.

Vision, clarity, wisdom, inspirational.

Vision and a willingness to be innovative even if this leads to short term 'pain'. This then needs to be coupled with an ability to persuade others of the validity of this vision by allowing – and listening to – open debate and constructive challenge to such innovations from those expected to implement change. Courage to follow through on 'painful' decisions.

A good role model and team player. To inspire others by example. Encourages other to reach their full potential. There is also a need for additional funding to enable staff to attend training on leadership issues.

Vision, empathy with front-line staff, experience of the sector, willingness to get involved with front-line activities (especially students) on a regular (preferably frequent) basis. Political nous and clout. Ability to survive in a poorly led, politically ineptly led, poorly planned sector.

Vision, fairness, influence, depth and breadth of understanding of the sector and deprivation factors, ability to communicate effectively to people at all levels and effective strategist. There must be enthusiasm for the future and for social justice. There must be support for ways of working which are less bureaucratic so that resources are well targeted at the needy.

Clear grasp of the landscape of FE followed through into a robust strategic direction which is effectively communicated to staff at all levels and facilitated through effective performance management with clear lines of accountability and reporting.

The courage to speak out against ill-conceived government policies and initiatives that are top-down and continually target-driven.

Figure 10.1: Leadership Survey results: question 14 (Jameson, 2006b)

leadership and 'hands-on' work, trust, courage, inspirational and encouraging role models, political 'nous' and clout, fairness, depth and breath of understanding of the LSC sector and deprivation issues, enthusiasm for the future, commitment to social justice and a clear, robust grasp of strategies for FE.

Responses for both 'strongly' and 'somewhat agree' outweighed those who disagreed with or were neutral to the statement in question 12: *Overall I have strong confidence in leadership in the learning and skills sector in the following areas.*

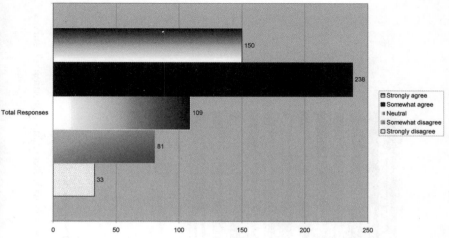

Figure 10.2: Strength of confidence in leadership across all areas in the learning and skills sector (Question 12)

'Neutral' responses were somewhat high, however, indicating possibly some reluctance to comment in areas of leadership with which respondents were less familiar (e.g. LSC sector external business leaders or union leaders, in some cases), or, in the case of some principals and other senior leaders, a conscientious wish to remain impartial in answering the survey. One principal commented that staff lower down in the hierarchy would not really know anything much about local or national LSC leadership, and therefore would be likely to remain neutral on that issue.

Figure 10.3 reports the detail regarding each area of leadership. The highest response count (37) was for the reply 'somewhat agree' in terms of having confidence in 'my institution – middle managers'. The second and third highest response counts, respectively, were 'somewhat agree' for 'my institution – academic teacher-leaders' (34) and 'my institution – governance' (30).

Next highest, in turn, was strong agreement with confidence in 'my institution – principal/CEO/head' (29) 'my institution – senior management' (28), and 'my own line manager' (26). Overall, the highest level of responses indicating strong agreement (29) was for 'my institution – principal/ CEO/ head',

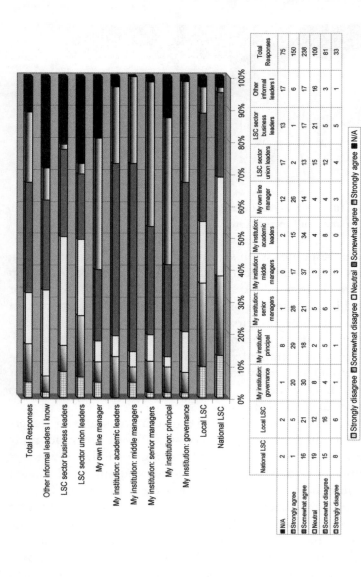

Figure 10.3: Analysis of responses to leadership survey regarding confidence in sector-wide leadership (Question 12, survey 1)

though the fact that the survey was distributed to senior managers and principals amongst other groups may or may not have introduced some bias, as indicated above. Assumptions cannot reliably be made that bias introduced would necessarily be in favour of leadership and management, however, as some senior managers, including principals, explicitly noted that they would be attempting to answer with a degree of objectivity.

Since responses are still being collected and the survey will remain open for some time to collect a wider range of responses, the results at this stage (autumn 2006) are illuminating rather than definitive: they do not constitute 'proof' that these views are representative of the majority of staff in the sector. The results do, however, provide useful indicative 'live' data from 79 respondents in or closely positioned to the sector, which we can use to consider our question about important factors affecting leadership and management in FE. An important factor to recognize in all research studies on the sector is the enormous complexity and diversity of local situations. As we noted above, there is no 'one size fits all' model of leadership and management that will suit all situations across the sector, and no one source that could necessarily accurately understand and report such a model, anyway, even if it did exist, so we always need to do the best with patchy elements of truth filtered through real-world complexities.

UK national standards for leadership and management in FE

Despite the myriad of local complexities, however, there is increasing UK government emphasis on providing a uniform structure of requirements for leaders and managers in the sector. A consultation by the Sector Skills Council for Lifelong Learning, Lifelong Learning UK (LLUK), was held on draft national standards for the role of FE principal. LLUK invited bids in 2006 for project management of the review and redevelopment of the national standards for leadership and management. In this project, the successful tender proposer will, with LLUK, and funded by DfES, develop professional occupational standards to cover all leadership and management roles in learning and skills within the 'FE system' defined by the FE White Paper (2006) (LLUK, 2006: 1).

These developments are linked to the revision of the national occupational standards for management in FE colleges (the NOS) launched in October 2001 by the former Further Education National Training Organisation (FENTO), now subsumed as part of Lifelong Learning UK. These early FENTO management standards were adapted for further education from generic national management standards produced by the Management Charter Initiative (MCI) (LLUK, 2006). A revision of the standards is now necessary, according to feedback from leaders in the sector. A number of reasons for this are cited by LLUK (LLUK, 2006:1). First, LLUK points out that FENTO has since been incorporated within it, and the LSC sector now includes adult and community learning, plus work-based training. Second, the Centre for Excellence in Leadership has been set up since the original standards were designed. The CEL *Leadership Qualities Framework* (CEL, 2004) was produced, now used sector-wide in training for UK leader-managers: the standards need to be reconciled with this framework. Third, new national standards for leadership and management have been produced by the Management Standards Centre (MSC). Fourth, LLUK notes:

LLUK: Review of the National Occupational Standards for Leadership (extract only – for original, see LLUK, 2006):
The role of the Principal is to:

- Anticipate the policy agenda and provide clear strategic leadership
- Lead the college with passion and energy, inspiring others
- Focus firmly on the mission and purpose of the college
- Promote the interests of students and employers within the college
- Set clear expectations to achieve high standards of quality
- Manage the college effectively

- Encourage all college staff to continually develop and improve
- Create positive relationships and develop collaborative working

The elements of the National Leadership and Management Standards are:

- Planning for the Future (strategic focus)
- Leading Learning and Teaching (learner focus)
- Recruiting and Developing People (people focus)
- Managing Operations, Finance and Resources (operational focus)
- Liability, Responsibility and Risk (accountability focus)
- Working with Partners, Employers and Networks (systems focus)

There is also an increasing emphasis on collaborative working within the sector and there is a clear need to address issues of equality and diversity and the skills to manage through periods of change. (LLUK, 2006:1)

And finally, from work with the Development Education Association (DEA) and consultant expert colleagues on global leadership for the lifelong learning sector, we observe that there is a need to incorporate within the standards additional factors relating to global leadership development, sustainability.

The attributes of good leadership

See also Chapter 2:

- Prioritization of student success as the core educational value of the sector
- Communicative clarity and coherence in influencing others
- A strong values-base
- Strategic thinking – big picture
- Capability to motivate others
- Capable of being people-centred/an emotionally intelligent leader

- Capable of authenticity
- Having passion and optimism
- Capable of teamwork
- Capable of building on and using others' perspectives
- Able to engage in self-development
- Able to be flexible and adaptable in renewing self and organizations

Prioritization of student success as the core educational value of the sector

The first essential element we identify is the need to prioritize student success, as discussed earlier in relation to Ofsted's findings for outstanding colleges. This is an absolutely indispensable element of good leadership, as it concentrates and focuses on the key purpose of educational institutions. Some of the outstanding colleges inspected by Ofsted and some of the successful leaders identified in Jameson (2006) have this, on its own, as their sole mission and purpose.

Communicative clarity and coherence in influencing others

The second essential element we pinpoint is clear, meaningful communication. To be effective, leaders must communicate well with people who work with and follow them. Such communication must also have an advantageous influence on others, if we are to take a more 'transformational' view of leadership, building on earlier theorists (Burns, 1978). Good communication can take many forms. It can be made evident through speech, actions, physical appearance, gestures and movements, writing, eye contact, silence, and through the creation of an enriching environment and/or atmosphere in the use of resources. Above all, however, effective communication by leaders must be appropriate to the people, time, place and situation in which the leader operates. It must also accurately address, listen to and respond in some way, even if instinctively and follower-defined, to the needs and characteristics of those following the leader. In educational institutions, effective communication is a two-way process: the leader must listen as well as talk, give as well as take, respond as well as lead, know when to be silent and when to be outspoken. Essentially it is balancing act, which those who are skilled in leadership perform with fluency.

An effective leader's communication will almost invariably have elements of clarity, astuteness, appropriacy, kindliness and inspirational influence, although these qualities may be expressed in many different forms and styles, may not instantly be recognized and may not always be present in the same degree or in the same ways as in other leaders. Good communication by leaders can be overt or subtle, enthusiastic or restrained, lengthy or terse, witty or serious, ostentatious or reserved, directed at one person or at many. The main thing, however, is that the leader must be understood clearly by followers, and, if we adopt a transformational view, must have a beneficial influence on them.

Successful leaders are usually also people who can express complex ideas in ways that are directly and immediately understood. Some leaders may instinctively use metaphors and images to convey their messages more candidly than ordinary words would do. All of the outstanding leaders I have met and interviewed in further education have been excellent at communicating with their followers. You could say that some winning leaders seem to light up a room when they walk into it, so that everyone in the room is aware that they are in the presence of an effective leader. They hold a relational power and a meaning-making ability that attracts people. However, rather than characterize this as an 'heroic' quality, it is useful to see such power as a potential attribute of everyone, and something that can be developed. All of the learning and skills sector interviewees reported here unanimously disagreed with the concept of 'heroic' leadership, or that power should ever be held by only one person. As Ruth Silver put it, 'I believe in leadership but I do not believe in leaders' (Jameson, 2006).

The kind of characteristic attraction some leader-managers stimulate in their followers through the way they communicate could be termed 'charismatic leadership'. However, charismatic leaders are not always beneficent. Hence there is danger in assuming that a strong presence, charm and good rhetorical skills are all that those in powerful positions need to be effective leaders. If that were the case, then many people in power who

---

Viewpoint 2.2: David Collins – metaphor for leadership

David: Yes, of course. I think the real role of a leader ... is to maintain the integrity of the mission, vision, values, structures, policies, systems, procedures, actions etc. So that the organization functions as a coherent and purposeful and successful unit. It is that *tying it all together* element which is key, I think, to a leader. Otherwise, you won't get the movement in a particular direction or the vision being achieved because there'll be too many pieces pulling in different directions.

Now this requires different emphases at different times and the ability to see what aspect of the organization's operation needs a particular focus or input. And giving you a metaphor within that, I've picked first of all on the *music hall novelty act*, going back a few years now, I can't, thank God, say I've seen it for a while, but the skill was to keep as *many plates spinning on a stick*, I think, if I remember rightly in motion and to be successful in doing this act you always had to be aware of one that was wobbling and get in there quick and give it extra attention.

I think the added complication that we seem to face in the real world, is that nowadays the environment is constantly changing and it's as if in that music hall act the stage is also moving and the audience also wants to see constant changes in the act. So you're not just spinning the plates, but you're spinning them in a very dynamic environment and it's receiving a very different action.

I think, to be a successful leader, you've got to ensure that all these extraneous movements on the organization are properly assessed and accommodated, so I think my first analogy would be *the plate spinner*.

---

have a charismatic style would automatically be good leaders. However, we know from prior negative examples such as Hitler, Papa Doc, Pol Pot, Mugabe and similarly tyrannical dictators, that charisma without a strong beneficent values-base can be deadly. Many years ago, Eisenhower wrote: 'The supreme quality for leadership is unquestionable integrity. Without it, no real success is possible, no matter whether it is on a section gang, a football field, in an army, or in an office' (cited in Covey, 2004: 146).

A strong values-base

The third essential element for good leadership that we could point out, therefore, is the need to have a strong values-base underpinning the vision and mission of the institution. David Collins was among the interviewees who demonstrated in his interview with me that a values-based culture is:

.... absolutely, almost absolutely essential, because I don't know of an organization that really succeeds without having implicit or explicit values that people hold in common. Otherwise, you are invariably going to get tensions with people operating in ways that they're not comfortable with or railling against ways in which things are being done. (see Viewpoint 2.2) (Dr David Collins, CBE, interview (Jameson, 2006))

Strategic thinking – big picture

It is important for leaders to work explicitly to outline and express the 'big picture' of strategic thinking for the institution as a whole, within the context of the learning and skills sector locally, regionally and nationally. What is a strategic plan? Essentially, it is a framework for the 'big picture' for the next several years of work for an FE institution. The strategic plan expands on the mission statement of the institution, outlining the key purposes and nature of the work of the learning and skills provision, the values that underpin the institution's operations, its understanding of the region in which it works and the needs of the main stakeholders involved, the benefits the institution hopes to provide, and its overall contribution to further education locally, regionally and nationally.

The strategic plan identifies clear priorities for the required period to achieve the mission and key purposes of the FE institution, to meet the needs of stakeholders in providing its core business. The strategic plan is underpinned by a more detailed operational plan outlining the processes and timescales by which the priorities identified in the strategic plan will be implemented and achieved within the organization, and the resources and personnel that will be deployed to achieve them.

As we noted earlier in the book, since 1993 colleges have been responsible for their own strategic planning, first to the FEFC (Further Education Funding Council) and, since 2001, to the LSC. Early strategic planning processes in FE were criticized as being either 'too inefficient' or 'too business-like' (Lumby, 1999), which suggests that you can't really win easily in this area. In 1999, Lumby carried out an analysis of 53 college strategic plans, and concluded that strategic planning occurred 'within a national strategic vacuum' using 'diverse plans and processes' (Lumby, 1999).

Since then, the picture has improved to some extent in terms of coherence, since greater attention has been paid to FE nationally in the recent Foster Review (2005) and White Paper on FE (2006). However, the overriding emphasis now on skills, vocational and work-based learning has perhaps created a new national coherence which is now rather too narrow, in terms of focus, to match either the diversity of what colleges actually do or the learners who need their provision. This narrowness has been pointed out in the House of Commons Education and Skills Committee *Fourth Report of the Session 2004–05* (House of Commons, 2006). Hopefully there may be some re-think of this for colleges, so that under-recognized elements of the work that is done in FE are preserved more effectively, in addition to the generally welcomed skills focus plus social inclusiveness agenda for the sector (DfES, 2006).

Recognizing the complexity of the above, and the need to juggle so many balls simultaneously in FE, while at the same time new ones are being thrown in the ring and others are disappearing, how can we win through on strategic planning? It is difficult. However, the *Essential FE Toolkit Series* provides leader-managers in FE with a helpful guide to strategic planning in David Collins's book, *Survival Guide for College Leaders and Managers*, which is highly recommended for those leader-managers who would like more detail on this area. A range of other recommended resources for strategic planning are also provided in the Appendices.

Capability to motivate others

As a leader-manager in FE, how do you motivate staff in institutions to achieve the best of which they are capable? Well, it's partly about offering people freedom within constraints, and managing diversity appropriately and responsively. It's about the 'deployment of discretions' to use Ruth Silver's phrase: enabling staff to select, for example, areas of freedom and agency they want for themselves, and allowing them to carry these out to develop local leadership, competence and skill. It's also about offering new, additional, supportive and interesting opportunities to staff, such as participation in external visits and conferences, lectures by visiting speakers, staff development courses, mentoring and peer support networks, recreational events such as staff parties and sports matches, and charity events, as well as specific opportunities for particular people to gain promotion, increases in salary or other rewards. It's about recognizing the needs of staff to gain support, structured assistance, reward, understanding feedback and 'critical friend' responsiveness for the work they do. Eliciting the views of staff via staff meetings, working parties, questionnaires, interviews, impromptu discussions and invited staff newsletter contributions is important. Rewards systems such as schemes for the 'best employee of the month' or 'best teacher of the year' can be highly valued by staff, and a feature can be made of the work that they do.

Capable of being people-centred

People need to feel they are valued, noticed and appreciated in their workplaces, or they may feel increasingly disconnected from institutions and start to plan ways to leave for another workplace in which they will be more appreciated. 'People-centred' leadership and management aims to focus on the needs, aspirations and talents of people in the organization, in contrast with 'task-focused' or 'systems-based' leadership and management. Even those leaders who prefer to focus mainly on tasks need to develop some people-centred skills and capability if they are to succeed in communicating effectively with followers and students.

Capable of authenticity

The concept of 'authenticity' in leadership is used to describe leaders who are operating genuinely and truthfully rather than as pseudo-leaders, manipulating and deceiving others. This is a key component of genuine benevolent leadership which distinguishes the fake from the real, particularly in relation to 'transformational leadership'. The criterion of 'authenticity' is discussed in more detail in a number of chapters in this book. It is suggested that leader-managers in FE should develop authenticity and fluidity in a living leadership context, rather than always allow themselves to be shaped by the external demands of agencies pulling and pushing for FE to be as they require it. This is also about developing and enabling confidence, so that students and staff can grow into being who they really want to be in ways that mutually benefit themselves and the institution.

This is discussed in more detail in relation to the development of a 'reflexive' (rather than resistant, accommodatory or over-compliant) response to policy demands in FE in Hillier and Jameson (2003: 29–33). In this publication, a typology of response patterns to policy initiatives in FE is outlined. Basically, the 'reflexive' response to policy in further education reaches a balance between rushing in over enthusiastically to implement every new initiative (over-compliant), and resisting angrily every new policy (resistant), while eschewing the wholesale watering down and swallowing up of policy (accommodatory). The reflexive response responds thoughtfully to policy changes, within the authentic context of the institution's own purposes, values and mission and its leaders' authentic priorities, fitted for the local environment. In this framework, leaders are encouraged to be courageous in identifying and developing distinctive and unique provision within the context of the institution's key interests and values. This kind of authentic 'distinctiveness' was mentioned in conversation with John Guy at Farnborough Sixth Form College. John said that at Farnborough they deliberately decided not to lose the distinctiveness of being a sixth form college, even when encouraged to do so in 1992:

> .... within the English system we're a sixth form college which, in 1992, when we transferred from the school sector to the college sector, was a risk really because a whole number of sixth form colleges wanted to ditch the title 'sixth form college' at that time. And it was a curious thing to do, because the mission of our colleges was about the 16 to 19 cohort, so we didn't ditch it because we thought it was something that actually parents and students valued..... So our mission really, our purpose is to provide the highest quality academic and vocation education to the young

people who live in the travel to study area centred on Farnborough. (Dr John Guy, OBE, interview 2005, Jameson, 2006)

Having passion and optimism

One of the reasons why people are persuaded by and influenced by leaders is that successful leaders are usually both passionate and optimistic about their work. This isn't necessarily obviously manifest in a Pollyanna-like fashion (though it may be). Sometimes people who are apparently externally dour and taciturn are, ultimately, the most quietly passionate and determined of all. Do not let external appearances mislead you either way in the analysis of whether leadership is genuinely passionate or optimistic. Try to see the results of people's leadership work and real actions rather than be swayed by superficial factors or by what may be ill-informed gossip. Remember that the quietest, most unassuming people may be effective leaders, just as the noisiest, most assertive people may also be. There is no 'one size fits all' model for leadership, as we have said a number of times in this book: but what is sometimes most important is that the 'fit' with the organization, in terms of the leaders' passion and purposes, is appropriate and achieves the best for students and staff, as Ruth Silver observed:

.... the *joy of the fit* ... is leadership's real skill ... it is social purpose, primary task and the world it finds itself in. Too often, my experience has been that when organizations get into difficulty, it's when they try and shut the work away and do their own thing, pretend that change isn't happening. We welcome change here and I think it's a very good. It's the aliveness of the institution. 'Fit' is the optimizing, and maximizing, of all of those things. (Dame Ruth Silver, DBE, interview 2005, Jameson, 2006)

Capable of teamwork

'Collaborative leadership', which builds strategy and operations for institutions in a spirit of teamwork, is increasingly at the forefront of leadership development programmes and research studies in further education. We live nowadays in a pluralistic, ever-changing global world in which no one person now can possibly have all the knowledge or abilities needed for an institution to keep up with changing events and to prosper. Leadership development to encourage teamwork at all levels is therefore strongly recommended in FE institutions.

Capable of building on and using others' perspectives

Within a teamwork perspective, leaders need to build on and use other people's perspectives in positive ways that acknowledge and give some power to all levels of institutional operation. There is a Japanese saying which goes, 'None of us is as smart as all of us.' There is quite a lot of truth in that. As a leader-manager, you will progress a lot further and faster in your college if you are able to tap into and use the collective knowledge and perspectives of all the staff. David Collins recommends this kind of perspective to us in his 'pictures on the walls story', (page 213) which he described as 'a very visual opportunity of showing the importance of team work and how important it was ... for everybody to realise that, yes, no matter how big the problem, if you've got four hundred people trying to solve it, you can solve it' (Jameson, 2006:190). If you build on and genuinely use the perspectives and energetic contributions of all of the staff in the institution, there will be almost nothing in the college mission that you cannot achieve together.

Able to engage in self-development

Leaders need to develop themselves all the time. This may sound like a truism, but it needs to be said, especially for older staff who may already be well-qualified, experienced and skilled, and may feel that they have reached the limit of their 'trainability'. Everyone can still improve their work, though, no matter how experienced and skilled they are, and therefore staff development programmes for leaders and managers at every level of the institution are necessary.

Summary

In Chapter 10, lessons from leaders, staff and some outstanding leader-managers in the FE system from interviews and a leadership survey are considered, as are leadership and management suggestions arising from research findings. The detailed results of the research survey are discussed. Some points relating to good leadership and management are outlined in relation to further education and the role of national agencies such as the Centre for Excellence in Leadership (CEL).

11: Bringing out the leader-manager within you

Whatever you can do, or dream you can do, begin it. Boldness has genius, power and magic in it. Begin it now.

Goethe

Some experiences of respondents in FE are reported here from various histories in senior management positions. This picks up on the kind of detailed situation reported in our story in the Introduction, and carries it forward. Some months or years ago (depending on the case study involved), these senior managers were working at Principal, Vice Principal, Director, Campus Manager or other senior level in an FE college not so far from you. These stories are here to tell you what happened in some challenging and difficult situations in which a leader-manager needed to act, and did act, decisively.

Our stories are reported in a series of Case Study boxes. When you've read them, we'll meet you at the end. The nature of these experiences might make your hair stand on end if you think you'll have to deal with all these on your own. Our aim is to alert you to some of the things that can happen in FE in a leader-manager's job, and to guide you in possible ways to cope with such incidents, including, notably, working as a team with others and using their strengths. We will also refer you to other books in the leadership and management series. The job of a leader-manager in FE can be wonderful, but also challenging: how will you develop yourself as a leader-manager?

Case Study 11.1: Challenging leadership situations reported by FE staff

While managing an FE college inner-city site, our respondents dealt with the following incidents as a college leader-manager. How would you deal with these? Do you think the leader-manager here acted in the best way or not? What else could have been done?

- *A gas leak* in a college building with 2,000 students required a full-scale evacuation. The director was called to deal with it. What would you do?
  Actions taken by leadership/management: The director evacuated the building and called emergency services. It turned out that the 'gas leak' was a chemical reaction caused by the interaction of large amounts of bleach with residual urine in the gents' loos – this was embarrassing for the facilities management. The incident was resolved successfully without problem, but with an apology and a lesson learnt by the (new) facilities staff.
- *A bomb scare* with a message sent to all students in the campus requiring an immediate negotiation with the police on whether to evacuate or not. What would you do?
  Actions taken by leadership/management: The campus manager called the police. He suspected a student prank and did not evacuate the building, acting on what the police said. The police warned him that they were not allowed to offer telephone advice in such situations, but that they could let him know that no code words for terrorist organizations had been used. He consulted with the ICT technical staff to examine the message. They both thought it looked suspiciously like a prank. They were right: it turned out that the bomb scare was a student hoax. The culprits were shame-facedly punished, but at the time, it seemed real enough – the incident was successfully handled.

- *A gunshot wound* to a local minority ethnic resident who fell into the college entrance bleeding profusely from a main artery, begging for help. What would you do?
  Actions taken by leadership/management: The director called the air ambulance rescue service, they arrived to take the patient to hospital; everything turned out OK. This is described in detail in the Introduction.

- *A suicide case:* The director was called because a young woman had threatened suicide and locked herself in the toilet. When he arrived, he discovered that teaching staff had persuaded the student to come out of the toilet, but she was sitting with a vacant look in her eyes in the carpeted corridor of the college building, saying she had nothing to live for and would commit suicide. This seemed to be more than a vain cry for attention: she seemed to have lost her will to live. What would you do?
  Actions taken by leadership/management: The director went to sit with the student to ensure this young person was protected from self-harm. From there, he immediately contacted the student counsellor and arranged for specialist treatment. It turned out later that the student was depressed and had made several suicide attempts already. A long-term course of counselling and medication was set up for the student. The incident was resolved satisfactorily.

Case Study 11.2: Challenging leadership situations reported by FE staff

Transforming college provision

Case study boxes 11.2–11.5 involve situations in which college leader-managers not only handled the immediate incident, but also set about a longer-term transformation of college provision. How would you deal with such situations? Do you think leader-managers here acted in the best way or not? What else could have been done to transform the situation in this situation and in 11.3? How are the examples cited in 11.4 and 11.5 useful for others?

- *A mini student protest* occurred in the college one afternoon, involving a group of 16–19-year-old students with generally low achievement and poor behaviour. They had ganged up together angrily because the canteen was temporarily closed. A group of about 20 were gathered outside the main building, shouting and complaining about not having any canteen services. The facilities staff called the vice principal, who was on duty. The security officers were concerned that an 'incident' might follow.
  Actions taken by leadership/management: The vice principal assessed the situation. Already the students, noisy and easily distracted at the best of times, were beginning to dissipate. She looked at the time: 5.30 pm. She judged they would soon be on their way. She had taught students like these in the past and knew the situation was likely to blow over soon: it was not worth having a confrontation. She stayed at the entrance, watching things develop. She was right. Within five minutes, the group became distracted by other things and left the premises. However, she was concerned about what had happened for the longer term future of the college. She contacted the canteen manager, asking if this canteen closure would be repeated. Having gained an assurance that this would not happen again during the college year (the closure was a one-off start-of-year stock-filling), she walked around that evening, consulting in an impromptu way with staff and students about the canteen.

It appeared things could be improved. The canteen manager agreed and said it would be OK to ask for student feedback. At the end of her walkabout, the vice principal sat down in her office and quickly designed a student questionnaire: *'Your views on the college canteen – Win an iPod!'*, offering a prize of an IPod for the best answer to a question at the end. The secretarial team picked up her urgent request to reproduce the questionnaires first thing the next morning. By 8.15 am, hundreds of copies were at the college entrance under a poster displaying an IPod. Within a few days, feedback was received from hundreds of students, necessary changes were made to the canteen, and one delighted 17-year-old student walked off with a new prize of an IPod. There were no more complaints from students about the canteen that year. In planning for the following year, the vice principal set up a task group to extend and improve the canteen facilities.

Case Study 11.3: Challenging leadership situations reported by FE staff

Transforming college provision

- *A knife attack threat* involving a black college student who travelled to a neighbouring school site weekly to study 'A' level Latin. This had been set up under the local 16–19 consortium agreement, as there was no provision for Latin at the college. The school rang the college principal to say the black student had threatened younger white pupils with a knife. No violence was involved, but the school head was concerned.

  Actions taken by leadership/management: The principal consulted the director of student services and asked her to handle the situation urgently and report back. The director consulted the school head. The student was summoned to meet the director immediately with his father.

In an interview with the student's father, the director discovered that the student had recently been threatened in a series of disturbing racist incidents in the area around the school. The young man was terrified and had carried a knife to defend himself. Some younger pupils had been joking around, calling out and laughing at him when he visited the school the next day. In what he thought was a defensive move, he pulled out a knife and shown it to them threateningly, telling them not to laugh at him. The pupils were terrified and reported the incident. The student's father was apologetic for his son's behaviour. He chastised him, saying he must never fight verbal racist situations with physical weapons or he might injure someone, get into trouble and end up in jail. The student was contrite. He apologized, saying he would try never to carry a knife again, but that he had been (and still was) frightened by what had happened in the environment around the school and did not know what to do. He was not strong physically and felt he needed a knife. He also said he thought school treatment of him was sometimes unsympathetic and that younger kids were rude to him. He was unhappy there, but wanted to finish his Latin, in which he was progressing well.

The director discussed the situation with the school head again. It was early summer. There were only a few lessons left before exams. She consulted with school staff and other students. It appeared that these younger pupils were rude to almost everyone, and needed disciplining for general behaviour as well as for this racist incident. The school head agreed that they would be suitably punished. Following further discussions with the head, the principal, the boy's father and the local police regarding both the knife-carrying and the racist incidents, it was agreed that some special sessions would be set up at the college for the student to have one-to-one tuition in the pre-exam. period so that he would not have to visit the school again. It was also agreed that, longer-term, the boy's father would take the young man to self-defence and assertiveness classes to learn how to defend himself without resorting to the use of weapons. The director set up a working group involving local police and community representatives to investigate the safety of local student travel-to-study routes. The principal was satisfied with the outcome. The student passed his exams at 'A' level. There were no more negative incidents involving him and he went on to university, where he continues to study. He never carried a knife again. The school staff, led by the principal and director, developed improved race equality policies and training for all staff, setting up some college-school events on race equality for students.

Case Study 11.4: Challenging leadership situations reported by FE staff

Transforming college provision

Lynne Sedgmore: It was a big watershed for me ... when I got promoted to the head of a business school [earlier in my career]. And that was such a diverse group of people. That was everything from bankers and accountants, through to the HR staff and the marketing people.

I'd mostly worked with, primarily, teachers up to that point, but here I got more ... these were management and leadership professionals who, of course, know it far better than any of the heads of department do, because they've all been out there, haven't they? And whether they've made it or not in the world, they know better. I mean the management team were just totally unmanageable. The social workers were quite difficult, the lawyers were all litigating, and it was absolutely fascinating. And I think that's when I really moved into being a leader, because of the relational side: we did the process stuff, but it really got me thinking about what being a leader was.

Because I had to, well I couldn't manage this lot, because they were totally unmanageable in the best sense, so it was herding cats of a certain kind and that was really when I started to think what is this leadership? How do I create relationships with a guy over here who's an accountant and a banker and then these incredibly creative people over here, these social workers and these MEd people and all the rest of it and that became like a playground, a whole kind of laboratory: and I used *collaborative inquiry* to engage with that, to understand ... A mix of Heron and Talbot and Peter Reason's work. I really got into human inquiry and all that collaborative inquiry, to really try and make sense of how you – have followers, or you generate followers – from people who didn't want to follow. They were a bunch of semi-anarchists. Highly professional and incredibly hard working.

And within four years, the Business School ... went from strength to strength. We over-achieved all our targets, we increased revenue three times. It was just a wonderful success story. But it was down to all of that relational stuff. So, it didn't change me – it formed my view, and I think in my model I went from managerial operational strategic really into the relational, and really understanding ... this was [in the early days] ... when ... 'leadership' hadn't really come to the fore in that sense. So I think that's what really formed my views ... I've kind of honed that and moved on.

Then when I went to [another appointment], to a very different environment, that was another major watershed. Because things that had worked well in [the earlier situation] weren't necessarily working well. And that's when I learnt [about] *contextual [leadership]*, the importance of the context and ... the situation. And who the followers are in relation to the leaders.

Because I'm just sitting there saying, 'Gosh, this worked really well in that context – why isn't it working here?' And again it was all in that relational [work] – and how people [reacted in different situations] – where they were coming from.

Case Study 11.5: Challenging leadership situations reported by FE staff

Transforming college provision

David Collins: I'll give you an example of something which probably of all the bits and pieces that I've done around the world, down through my life and wherever in the world, I'm probably most proud of, and it's just an idea that came to me in the middle of the night.

I was at one failing college as an acting principal to sort out or help them sort out, obviously, fairly major financial positions and some issues of quality, etc. ... I was brought in shortly before Christmas, about three weeks before Christmas, to an institution that was in a pretty big mess. Staff were very demoralized. In fact, I think the week before, they had had placards with the management team's (who were there, then) photographs on them being paraded around the building, blaming them for the mess that the college was in.

I had a staff meeting straight away and outlined how bad the problem was and said, 'This is how much money we've got to save. Provided we've got cooperation and everybody is on the same side, we can do this without compulsory redundancies and we can make sure that the college has a firm future.' And then the idea which came to me in the middle of the night. I said, 'We can only do this if we've got everybody working in the same direction and everybody is part of that team, because it's not something that one person can do. It's something that needs all three hundred and eighty of you', or whatever the number was, 'to do it.' So I said, I'm not in college tomorrow, I'm coming back on Thursday and I will tell you on Thursday, what the percentage chances of this college surviving are – precisely. I will work this out to a figure out of a hundred per cent and this is how I will do it. The walls of this campus . . .', and I was pointing particularly at one particular campus '. . . are completely bare. You all have in your garage or in your house somewhere a picture, which you do not want or you could do without. Tomorrow, put them on the walls of the college and I will come in on Thursday morning and count the number of pictures on the walls and the proportion out of three hundred and eighty that we have on the walls, will be our chances of survival.'

I came in on the Thursday and there were something like four hundred and twenty pictures on display, because some people had brought two just in case somebody had forgotten. So it was a fantastic opportunity and also a very visual opportunity of showing the importance of team work and how important it was for that particular organization, for everybody to realise that yes, no matter how big the problem, if you've got four hundred people trying to solve it, you can solve it. And over the rest of the year, people worked very hard, they were very flexible, and that particular college, as it now is, under its new principal is a successful and developing institution.

Questions

This is a true incident that occurred in an FE college. Although we have reported this verbatim from an interview with Dr David Collins, CBE, by kind permission, other names have been removed. What do you think of the incident? What leadership and management characteristics can you identify in David's words? What do you think of the reactions of staff? Can you identify situations like this in your own environment in which you could have an influence in a similar sort of way as David, by getting the staff to rally together around a common cause? How would you react if this kind of situation (financial mess, threat of closure) happened in an institution you work for? In what ways did leadership act to turn this situation around?

Case Study 11.6: Challenging leadership situations reported by FE staff

Transforming college provision

Lynne Sedgmore (In response to the question from Jill Jameson: *What was the most important thing, then, do you think, in terms of what made you achieve success at that point?* [at a challenging point in her career development]): It was learning to be *authentic and vulnerable*, while also being *competent and adding value*. That was the really big lesson there. Because I was still coming at 'management' and all that, a lot from my head ... I didn't feel such an experienced practitioner and – there was a lot of mistrust when I went there, because I was a young woman and they were all men in their 40s and 50s. And there was this 32-year-old woman came along (and I looked younger actually). So it was sort of, 'What can *she* tell us?' They'd all got MBAs ... and I was terrified. I was thinking they'd all be these strategic thinkers and all of that so ... But ... I learnt ... by being really honest, really being clear and having a vision that I shared with them, and really knowing what I was doing as well. ... The big turning point

– when I went there [was when] ... I made a couple of mistakes early on. And I went out and I publicly apologized and explained how we'd got there.

They weren't massive blunders or anything, they were about – one was about trying to reduce course hours quicker than they were ready for – and they were up in arms. Now, I'd do it much more incrementally, but it was like, 'Come in, let's do that, got to make my mark.' And going out and then actually saying to them, 'Hang on, I think I got this wrong, let me talk you through where I was coming from. The way I saw it was this. I was under these incredible pressures to try and impress you all and to ...' And I was just really honest with them and [said], 'Actually, I'm changing my decision on that now, I'm publicly acknowledging that, I've listened to what's been said, I've heard, so we're going to change that and I just hope you can hear that in the spirit in which it's given. Now if I make a mistake everyday, then I think I should resign, but ...' And it wasn't easy – it was hard.

It's being *very authentic*. ... My experience is that if you do that *very honestly*, it's amazing. It's almost like *people want the leader not to be perfect*, either, do you know what I mean? I mean, you can't set that up, actually, you can't kind of go, 'I'll make a couple of mistakes and I'll go and apologize, then they're all trust me or whatever.'

But they were very real. I mean, I'm like *agonizing* over this and losing sleep and, 'What do I do with this?' ... Now, I'd ... have much more courage through experience, that actually the more open you are ... and you show that. It's a form of – it's not weakness you're showing – it's *vulnerability* and I think it's different. But it took me a while to understand what that difference is. Those were the turning points.

Bringing out the leader-manager in you

We meet you, as promised, on the other side of the case studies. Having looked at a few of these practical, somewhat challenging examples of what Iszatt White, Kelly and Rouncefield (2005) describe as the 'mundane' work of daily leader-manager tasks in FE colleges, how can we use these to help bring out the leader-managers within ourselves? Well, first of all, we can learn from prior leaders who have carried out the processes involved in 'doing leadership work' effectively in FE colleges. Read through the case studies again. Consider how and why leadership was effective in these cases and whether you would agree or disagree with the actions taken. What can we learn from the 'meaningful moments' of leadership reported here?

Developing situation–specific leadership and management skills

First, from Lynne Sedgmore, we can learn the importance of relational work, collaborative inquiry, being authentic and honest, demonstrating vulnerability and allowing followers to see that you are not perfect. Next, we can learn the importance of effective leadership work which relates to the particular context, culture and situation you find yourself in. In Lynne's Case Study 11.4, the highly successful strategies employed in the first situation did not work in the second situation. The people, place, work demands and circumstances were different. The prevailing ethos had its own peculiarities which did not 'fit' with earlier strategies, so she needed to change, re-think, and learn adaptability and flexibility – several of the hallmarks of successful leadership work.

Second, from David Collins, we can learn how essential and useful it is to engage the whole staff in the mission, achievement and development of an institution, getting every single member of staff to sacrifice a bit of themselves for the good of the whole, so that no one person has to suffer from being made redundant. We can learn from this how helpful it is to give people a vision and means of actively securing a potentially safe future for themselves and the institution, in the context of a failing college, i.e. how important it is to bring all staff 'on board' in rescuing the institution.

Third, from the more general case studies reported earlier, we can learn how important it is to be 'street-wise', focused and practical in the job of leadership, to concentrate on the task in hand and solve each problem with confidence and skill in a realistic, appropriate way. In each of the somewhat scary situations reported here, the leader-manager did not know the answer immediately, but through focused attention, clever thinking and team-work, each one managed successfully to resolve the challenges of the situation. You too can achieve success if you are determined to learn how to be a good leader-manager in FE.

Prioritizing between the multiple challenges of leader-managers

It can seem sometimes that the job of a leader-manager in FE is never done. When you are a senior manager operating at executive level in colleges, there often seem to be not enough hours in the day to cope with all the competing priorities of the above kinds of internal and external requirements. And yet colleagues working in FE institutions do cope well enough – in some cases, spectacularly well. Sometimes college leaders achieve amazing things that at first appear to be impossible. Sometimes we do not achieve everything we set out to do, and have to pick ourselves up, dust ourselves off, learn from our mistakes, grow in our thinking and adjust to new realities. Anyone who says they have never failed at anything is, in our view, unlikely to be telling the full truth.

To consider how leader-managers can realistically determine the most important aspects of their role, how best to tackle the plethora of tasks facing them, and how best to cope with changing situations in FE are some of the aims of this book. We provide here a suggested framework for coping with multiple responsibilities in leadership and management in FE, gaining the trust of staff, and achieving a good percentage of the tasks you set out to do.

Reflect on your role and values
One of the first priorities is to reflect on your role and work-load, to ensure that you are aware of the overall purpose you serve, your own identity in relation to this, and the values which underpin your work. Reflection before the outset of

each year and each week is helpful, in the spaces all of us have during holiday time and weekends. Reflection is important. Give yourself some space to think away from the rush of competing demands at work, to make sure you have had time to consider the real nature of your job in the organization, your role, place within the institution, and the ways in which your own professional and personal motivation, qualifications, skills and interests interact with the demands upon you.

To build on your own personal reflections, if you have an opportunity for a non-confrontational appraisal process to be carried out with your line manager, ensure that you take this up. Within the margins of safety regarding organizational culture, be as honest as you can about what you really feel about the institution (caveat for those with highly negative views: beware of potential outfalls from rocking the boat – could be bad for career health and not worth it, unless you are absolutely sure there is no other way of getting hard truths told and you feel you must be the one to reveal them). Being *authentic* in relation to your own values and motivations through reflection, appraisal and self-development should hopefully be a positive process that should enrich your day-to-day working practice as a leader-manager and make it somewhat easier to cope with the difficult demands you face at work. If you feel safe enough to be honest with your line manager about your reflections, then this process may enable her/him to understand and facilitate improvements in your working conditions and staff development opportunities.

Develop trust

One of the most important factors for leaders is to develop trust and confidence, not only in yourself but in the whole leadership team, staff body and students in an institution. It can be difficult to develop trust when there seems to be none. It requires time, patience, persistence and hard work, following up on little things and continuously making investments in people and processes. It is, however, worth it in the long run.

Remember the tortoise – be persistent and steadfast

The tortoise won in the race against the hare because it carried on steadily along the same path, did not despair, did not give up, but just continue to plug away, on and on, relentlessly progressing until it reached the finish line. Genius mainly consists in hard work, persistence and tenacity, as Thomas Edison famously said: 'Genius is one per cent inspiration and 99 per cent perspiration.' Expelled from school at the age of twelve because the teachers thought he was educationally subnormal, Edison used this apparent failure as a new opportunity to start a paper round. He then created his own newspaper and finally his own laboratory, inventing, amongst other things, the gramophone and lightbulb. After more than 10,000 failures, Edison was still doggedly enthusiastic in pursuing his projects: his relentless creative, systematic persistence and sheer hard work enabled him to enjoy, in the final analysis, many successes. We would all do well to emulate Thomas Edison in the development of these qualities.

Prioritize urgent matters without jeopardizing your own health

It goes without saying that urgent tasks always need to be prioritized and must be dealt with as soon as possible. However, as leader-managers in FE we often need to be reminded to take care of our health and to ensure we get enough rest and relaxation, as the job can be very taxing and stressful, particularly when important deadlines are coming up or there is a major challenge, like an inspection, on the horizon. Unless it's a life-and-death health and safety situation as in our story in the Introduction, though, you need to remember that in most cases in education and training, the question of 'urgency' is relative. Most things will keep until tomorrow, or another suitable deadline, as necessary.

Do not neglect your health, family and happiness by over-working to the point of excessive strain, if you can possibly avoid this. Try to schedule tasks in ways that allow you to get some recreation and enough sleep during the working week. Try to put aside a bit of time for exercise at least once a day, even if this is only walking around the block for ten minutes, walking or running up the stairs instead of taking the lift, or doing a few yoga stretches.

Eliminate entirely or cut down on things that you know are bad for your health, like alcohol, tobacco, caffeine, sugary foods, fizzy drinks, junk foods and other indulgences. Part of the job of being a leader–manager is achieving a balanced and realistic working pattern and lifestyle. Your staff will expect this, to the extent that this allows or impinges on your ability to perform your job effectively. Beyond that, ensure you have also, beyond work, some spaces and freedoms in your life in which work does *not* intrude and has no place, so that you also give yourself respite, freedom, time for contemplation and leisure, and an escape from constantly being at everyone's beck and call. No one should ever expect you to be working at your job 24/7, so if they do, it is time to make a complaint . . .

Develop good judgement by learning from mistakes and failures

Ruth Silver reminded us earlier in the book that 'obstacles are our teachers'. The development of good judgement skills is one of the most difficult challenges facing us in our working lives, whether this is in FE leadership and management or in another role. As a species, human beings often get this wrong. Our tendency to appoint an inappropriate person to a job, not separate the chaff from the wheat, bury the needle firmly in the haystack, be taken in by imposters and fail to recognize true talent is manifested daily. History is full of legendary blunders. Let us consider just a few examples of famous mistakes in judgement (see Figure 11.1).

The writer James Joyce said that 'Mistakes are the portals of discovery'. Without making mistakes sometimes, we do not give ourselves the freedom to take risks and to learn from failure. In the development of innovatory leadership, to allow and forgive mistakes, especially when employees are at the start of a new job or in the early processes of a new venture, is essential in order that people can learn and grow. Bearing in mind the classic examples of legendary blunders overleaf and others of this ilk, can you see any characteristics which describe these kinds of errors of judgement? 'Blind spots', wrong

- In a Western Union internal memo dated 1876, a member of staff wrote, 'This "telephone" has too many shortcomings to be seriously considered as a means of communication. The device is inherently of no value to us.'
- In 1895, the Federal Swiss Polytechnic University rejected an application for entrance from a young man called Albert Einstein. In the same year, Albert's teacher said to the boy's father, 'It doesn't matter what he does, he will never amount to anything.' Ten years later, Einstein gained his doctorate from Zurich University and by 1921 had been awarded the Nobel Prize for Physics, on his way to lasting success as one of the greatest scientists in history.
- In 1897, Lord Kelvin, Victorian physicist and President of the Royal Society, pronounced solemnly that 'Radio has no future'.
- In 1962, an executive at Decca Records rejected a group called The Beatles, telling their manager Brian Epstein, 'I don't like their sound and guitar groups are on the way out, Mr Epstein', signing up local group Brian Poole and the Tremeloes instead. By 1963, the 'Beatlemania' craze began in England: the group rocketed its way to worldwide stardom and became millionaires. The division that let this slip past them must have been shooting itself in the foot ever since.
- In 1974, Margaret Thatcher said, 'It will be years – not in my time – before a woman will become Prime Minister.' She went on to become the first female UK Prime Minister just five years later, in 1979.
- In 1991, Gerald Ratner, owner of Ratner's Jewellery, made a speech in which he rubbished one of his own company's products. By implication, his speech also rubbished Ratner's entire range of jewellery. The result of this monumental error was that he lost his job, and the company went bankrupt and had to re-brand. The expression *Doing a Ratner* lived on to describe a legendary blunder in the making.

Figure 11.1: Some famous mistakes in judgement.

judgement, closed-mindedness, perhaps a range of different kinds of weaknesses in vision and understanding? It is worth pondering on the mistakes made by yourself as well as others in FE in the past to avoid repeating historical errors. In my interview with David Collins he also reminded us of the way in which we can learn from mistakes made in colleges, and put these into perspective. David said that he regarded mistakes as 'learning opportunities', putting these into context in the development of success:

> Certainly, we're quite happy with mistakes and again, that's something that evolves over time. I think when you're younger, you worry about making mistakes and you worry about other people making mistakes. And as you get older, you see them as learning opportunities and you're happy to encourage other people to make them if you have to, not encourage them to make them willy-nilly, but it's not exactly a disaster usually if a mistake is made. So – not to condemn failure or not to be too hard on people who get things wrong. (David Collins, CBE, Principal South Cheshire College, interview 2005)

Develop a set of values for the institution/department and stick by them

In our development as leaders and managers, perhaps the most important thing of all is to develop a set of values for our institution/department or other unit in consultation with others, and to stick by them. We are leaving the most important thing until last in this short guide to bring out the leader-manager in you, because it is the one main issue to remember for the future.

We could begin this important topic by considering the values appropriate for the learning and skills profession as a whole, in terms of the key role of teaching and learning. The Institute for Learning (IfL) wrote about key values for teacher professionals in its recent response to the government White Paper on FE (IfL, 2006: 15):

Ethics and Respect

Teachers recognise the fundamental role they play in developing individuals and the responsibility inherent in teaching learners to learn, helping them acquire the skills to question rather than accept, and to challenge within a process of gaining a greater depth of understanding.

Teachers welcome the fact that whilst having subject expertise there are always alternative solutions and often adult learners will already have an understanding of these. An enhanced level of exchange is achieved when both acknowledge and respect their existing skills, knowledge and expertise, leading to mutual benefits for both teacher and learner.

Five essential ethics underpin professional teaching practice:

- *Truth disclosure* – which must override personal advantage
- *Subjectivity* – where individuals recognise the limits of their perceptions and the individuality of their values
- *Reflective integrity* – where professionals recognise the limits of their personal perceptions and the need to incorporate many understandings of a situation
- *Humility* – where professionals recognise that such sub-jectivity means that personal fallibility is part of the human condition and not a failing
- *Humanistic education* – where it is the duty of the profes-sional to help the learner help themselves

As leader-managers in the sector, we need to be aware of these but also to incorporate values additional to these in terms of leadership and management responsibilities, so this is a good start. Now let's consider also the views of some leader-managers in FE on this question of having a values-base.

John Guy at Farnborough Sixth Form College talked about the importance of values and the maintenance and upkeep of these, using the model of the sigmoid curve as an example:

You've got to balance the notion of leadership within a value system which enables you to be followed but also to set standards as well. . . . You can't expect to lead, unless people actually feel secure in the leadership. And I suppose it's my view that when organizations and institutions go wrong it's because there's a rebellion in the ranks and people no longer want to be led by that leader. And what we try to do in college is ... follow the sigmoid curve ... it's sort of like this.... Things are going well. And then if you don't change, they begin to drop off ... for all sorts of reasons. And the idea is to begin to feel when it's going to do that and then you introduce a new change to improve things, so that the net effect is that, even though when you introduce a change, you get a dip, because you're still on the up, on the whole, you get that sort of movement (demonstrating a new wave of upward movement to counteract the depression of a natural decline in fortunes). (Dr John Guy, OBE, Principal of Farnborough College, interview 2005)

In order to help you continue to progress, update your strategy and make progress as a leader-manager, to abide by a set of common values agreed in the institution is very helpful. An example set of values for an FE college is included here in the case study supplied from South Cheshire College. Discussing these values, and the importance of living with these proactively, in an interview on leadership, David said:

I'd like to go back to a time before I was principal, when I went to a number of community colleges in America. For the first time I came across a college that spent some time defining its values. I was very much struck by how 'different' that organization felt from the others that I visited and it made me much more aware of the importance, I think, of a successful organization having a clear and accepted value-based culture. So when I became principal, one of the first things I did was to draft a set of values for the college that reflected what I believed in. These then became the agreed values on which the new incorporated organization, back in 1993, would be based. Every year since then, as part of our planning process, we review the values, but in essence, they've remained unchanged for the past 12 years ... (David Collins, CBE, Principal South Cheshire College, interview 2005)

The purpose of these values are:

... to create a corporate approach to *how* we do things rather than what we do. I think a values–driven culture is absolutely essential. I don't know of an organization that really succeeds without implicit or explicit values people hold in common . . . as a principal, or leader, you have to be able to show that your words and your actions have a *congruence* and you are setting the example for others to follow. There's perhaps no better way to doing this than by showing values in action (*ibid.*).

We can think of no better way to end this chapter than to quote the values system adopted by South Cheshire College as an example to the FE sector (Case Study 11.7). Our thanks to South Cheshire College staff and to David for their fine work in allowing readers from across the sector to benefit from these recommendations.

Case Study 11.7: The values of South Cheshire College

1. South Cheshire College exists to serve its community; each member is a valued asset.
2. Everyone will be treated with care and consideration as an individual whose contribution to the college is recognized.
3. Management is more concerned with guidance and support than with regulation and control.
4. All members of the college are partners in the success or failure of the organization, each one is accountable for results.
5. Quality is at the heart of all we do; in our pursuit of excellence we recognize that individually and collectively we can always improve.
6. The willingness to contribute to and respond to change is fundamental to our success.
7. Within the college, integrity and commitment are as highly valued as enterprise and creativity.
8. Clarity and openness of communication are considered essential to both our stability and our success.
9. Cooperation is preferred to competition and partnerships will be encouraged with both education or location providers to develop our provision.

10. Perhaps the most important of all, equality of opportunity is a commitment which all members of the college will actively pursue.

Interview with Dr David Collins, CBE, Principal of South Cheshire College – see also David's book in the *Essential FE Toolkit Series: A Survival Guide for College Leaders and Managers* (2006).

Summary

Chapter 11 provides a guide to bring out the leader-manager within you for your role working in further education. Suggestions for developing situation-specific leadership and management skills are outlined in the context of challenges facing leaders and managers in the sector, drawing on experience and findings from the field. A range of case studies and challenging situations is presented, and leaders are invited to consider the way in which these were dealt with by the respondents reporting them. Finally, the chapter considers the values and ethics that leader-managers can adopt in their work, and provides an example of whole college values adopted by South Cheshire College, for leader-managers in the sector to consider.

12: Conclusion

In times of change, learners inherit the Earth, while the learned find themselves beautifully equipped to deal with a world that no longer exists.

Eric Hoffer

In this book we examined the national leadership and management position in further education, current tensions and government priorities. We considered the differences and overlapping areas between 'leadership' and 'management' and between 'professionalism' versus 'managerialism'. Aiming to go beyond the 'performativity' and scrutiny of a targets-based culture, we discussed distributed and emotionally intelligent leadership and management of FE institutions. Staff perspectives on leadership and management in FE were discussed. Results from an ongoing leadership survey with staff in or linked with the learning and skills sector and related agencies were reported and analysed.

We examined leadership definitions, considering perspectives on the way some outstanding leaders operate. We reported on definitions of management in FE, reflecting on business approaches applied to educational management. We described 'senior', 'middle' management and 'executive' roles and line management roles and duties in further education. We looked at problems with leadership and management, providing a guide for spotting rotten managers and leaky leaders. We discussed scandals, messes and scapegoats, the loss of staff in constant restructurings and amanesiac organizations, and the way to avoid this.

In section two, we examined formal and informal models of leadership, positional authority and formal hierarchical models, including structural, systems, bureaucratic, rational models and trait, behavioural and situational theories. Transformational, distributed, team and ambiguity theories were debated alongside emerging models of leadership such as servant leadership, creative and quantum leadership. We examined links between theory and practice in leadership in FE and identified characteristics of good leaders.

In section three, attributes of excellent management were discussed. Strategic planning, finance, audit, quality assurance and governance functions were outlined. Values-based ethical management and tools and techniques for managers are described. We looked at 360° feedback, 3 Cs, 7 Ps and 'guru' models of management. We considered ways in which to measure the difference between good and poor management.

Diversity and authenticity in management were considered alongside the development of 'authentic' situation-specific management. Recognizing the need for diversity and the relative lack of this at senior management levels in FE, we recommended the implementation of policies for inclusion. Facts on the representation of women, black and ethnic minority groups and disabled staff in leadership and management were reported. The question of authenticity in management and leadership was discussed.

In section four we considered how to be a good leader-manager in FE, looking at lessons from leader-managers and leadership and management suggestions from outstanding leaders in further education. We gave examples from a research survey on leadership and management in FE and quoted from interviews with some outstanding leaders in the sector.

We then presented a brief guide to 'bring out the leader-manager within you'. Suggestions for developing situation-specific leadership and management skills were outlined to address the multiple challenges facing leaders and managers. Case study examples were provided regarding appropriate responses in challenging situations. Leader-managers were encouraged to develop their skills and undertake further practical leadership development and training.

Key leadership techniques

To conclude, we recommend the following key tasks for good practice in leadership and management (Kouzes and Posner, 1987), which are relevant for all leaders and managers:

- Envision the future
- Search for opportunities
- Experiment and take risks
- Enlist others
- Foster collaboration
- Strengthen others
- Set the example
- Plan small wins
- Recognize individual contributions
- Celebrate accomplishments
- Be positive, enjoy and appreciate your own role

I hope our wisdom will grow with our power and teach us that the less we use our power the greater it will be.

Thomas Jefferson

References

Ackoff, R.L. (1998) 'A systemic view of transformational leadership', *Systemic Practice and Action Research*, 11, 1:23–36.

Acton, Lord, J.E.E. (1887) *Letter to Bishop Mandell Creighton*, 3 April, in Dalberg-Acton, J.E.E., First Baron Acton (1948), *Essays on Freedom and Power*. Boston: Beacon Press: 264.

Adair, J. (2002) *Effective Strategic Leadership*. London: Pan Books.

Adams, S. (1996) *The Dilbert Principle: A Cubicle's-Eye View of Bosses, Meetings, Management Fads and Other Workplace Afflictions*. New York: HarperCollins.

Ainley, P. (2003) 'Towards a seamless web or a new tertiary tripartism? The emerging shape of post-14 education and training in England', *British Journal of Educational Studies*, 51, 4: 390.

—— and Bailey, B. (1997) *The Business of Learning: Staff and Student Experiences of Further Education in the 1990s*. London: Cassell Education.

ALI (Adult Learning Inspectorate) (2002) *Annual Report of the Chief Inspector 2001–02*. Coventry: ALI.

ALI/Ofsted (Office for Standards in Education) (2001) *The Common Inspection Framework for Inspecting Post-16 Education and Training*. Coventry: ALI and Ofsted.

Alimo-Metcalfe, B. and Alban-Metcalfe, J. (2005) 'Leadership: time for a new direction?', *Leadership*, 1, 1: 51–71.

Alvesson, M. and Sveningsson, S. (2003) 'Good visions, bad micro-management and ugly ambiguity: contradictions of (non-)leadership in a knowledge-intensive organization', *Organization Studies*, 24, 6: 961–88.

AoC (Association of Colleges) (2001) *Association of Colleges and Joint Unions National Review of Staffing and Pay in Further Education*. London: OCR International.

—— (2004) *Ofsted college criticisms 'inappropriate'*. Press release. London: AoC, 26 November.

Argyris, C. and Schön, D. A. (1978) *Organisational Learning*. Reading, MA.: Addison Wesley.

Austin, M. (2006) 'No more heroes any more', *Times Educational Supplement* (TES), June 23.

Avis, J. (2002) 'Imaginary friends: managerialism, globalism and post-compulsory education and training in England', *Discourse Studies in the Cultural Politics of Education*, 3, 3: 3–42.

—— (2003) 'Rethinking trust in a performative culture', *Journal of Education Policy*, 18: 315–32.

—— and Bathmaker, A-M. (2004) 'Critical pedagogy, performativity and a politics of hope: trainee further education lecturer practice', *Research in Post-Compulsory Education*, 9, 2: 301–12.

Ball, S. (2003) 'The teacher's soul and the terrors of performativity', *Journal of Education Policy*, 18: 215–28.

Bascia, N. and Hargreaves, A. (eds) (2000) *The Sharp Edge of Educational Change: Teaching, Leading and the Realities of Reform.* London: Falmer Press.

Bass, B.M. (1998) *Transformational leadership: Industry, military, and educational impact.* Mahwah, NJ: Lawrence Erlbaum Associates.

—— (1990) 'From transactional to transformational leadership: Learning to share the vision', *Organizational Dynamics* (winter): 19–31.

—— and Avolio, B.J. (1990a) 'The implications of transactional and transformational leadership for individual, team, and organizational development', in *Research in Organizational Change and Development*, vol. 4, R.W. Woodman and W.A. Passmore (eds), Greenwich, CT: Jai Press: 231–72.

—— and Avolio, B.J. (1990b) 'Training and development of transformational leadership: looking to 1992 and beyond', *Journal of European Industrial Training*, 14, 5: 21–37.

—— and Avolio, B.J. (1994) *Improving organizational effectiveness through transformational leadership.* Thousand Oaks, CA: Sage Publications.

—— and Avolio, B.J. (2000 [1995]) *Technical Report for the Multifactor Leadership Questionnaire.* San Francisco, CA: Mind Garden.

—— and Steidlmeier, P. (1998) *Ethics, Character and Authentic Transformational Leadership.* Available online: cls.binghamton.edu/ BassSteid.html.

—— and Steidlmeier, P. (1999) 'Ethics, character, and authentic transformational leadership behavior', *Leadership Quarterly*, 10: 181–217.

Bauman, Z. (2001) *The Individualized Society.* Cambridge: Polity Press.

Beck, U. and Beck-Gernsheim, E. (2002) *Individualization.* London: Sage Publications.

Bedeian, A.G. and Armenakis, A.A. (1998) 'The cesspool syndrome: how dreck floats to the top of declining organizations', *Academy of Management Executive*, 12: 58–63.

Bell, D. (2005) 'What makes a college successful?', Speech by David Bell, Her Majesty's Chief Inspector of Schools, annual conference of the Principals' Professional Council, 15 September.

Bennis, W. (1994) *On Becoming a Leader*. Reading, MA: Addison-Wesley.

—— and Nanus, B. (1985) *Leaders: The Strategies for Taking Charge*. New York: Harper & Row.

Bernstein, B. (1996) *Pedagogy Symbolic Control and Identity*. London: Taylor and Francis.

Binney, G., Wilke, G. and Williams, C. (2005) *Living Leadership: A Practical Guide for Ordinary Heroes*. Harlow: Pearson Education.

Blackmore, J. (2004) 'Leading as emotional management work in high risk times: the counterintuitive impulses of performativity and passion', *School Leadership and Management*, 24, 4: 440–59.

Blake, R.R. and Mouton, J.S. (1964) *The Managerial Grid*. Houston, TX: Gulf Publishing.

—— and Mouton, J.S. (1978) *The New Managerial Grid*. Houston, TX: Gulf Publishing.

—— Mouton, J.S. and McCanse, A.A. (1989) *Change by Design*. Reading, MA: Addison-Wesley.

Blanchard, K. and Johnson, S. (1983) *The One Minute Manager*. London: Fontana.

—— Zigarmi, P. and Zigarmi, D. (1986) *Leadership and the One Minute Manager* (first published 1985). London: HarperCollins.

Blank, W. (1995) *The 9 Natural Laws of Leadership*. New York: AMACOM.

Blase, J. and Anderson, G.L. (1995) *The Micropolitics of Educational Leadership: From Control to Empowerment*. London: Cassell.

Block, P. (1987) *The Empowered Manager: Positive Political Skills at Work*. San Francisco, CA: Jossey-Bass.

—— (1993) *Stewardship: Choosing service over self-interest*. San Francisco, CA: Berrett-Koehler.

Bloomer, M. and Hodkinson, P. (1997) *Moving into FE: The Voice of the Learner*. London: Further Education Development Association.

—— and Hodkinson, P. (1999) *College Life: The Voice of the Learner*. London: FEDA.

Blunt R. (2001) *Organisations Growing Leaders: Best Practices & Principles in the Public Service*. Washington DC: The Price Waterhouse Coopers Endowment for the Business of Government.

Bolden, R. (ed) (2005) *What is Leadership Development? Purpose and Practice*, Leadership South West Research Report 2, June, Exeter: University of Exeter.

Bolman, L.G. and Deal, T.E. (1993) *The Path To School Leadership: A Portable Mentor*. Newbury Park, CA: Corwin Press.

—— and Deal, T.E. (1995) *Leading With Soul: An Uncommon Journey of Spirit*. San Francisco, CA: Jossey-Bass.

—— and Deal, T.E. (1997) *Reframing Organizations: Artistry, Choice, and Leadership*. San Francisco, CA: Jossey-Bass.

Bosworth, D. (1999) *Empirical Evidence of Management Skills in the UK*. National Skills Task Force. Research paper 18, Department for Education and Employment.

Brennan, J. (2004) Letter to David Bell, HMCI, on 'Why Colleges succeed' and 'Why Colleges Fail'. *AoC Briefing* CE 24/04, London: AoC.

Briggs, A.R.J. (2001a) 'Academic managers in further education: reflections on leadership', *Research in Post-Compulsory Education*, 6, 2: 223–36.

—— (2001b) 'Middle managers in further education: exploring the role', *Management in Education*, 15, 4: 12–15.

—— (2002) 'Facilitating the role of middle managers in further education', *Research in Post-Compulsory Education*, 7, 1: 63–78.

—— (2005a) 'Middle managers in English further education colleges: understanding and modelling the role', *Educational Management and Administration*, 33, 1: 27–50.

—— (2005b) 'Making a difference: an exploration of leadership roles within sixth form colleges in maintaining ethos within a context of change', *British Educational Research Journal*, 31, 2: 223–8.

—— (2005c) 'Modelling the muddle – making sense through research', in *Readings in post-compulsory education*, Y. Hillier and A. Thompson (eds), London: Continuum: 109–25.

—— (2006) *Middle Management in FE*. London: Continuum.

Bruner, J.S. (1986) *Actual Minds, Possible Worlds*. Cambridge, MA: Harvard University Press.

—— (1996) *The Culture of Education*. Cambridge, MA: Harvard University Press.

Bryman, A. (1992) *Charisma and Leadership in Organisations*. London: Sage.

—— (1996) 'Leadership in organizations', in *Handbook of Organization Studies*, S.R. Clegg, C. Hardy and W.R. Nord (eds). London: Sage Publications: 276–92.

Burchill, F. (1998) *Five Years of Change: A Survey of Pay, Terms and Conditions in FE Five Years after College Incorporation*. London: NATFHE (University and College Lecturers' Union).

Burgoyne, J. (2004) 'How certain are we that management and

leadership development is effective?', Presentation at the Centre for Excellence in Leadership First Annual Conference, 30–31 March.

——— Hirsh, W. and Williams, S. (2004) *The Development of Management and Leadership Capability and its Contribution to Performance: The Evidence, the Prospects and the Research Need.* DfES Research Report 560, Lancaster: Lancaster University. Available online: www.dfes.gov.uk/ research/data/uploadfiles/RR560.pdf. Accessed 6 November 2006.

Burns, J.M. (1978) *Leadership.* New York: Harper and Row.

Bush, T. (1995), *Theories of Educational Management* (2nd ed). London: Paul Chapman.

——— (2003) *Theories of Educational Leadership and Management* (3rd ed). London: Paul Chapman and Sage Publications.

——— (2006) *Theories of Educational Management.* Connexions website creative commons article, 15 Sept 2006. Available online: cnx.org/ content/m13867/latest/.

——— and Bell, L. (eds) (2002) *The Principles and Practice of Educational Management.* London: Paul Chapman and Sage Publications.

——— and Glover, D. (2003) *Leadership Development: Evidence and Beliefs,* Nottingham: National College for School Leadership.

——— and West-Burnham, J. (1994) *The Principles of Educational Management.* London: Pearson Education.

Busher, H. and Harris, A. (2000) *Leading Subject Areas Improving Schools.* London: Paul Chapman.

Caldwell, B.J. and Spinks, J.M. (1992) *Leading the Self-Managing School.* London: Falmer Press.

Campbell M. (2001) *Skills in England 2001: Key Messages.* London: Department for Education and Skills.

——— (2002) *Learn to Succeed: The Case for a Skills Revolution.* Bristol: Policy Press.

CEL (Centre for Excellence in Leadership) (2004) *The Leadership Qualities Framework. London: Centre for Excellence in Leadership.* Available in summary form online: www.centreforexcellence.org.uk/UsersDoc/ LQFintrodoc.pdf. Accessed 6 August 2006.

——— (2004a) *Leading Learning and Skills.* Newsletter. London: CEL, autumn.

——— (2004b) *Leading the Way 2004–06: Leadership for the Learning and Skills Sector.* London: CEL.

——— (2005) *Hints and Tips: career insights from successful leaders in the learning and skills sector.* London: CEL.

CEML (Council for Excellence in Management and Leadership) (2002) *Managers and Leaders; Raising our Game.* Final Report. London: CEML.

Chater, M. (2005) 'Archetypes of destruction: notes on the impact of distorted management theory on education communities', *International Journal of Leadership in Education*, Jan–March, 8, 1: 3–19.

Chuan Zhi Shakya (2005) *Eating the Menu. Dharma Talks by Chuan Zhi Shakya 2002–2005*, Zen Buddhist Order of Hsu Yun. Available online: www.hsuyun.org/Dharma/zbohy/Literature/essays/czs/czs-essays-home.html. Accessed 3 October 2006.

Clancy, J. (2005) 'Race chief threat to colleges', *Times Educational Supplement*, 28 January. Available online: www.tes.co.uk/search/story/?story_id=2069038. Accessed 6 November 2006.

Clarke, C. (2004) 'Developing the learning and skills sector – next stage of reform', keynote address presented to the Learning and Skills Development Agency Summer Conference, 15 June.

Clegg, S. (1999) 'Professional education, reflective practice and feminism', *International Journal of Inclusive Education*, 3, 2: 167–79.

Clements, C. and Washbush, J.B. (1999) 'The two faces of leadership: considering the dark side of leader-follower dynamics', *Journal of Workplace Learning*, 11, 5: 170–1.

Codd, J. (1999) 'Educational reform, accountability and the culture of distrust', *New Zealand Journal of Educational Studies*, 34: 45–53.

Cohen, S. and Eimicke, W. (1995) *The New Effective Public Manager: Achieving Success in a Changing Government*. San Francisco, CA: Jossey-Bass.

Cole, M. (2000) 'Learning through reflective practice: A professional approach to effective continuing professional development among health care professionals', *Research in Post-Compulsory Education*, 5, 1: 23–38.

Coleman, M. and Briggs, A.R.J. (eds) (2002) *Research Methods in Educational Leadership and Management*. London: Paul Chapman and Sage Publications.

Colley, H. (2002) 'From childcare practitioner to FE tutor: Biography, vocational culture and gender in the transition of professional identities', paper presented to the British Education Research Association Conference, University of Exeter, 12–14 September.

Collins, D. (2006) *Survival Guide for College Managers and Leaders*. London: Continuum.

Collins, M. (1991) *Adult Education as Vocation. A critical role for the adult educator*. London: Routledge.

Collinson, D. (2006) 'Appeal of the roller-coaster job', *Times Educational Supplement*, 18 August: 30.

Collinson, M. and Collinson, D. (2005a) *The nature of leadership: Leader-led relations in context*. Lancaster: Centre for Excellence in Leadership.

—— and Collinson, D. (2005b) *The nature of leadership: Leadership challenges*. Lancaster: Centre for Excellence in Leadership.

Commission for Black Staff in Further Education (2002a) *Challenging Racism: Further Education Leading the Way*. London: AoC.

—— (2002b) *Black Staff in Further Education: An Agenda for Action?* London: AoC.

Covey, S.R. (1991) *Principle-Centered Leadership*. New York: Summit Books.

—— (2004) *The 8th Habit: From Effectiveness to Greatness*. London: FranklinCovey, Simon & Schuster.

Crowther, F. and Olsen, P. (1997) 'Teachers as leaders – an exploratory framework', *International Journal of Educational Management*, 11, 1: 6–13.

Cummings, T.G. and Worley, C.G. (2001) *Organization Development and Change* (7th edn). Cincinnati, OH: South-Western College Publishing.

Curtis, P. (2004) 'Colleges branded a "national disgrace" ', *Guardian*, 29 November 2005. Available online: education.guardian.co.uk/ofsted/story/0,,1362030,00.html. Accessed 6 November 2006.

Davidson, M. (1997) *The Black and Ethnic Minority Woman Manager: Cracking the Concrete Ceiling*. London: Paul Chapman.

Dawoody, A. (2003) *The Matriarch as a Leader and the Metaphors of Chaos and Quantum Theories*. Bloomington, IN: 1st Books.

Deem R., Ozga J.T. and Pritchard G. (2000) 'Managing further education: is it still men's work too?', *Journal of Further and Higher Education*, 24, 2: 231–51.

De Pree, M. (1987) *Leadership is an Art*. East Lansing, MI: Michigan State University Press.

—— (1992) *Leadership Jazz*. New York: Dell.

Dewey, J. (1897) 'My pedagogic creed: Article 1: What Education Is', *The School Journal*, vol. LIV, No. 3 (16 January 1897): 77–80. Available online: www.infed.org/archives/e-texts/e-dew-pc.htm. Accessed 23 September 2006.

—— (1916) *Democracy and Education: An introduction to the philosophy of education*. New York: Macmillan. Available online: xroads.virginia.edu/~HYPER2/dewey/header.html. Accessed 24 September 2006.

DfES (Department for Education and Skills) (2002) *Success for All: Reforming Further Education and Training*. London: DfES.

—— (2002a) *Chart A: Education and Training Structure*. Available online: www.dfes.gov.uk/trends/index.cfm?fuseaction=home.showChart&cid=1&iid=1&chid=1. Accessed 6 November 2006.

—— (2006a) *Further Education White Paper: Further Education: Raising Skills, Improving Life Chances*. 27 March 2006. White Paper and DfES

238 ULTIMATE FE LEADERSHIP AND MANAGEMENT HANDBOOK

Press Release. Available online: www.dfes.gov.uk/pns/DisplayPN. cgi?pn_id=2006_0045. Accessed 6 May 2006.

—— (2006b) *Extract: DfES Notice: 'Thinking of Becoming a Governor'*. Available online: www.dfes.gov.uk/furthereducation/index.cfm? fuseaction=content.view&CategoryID=15. Accessed 6 October 2006.

Dodgson, M. (1991) 'Technological learning, technology strategy and competitive pressures', *British Journal of Management*, 2, 2: 133–49

Dourado, P. and Blackburn, P. (2005) *Seven Secrets of Inspired Leaders: How to Achieve the Extraordinary, by the Leaders Who Have Been There and Done it*. Chichester: Capstone.

Downton, J.V. (1973) *Rebel Leadership: Commitment and Charisma in the Revolutionary Process*. New York: Free Press.

Doyle, M.E. and Smith, M.K. (2001) 'Classical leadership' in *The Encyclopaedia of Informal Education*. Available online: www.infed.org/leadership/traditional_leadership.htm. Accessed 6 November 2006.

Duigan, P.A. and Macpherson, R.J.S. (eds) (1992) *Educative Leadership: A Practical Theory for New Administrators and Managers*. London: Falmer Press.

Eagly, A.H. and Carli, L.L. (2003) 'The female leadership advantage: an evaluation of the evidence', *Leadership Quarterly*, 14: 807–34.

Ecclestone, K. (2003) 'From Freire to fear: the rise of low self-esteem in British post-16 education', paper presented to the British Educational Research Association Annual Conference, Heriot-Watt University, Edinburgh, 11–13 Sept.

Elliott, G. (1999) *Lifelong Learning: The Politics of the New Learning Environment* London: Jessica Kingsley.

English, F.W. (1994) *Theory in Educational Administration*. New York: Harper Collins College Publisher.

FEFC (Further Education Funding Council) (1998) *Management Statistics 1995–96*. Coventry: FEFC.

FENTO (Further Education National Training Organisation) (1999) *Standards for Teaching and Supporting Learning in Further Education in England and Wales*. London: FENTO.

—— (2002) *Skills Foresight for Further Education in 2002: England Supplement*. Available online. www.lifelonglearninguk.org/research/skills_foresight_and_dev_plans.html.

Ferreday, D., Hodgson, V. and Jones, C. (2005) *'It's a fairly lonely job': the benefits of a networked approach to leadership learning for the learning and skills sector*. Centre for Excellence in Leadership working paper series. Lancaster: CEL.

Fiedler, F.E. (1964) 'A contingency model of leadership effectiveness', in

Advances in Experimental Social Psychology, vol I, L. Berkowitz (ed), New York: Academic Press.

—— (1967) *A Theory of Leadership Effectiveness*. New York: McGraw Hill.

—— (1997) 'Situational control and a dynamic theory of leadership', in *Leadership: Classical, Contemporary and Critical Approaches*, K. Grint (ed), Oxford: Oxford University Press: 126–48.

—— and Garcia, J.E. (1987) *New Approaches to Effective Leadership*. New York: John Wiley.

Field, R.H.G. (2002) 'Leadership defined: web images reveal the differences between leadership and management', paper submitted to the Administrative Sciences Association of Canada annual meeting, Winnipeg, Manitoba, Jan.

Field, T. (1996) *Bully In Sight*. Oxfordshire, UK: Success Unlimited. Linked to Tim Field's online resource, *Bully on Line*, The Field Foundation (www.thefieldfoundation.org/).

Fiol, C.M. and Lyles, M.A. 1985. 'Organizational learning', *Academy of Management Review*, 10, 4: 803–13.

Fisher, D. and Torbert, W.R. (1995) *Personal and Organisational Transformation: The True Challenge of Continual Quality Improvement*. London: McGraw Hill.

Fisher, J.L. (1994) 'Reflections of transformational leadership', *Educational Record*, 75, 3: 60–5.

Foster, Sir Andrew (2005). *Realising the potential. A review of the future role of further education colleges*. London: DfES.

Foucault, M. (1997) *Discipline and Punish: The Birth of the Prison* (NY: Vintage Books 1995):195–228. Translated from the French by Alan Sheridan. Section III. *Discipline 3. Panopticism*. Available online: www.foucault.info/documents/disciplineAndPunish/foucault. disciplineAndPunish.panOpticism.html. Accessed 30 September 2006.

Fox, S., Kerr, R., Collinson, M., Collinson, D. and Swan, E. (2005) *Foster Review of FE 'think piece': Local management and leadership: Final Draft*. DfES. Available online: www.dfes.gov.uk/furthereducation/fereview/downloads/local_management_leadershipthinkpiece_final2. doc. Accessed 14 May 2006.

Fox, S., Hughes, J., Iszatt White, M., Kelly, S., Randall, D. and Rouncefield, M. (2005) 'Talking leadership', paper presented at the 4th International Critical Management Studies Conference 'Critique and Inclusivity: Opening the Agenda', 4–6 July 2005. Judge Institute of Management, University of Cambridge, Cambridge, UK.

Frearson, M. (2002) *Tomorrow's Learning Leaders: Developing Leadership and Management for Post-compulsory Learning: 2002 Survey Report*. London: Learning and Skills Development Agency (LSDA).

—— (2003a) *Tomorrow's Learning Leaders: Developing Leadership and Management for Post-compulsory Learning*. London: LSDA.

—— (2003b) *Leading Learning Project, Work Package 1: International Comparator Contexts*, LSRC. Research findings report. London: LSDA (also listed as LSDA, 2003).

Friedman, A.A. (2004) 'Beyond mediocrity: transformational leadership within a transactional framework', *International Journal of Leadership in Education*, 7, 3: 203–24.

Freire, P. (1972) *Pedagogy of the Oppressed*. Harmondsworth: Penguin.

Gardner, H. (1975) *The Shattered Mind*. New York: Knopf.

—— (1993 [1983]) *Frames of Mind: The Theory of Multiple Intelligences*. New York: Basic Books.

—— (1995) *Leading Minds: An Anatomy of Leadership*. London: HarperCollins.

Gardner, J. (1989) *On Leadership*, New York: Free Press.

Gardner, W.L. and Schermerhorn, J.R., Jnr. (2004) 'Unleashing individual potential: performance gains through positive organisational behavior and authentic leadership', *Organizational Dynamics*, 33, 3: 270–81.

Glatter, R. and Kydd, L. (2003) ' "Best practice" in educational leadership and management: can we identify and earn from it?', *Educational Management and Administration*, 31, 3: 231–43.

Gleeson, D. (2001) 'Style and substance in education leadership: further education (FE) as a case in point', *Journal of Education Policy*, 16, 3: 181–96.

—— and Shain, F. (1999) 'Managing ambiguity: between markets and managerialism – a case study of "middle" managers in further education', *Sociological Review*, 47: 461–90.

Glover, D. and Law, S. (2000) *Educational Leadership and Learning*. Milton Keynes: Open University Press.

Goddard-Patel, P. and Whitehead, S. (2001) 'The Mechanics of "Failure" in Further Education: The Case of Bilston Community College', *Policy Studies*, 22, 3–4, 1: 181–95.

Goldstein, H. (1990) *Problem-oriented policing*. New York: McGraw Hill.

Goleman, D. (1995) *Emotional Intelligence*. New York: Bantam Books.

—— (1996) *Emotional Intelligence: Why it can matter more than IQ*. London: Bloomsbury.

Goswami, A. (2003) *Quantum Mechanics* (2nd edn). Prospect Heights, IL.: Waveland Press.

Greenleaf, R.K. (1970) *The Servant as Leader*. Newton Centre, MA: Robert K. Greenleaf Center.

—— (1977) *Servant Leadership: A Journey into the Nature of Legitimate Power and Greatness*. New York: Paulist.

Gregory, M. (1996) 'Developing effective college leadership for the management of educational change', *Leadership and Organization Development Journal*, 17, 4: 46–51.

Grint, K. (2000) *The Arts of Leadership*. Oxford: Oxford University Press.

—— (2005) *Take me to your leader*. Small Business School Series, PBS, Worldnet and online.

—— (2005a) *Leadership: Limits and Possibilities*. Basingstoke: Palgrave Macmillan.

—— (2005b) 'Leadership limited: white elephant to wheelwright', *Ivey Business Journal*, 69, 3:1–4.

Gronn, P. (1995) 'Greatness re-visited: the current obsession with transformational leadership', *Leading and Managing*, 1, 1: 14–27.

Guardian (2003) 'FE college managers given pay cut', 3 January.

Gunter, H.M. (2001) *Leaders and Leadership in Education*. London: Paul Chapman and Sage Publications.

Handy, C. (1981 [1976]) *Understanding Organizations*. Harmondsworth: Penguin.

—— (1989) *The Age of Unreason*. London: Pan.

—— (1994) *The Empty Raincoat: Making Sense of the Future*. London: Hutchinson.

—— (1995) *The Age of Paradox*. Cambridge, MA: Harvard Business School Press.

Hargreaves, D. (2003) *Education Epidemic: Transforming Secondary Schools through Innovative Networks*. London: Demos.

Harper, H. (2000) 'New college hierarchies: towards an examination of organisational structures in further education in England and Wales', *Educational Management and Administration*, 28: 433–46.

Hay Group (2002) *Further Lessons of Leadership: How Does Leadership in Further Education Compare to Industry*. London: Hay Group.

Hay Group for the National College for School Leadership (2006) *Models of Excellence for School Leadership: Raising Achievement in Our Schools: Models of Excellence for Headteachers in Different Settings, Part 3*. Hay Group. Available online: www.ncsl.org.uk/media/F7B/52/kpool-hay-models-ofexcellence-part–3.pdf. Accessed 6 November 2006.

Hay McBer (2000a) *Models of Excellence for School Leadership: Raising Achievement in Our Schools: Models of Excellence for Headteachers in Different Settings, Parts 1 and 2*. Hay Group for the National College for School Leadership. Available online: www.ncsl.org.uk/the_knowledge_pool/foundations/kpool-foundations-index.cfm Part 3. Accessed 6 November 2006.

Hay McBer (2000b) *Research into Teacher Effectiveness: A Model of Teacher Effectiveness*. DfEE Research Report 216. London: DfEE. Available online: www.teachernet.gov.uk/teachinginengland/detail.cfm?id–521. Accessed 9 September 2006.

Hayes, D. (2003) 'New Labour, New Professionalism', in *Discourse, Power Resistance: Challenging the Rhetoric of Contemporary Education.* J. Satterthwaite, E. Atkinson and K. Gale (eds), Stoke-on-Trent: Trentham Books, 27–42.

Heifetz, R.A. (1994) *Leadership without Easy Answers.* Cambridge, MA: Harvard University Press.

—— and Laurie, D.L. (1997) 'The work of leadership', *Harvard Business Review*, 75, 1:124–34.

Hersey, P. and Blanchard, K. H. (1977) *The Management of Organizational Behaviour* (3rd ed). Upper Saddle River, NJ: Prentice Hall.

Hill, R. (2000) 'A study of the views of full-time further education lecturers regarding their college corporations and agencies of the further education sector', *Journal of Further and Higher Education*, 24, 1: 67–75.

Hillier, Y. and Jameson, J. (2003) *Empowering Researchers in FE.* Stoke-on-Trent: Trentham Books.

Hochschild, A.R. (1983) *The Managed Heart: Commercialisation of Human Feeling.* Berkeley, CA: University of California Press.

—— (2003) *The Commercialisation of Intimate Life: Notes from Home and Work.* Berkeley, CA: University of California Press.

Hodge, M. (1998) *House of Commons Select Committee on Education and Employment: Sixth Report (Further Education).* London: HMSO.

Hollinshead, A. (2003) *Quality control, autonomy, accountability: lecturers' perception of their working lives in the changing context of HE.* Unpublished EdD thesis, Open University.

Horsfall, C. (ed) (2001) *Leadership Issues: Raising Achievement.* London: Learning and Skills Development Agency.

House, R. (1971) 'A path-goal theory of leadership effectiveness', *Administrative Science Quarterly*, 16: 321–38.

House, R.J. and Baetz, M.L. (1979) *Leadership: Some Empirical Generalizations and New Research Directions.* New York: Academic Press.

House of Commons (2006) *Fourth Report of Session 2005–06 Report, together with formal minutes, oral and written evidence paragraph 22 HC 649*, 12 September 2006. London: House of Commons: The Stationery Office.

Howell, J.M. and Hall-Meranda, K.E. (1999) 'The ties that bind: the impact of leader-member exchange, transformational and transactional leadership, and distance on predicted follower performance', *Journal of Applied Psychology*, 84, 5: 680–94.

Howells, R. (2000) *Team Management Profile and Emotional Intelligence:*

More than the Sum of their Parts. Available online: www.tms.com.au/ tms12–1s.html. Accessed 6 November 2006.

IfL (Institute for Learning) (2006) *The IfL Response to the Government White Paper on Further Education: Further Education: Raising Skills, Improving Life Chances*. London: Institute for Learning. Available online: www.ifl.ac.uk/documents/ifl_fe_white_paper_response.doc. Accessed 2 October 2006.

Irby, B.J., Brown, G., Duffy, J. and Trautman, D. (2002) 'The synergistic leadership theory', *Journal of Educational Administration*, 40, 4: 304–22.

Iszatt White, M. (2005) 'Tough at the top, even tougher at the bottom: the role of leadership in making staff feel valued'. Paper presented at Rethinking Leadership: New Directions in the Learning and Skills Sector, 27–29 June 2005, Lancaster University, UK. Available online: www.comp.lancs.ac.uk/computing/research/cseg/projects/ explicating/Explicating_leadership/Papers/feelingvalued.pdf. Accessed 6 November 2006.

——, Kelly, S. and Rouncefield, M. (2005) 'The nature of leadership: Leadership as Mundane Work', *Research Summaries*. Centre for Excellence in Leadership, Lancaster. Available online: www.lums. lancs.ac.uk/files/cel/7905/download/. Accessed 1 November 2006.

Jameson, J. (2005a) 'Inspiring leaders for the future of lifelong learning', paper presented at the Twelfth International Conference on Learning, University of Granada, Spain, 11–14 July.

—— (2005b) 'Metaphors of leadership in post-compulsory education', *Proceedings of the Re-thinking Leadership: New Directions in the Learning and Skills Sector?* CEL Research Conference, University of Lancaster, 26–27 June.

—— (2006) *Leadership in Post Compulsory Education: Inspiring Leaders of the Future*. London: David Fulton.

—— (2006a) 'Metaphors of Leadership in Post-Compulsory Education', *The International Journal of Knowledge, Culture and Change Management*, vol. 6.

—— and Hillier, Y. (2003) *Researching Post-Compulsory Education*. London: Continuum.

Jarvis, P. (ed) (1987) *Twentieth Century Thinkers in Adult Education*. London: Routledge.

Johnson, J. and Winterton, J. (1999) *Management Skills. National Skills Task Force*. Research Paper 3, Department for Education and Employment, 35.

Kellerman, B. (2004) *Bad Leadership: What it is, How it Happens, Why it Matters*. Boston, MA: Harvard Business School Press.

Kelly, S., Iszatt White, M., Randall, D. and Rouncefield, M. (2004)

'Educational leadership as mundane work', *Proceedings of the 2004 Commonwealth Council for Educational Administration and Management (CCEAM) Conference on Educational Leadership in Pluralistic Societies*, 20–27 October 2004. Hong Kong and Shanghai. Available online: www.comp.lancs.ac.uk/computing/research/cseg/projects/explicating. Accessed 1 October 2006.

——, White, M.I., Randall, D. and Rouncefield, M. (2004) 'Stories of educational leadership', CCEAM Conference on Educational Leadership in Pluralistic Societies, Hong Kong and Shanghai, 20–27 October 2004.

—— Iszatt White, M., Rooksby, J. and Rouncefield, M. (2005) 'Storytelling and design: the problem of leadership', *Proceedings of the Rethinking Leadership: New directions in the learning and skills sector? CEL Research Conference*, 27–29 June 2005. Lancaster University, UK. Centre for Excellence in Leadership. Available online: www.comp. lancs.ac.uk/computing/research/cseg/projects/explicating/Explicating_leadership/Papers/storytelling_leadership.pdf. Accessed 1 October 2006.

—— Iszatt White, M. and Rouncefield, M. (2005) *The Nature of Leadership: Storytelling and Leadership.* Lancaster: Centre for Excellence in Leadership.

Kennedy, H. (1997) *Learning Works: Widening Participation in FE.* Coventry: FEFC.

Kerfoot, D. and Whitehead, S. (1998) ' "Boys own stuff" ': masculinity and the management of further education', *Sociological Review*, 46, 3: 436–55.

Killian, R. (2004) *Ethical Leadership.* Business presentation at the University of Colorado, J. Luftig (ed). Boulder, CO: University of Colorado.

Kilmann, R.H. (2001) *Quantum Organizations: A New Paradigm for Achieving Organizational Success and Personal Meaning.* Palo Alto, CA: Davies-Black.

Kingston, P. (2003) 'Has the FE management crisis solution come too late?', *Guardian*, 15 July.

Kotter, J.P. (1990) *A Force for Change: How Leadership Differs from Management.* New York: Macmillan.

Kübler-Ross, E. (1985) *On Death and Dying.* London: Tavistock Publications.

Kugelmass, J.W. (2003) *Inclusive Leadership; Leadership for Inclusion.International Practitioner Inquiry Report.* Nottingham: National College for School Leadership.

Lao-Tzu (also known as 'Lao Tze') (1996) *Tao Te Ching.* A translation for the public domain by J.H. McDonald. Available online: www.wam.umd.edu/~stwright/rel/tao/TaoTeChing.html.

Lave, J. and Wenger, E. (1990) *Situated Learning: Legitimate Peripheral Participation*. Institute for Research on Learning (IRL) Report 90–0013, Palo Alto, CA: IRL.

Leader, G. (2003) 'Lifelong learning: policy and practice in further education', *Education + Training*, 45, 7: 361.

—— (2004) 'Further Education Middle Managers: Their Contribution to the Strategic Management Decision Process', *Educational Management and Administration*, 32, 1: 67–79.

Leonard, L. and Leonard, P. (1999) 'Reculturing for collaboration and leadership', *Journal of Educational Leadership*, 92, 4: 235–42.

Leonardo, Z. (2003) 'Discourse and critique: outlines of a post-structural theory of ideology', *Journal of Education Policy*, 18: 203–14.

Lester, S. (1994) 'Management standards: a critical approach', *Competency*, 2, 1: 28–31, October.

Lifelong Learning UK (LLUK) (2005) *National Occupational Standards for Leadership and Management in the Post-Compulsory Learning and Skills Sector*. London: LLUK.

—— (2006) *Invitation to Tender: Project management of the review and redevelopment of the national standards for leadership and management*. Tender invitation. London: LLUK. Available online: www.lifelong learninguk.org/documents/tenders/tender_lm_standards_proj_man.doc. Accessed 28 August 2006.

Lingard, B., Hayes, D., Mills, M. and Christie, P. (2003) *Leading Learning*. Maidenhead: Open University Press and McGraw-Hill Education.

Loots, C. and Ross, J. (2004) 'From academic leader to Chief Executive: altered images', *Journal of Further and Higher Education*, 28, 1: 19–34.

LSC (Learning and Skills Council) (2002) *Leadership and Management in Work-Based Learning*. Coventry: LSC.

—— (2005) *LSC statistical release*, AoC FE Postbag, 13 December 2005. Available online: www.lsc.gov.uk/National/Partners/Data/Statistics/LearnerStatistics/StatisticalFirstReleases/StatisticalFirstRelease200405. htm. Accessed 6 May 2006.

—— (2006) *LSC statistical release*, April, 2006. Available online: www.lsc.gov.uk/National/Partners/Data/Statistics/LearnerStatistics/StatisticalFirstReleases/StatisticalFirstRelease200405.htm. Accessed 6 May 2006.

—— (2006a) *LSC Update January 2006*. Available online: http://reading room.lsc.gov.uk/LSC/2006/externalrelations/newsletters/lsc-update-january–2006.pdf. Accessed 6 May 2006.

—— (2006b) *National Learner Satisfaction Survey* (NLSS) Coventry: LSC. Available online: readingroom.lsc.gov.uk/Lsc/2006/research/consultation/nat-nationallearnersatisfactionsurveyhighlights200405-re-june2006.pdf. Accessed 2 October 2006.

LSDA (Learning and Skills Development Agency) (2003) *Leading Learning Project Work Package 1: International Comparator Contexts.* Research findings report, London: LSDA, July.

Lucas, N. (2004) 'The "FENTO Fandango"': national standards, compulsory teaching qualifications and the growing regulation of FE college teachers', *Journal of Further and Higher Education*, 28, 1: 35–51.

Lumby, J. (1997a) 'Developing managers in further education. Part 1: the extent of the task', *Journal of Further and Higher Education*, 21, 3: 345–54.

—— (1997b) 'Developing managers in further education. Part 2: the process of development', *Journal of Further and Higher Education*, 21, 3: 355–64.

—— (1999) 'Strategic planning in further education: the business of values', *Educational Management Administration and Leadership*, 27, 1: 71–83.

—— (2000) 'Funding Learning in Further Education', in *Managing Finance and Resources in Education*, M. Coleman and L. Anderson (eds): London: Paul Chapman: 81–98.

—— (2001) *Managing Further Education: Learning Enterprise.* Education Management: Research and Practice Series. London: Paul Chapman.

—— (2002) 'Distributed leadership in colleges: leading or misleading?', keynote paper presented at the British Educational Leadership and Management Association Annual Conference, Leaders and leadership: leadership teams, team leaders and middle managers, 20–22 September, Birmingham.

—— (2003a) 'Distributed leadership in colleges? Leading or misleading?', *Educational Management and Administration*, 31, 3: 283–93.

—— (2003b) 'Constructing culture change: the case of sixth form colleges', *Educational Management and Administration*, 31, 2: 157–72.

—— and Simkins, T. (2002) 'Researching Leadership and Management', *Research in Post-Compulsory Education*, 7, 1: 5.

—— and Tomlinson, H.T. (2000) 'Principals speaking: managerialism and leadership in further education', *Research in Post-Compulsory Education*, 5, 2: 139–51.

—— Briggs, A.R.J. with Wilson, M., Glover, D. and Pell, A. (2002) *Sixth Form Colleges: Policy, Purpose and Practice.* Research report. Leicester: Leicester University.

—— Harris, A., Morrison, M., Muijs, D. and Sood, K. with Briggs, A., Glover, D., Middlewood, D. and Wilson, M. (2004) *Leadership,*

Development and Diversity in the Learning and Skills Sector. London: LSRC (draft copy).

—— Harris, A., Morrison, M., Muijs, D. and Sood, K. with Briggs, A., Glover, D., Middlewood, D. and Wilson, M. (2005) *Leadership, Development and Diversity in the Learning and Skills Sector*. London: LSRC.

Luthans, F. and Avolio, B.J. (2003) 'Authentic leadership: a positive development approach', in *Positive Organizational Scholarship*. K.S. Cameron, J.E. Dutton and R.E. Quinn (eds). San Francisco, CA: Berrett-Koehler: 241–58.

McGinty, J. and Fish, J. (1993) *Further Education in the Market Place*. London: Routledge.

McGregor, D. (1960) *The Human Side of Enterprise*. New York: McGraw Hill.

McNay, I. (1998) *The Reality of College Management*. York: Longman/ Futher Education Unit (FEU).

—— (1995) 'From the collegial academy to corporate enterprise: the changing cultures of universities, in Tom Schuller (ed.) *The Changing University?*, Buckingham: Open University Press.

—— (ed.), (2000) *Higher education and its communities*. Maidenhead: SRHE/Open University Press.

—— (2002) *Governance and Decision-Making in Smaller Colleges*. *Higher Education Quarterly*, 56(3), pp. 303–15.

—— (2005) 'Managing institutions in a mass higher education system', in McNay, I. (ed), *Beyond Mass Higher Education: building on experience*, Maidenhead, SRHE/Open UP (chapter 12).

—— and Ozga, J. (eds) (1985) *Policy-Making in Education: The Breakdown of Consensus*. Oxford: Pergamon.

McTavish, D. (1998) 'Strategic management in further education colleges. A pilot study', *Scottish Educational Review* 30(2): 125–37.

—— (2003) 'Aspects of public sector management. A case study of further education, ten years from the passage of the Further and Higher Education Act', *Educational Management and Administration*, 31, 2: 173–85.

—— (2006) 'Further education management strategy and policy institutional and public management dimensions', *Educational Management Administration and Leadership*, 34, 3: 411–28.

Maccoby, M. (2005) 'Narcissistic leaders: the incredible pros, the inevitable cons', in *Harvard Business Review* on *The Mind of the Leader*. Boston, MA: Harvard Business School Publishing Corporation.

Maginn, A. and Williams, W. (2002) *An assessment of skill needs in post-16 education and training*. London: Institute for Employment Studies, Department for Education and Skills.

Manklelow, J. (2005) *SWOT Analysis: Discover new opportunities: Manage and eliminate threats.* Mindtools article online: www.mindtools.com/pages/article/newTMC_05.htm. Accessed 12 January 2007.

——— (2006) 'Swot Analysis and Time Management Blog', *It's about the Journey.* Available online: threesummits.typepad.com/journey/leadership_tools/index.html. Accessed 9 October 2006.

Mann, R. D. (1959) 'A review of the relationship between personality and performance in small groups', *Psychological Bulletin*, 66, 4: 241–70.

Matteson, J.A. and Irving, J.A. (2005) 'Servant versus self-sacrificial leadership: commonalities and distinctions of two follower-oriented leadership theories', Servant Leadership Research Roundtable, Regent University, August.

May, D., Chan, A., Hodges, T. and Avolio, B. (2003) 'Developing the moral component of authentic leadership', *Organizational Dynamics*, 32(3): 247–60.

MCI (Management Charter Initiative) (1997) *National Occupational Standards in Management.* London: MCI. Available online: www.management-standards.org.uk. Accessed 6 November 2006.

Merrick, N. (2004) 'Lessons learnt?', *Independent*, Independent Digital (UK) Ltd, 1 July.

Michie, S. and Gooty, J. (2005) 'Values, emotions and authenticity: will the real leader please stand up?', *Leadership Quarterly*, 16, 3: 441–57.

Millar, M. (2005) 'Lack of faith in senior managers is exposed', *Personnel Today*, 12, 22 February.

Moore, A., Edwards, G., Halpin, D. and George, R. (2002) 'Compliance, resistance and pragmatism: the (re)construction of school-teacher identities in a period of intense educational reform', *British Educational Research Journal*, 28: 551–65.

Morrison, M. (2006) 'Constructions of diversity. Research among staff leaders in the learning and skills sector', *Journal of Further and Higher Education*, 30, 2: 169–80.

MSC (Management Standards Centre) (2004) *Draft National Occupational Standards in Management and Leadership.* Working document. Available online: www.management-standards.org. Accessed 19 May 2006.

Mullen, C.A. and Kochan, F.K. (2000) 'Creating a collaborative leadership network: an organic view of change', *International Journal of Leadership in Education*, 3, 3: 83–200.

Mumford, M.D., Zaccaro, S.J., Connelly, M.S., and Marks, M.A. (2000) 'Leadership skills: conclusions and future directions', *Leadership Quarterly*, 11(1): 155–70.

NAO (National Audit Office) (1999) *Value for Money Report: Education and Employment: Investigation of Alleged Irregularities at Halton College.*

House of Commons Paper HC 357, 1998–99. London: The Stationery Office.

—— (2005) *Securing strategic leadership for the learning and skills sector in England*. Report by the Comptroller and Auditor General. HC 29 Session 2005–6, 18 May 2005, National Audit Office. Available online: www.nao.org.uk/publications/nao_reports/05-06/050629es.pdf. Accessed 6 October 2006.

NCSL (National College for School Leadership) (2003) *Leadership Development Framework*. Available online: www.ncsl.org.uk/index.cfm?pageid=ldf. Accessed 19 May 2005.

Nolan Committee on Standards in Public Life (1995) *First Report of the Committee on Standards in Public Life*, vol. 1: Report Command Paper No Cm 2850-I. Available online: www.public-standards.gov.uk/publications/reports/1st_report/index.asp. Accessed 6 October 2006.

Northouse, P.G. (2004) *Leadership Theory and Practice* (3rd ed). London: Sage Publications.

OECD (Organisation for Economic Cooperation and Development) (2001) 'Investment in human capital through post compulsory education and training', *Economic Outlook*, 70, Ch. V. Paris: OECD.

Ofsted (2003) *Annual Report of Her Majesty's Chief Inspector of Schools 2001/02*. Norwich: The Stationery Office.

—— (2004a) *Chief Inspector's Report*, London, Ofsted, *Annual Report of Her Majesty's Chief Inspector of Schools 2003/04*. Norwich: The Stationery Office.

—— (2004b) *Why Colleges Succeed*. London: Ofsted.

—— (2004c) *Why Colleges Fail*. London: Ofsted.

—— (2004d) *The Common Inspection Framework for Inspecting Education and Training*, HMI 2434. London: Ofsted.

—— (2005) *Annual Report of Her Majesty's Chief Inspector of Schools 2003/04*: 9. Norwich: The Stationery Office.

Ogawa, R.T. and Bossert, S.T. (1997) 'Leadership as an organisational quality', in M.Crawford, L.Kydd and C. Riches (eds), *Leadership and Teams in Educational Management*. Buckingham: Open University Press: 9–23.

Olssen, M. (2003) 'Structuralism, post-structuralism, neo-liberalism: assessing Foucault's legacy', *Journal of Education Policy*, 18: 189–202.

Pascale, R. (1990) *Managing on the Edge*. London: Penguin: 65.

Patterson, K. (2003) *Servant leadership: a theoretical model*. Dissertation Abstracts International, 64, 2: 570 (UMI 3082719).

Pedler, M., Boydell T. and Burgoyne J. (1988) *Learning Company project: A Report on Work undertaken October 1987 to April 1988*. Sheffield: Training Agency.

—— (1997, 1991) The Learning Company Strategy for Sustainable Development (2nd edn). London: McGraw Hill.

Peters, L.J. and Hull, R. (1969) *The Peter Principle: Why Things Always Go Wrong.* New York: Morrow.

Pfeffer, J. and Viega, J.F. (1999) 'Putting people first for organizational success', *Academy of Management Executive*, 13: 37–48.

Podsakoff, P.M., Todor, W.D., Grover, R.A. and Humber, V. (1984) 'Situational moderators of leader reward and punishment behaviours: factor or fiction?', *Organizational Behavior and Human Performance*, 34: 21–63.

Powell, S. (2000) 'Great groups and leaders: Warren Bennis', *Team Performance Management*, 6,1–2, 34.

Preedy, M., Glatter, R. and Wise, C. (2003) *Strategic Leadership and Educational Improvement.* London: Paul Chapman and Sage Publications.

Price, H. (2001) 'Emotional labour in the classroom: a psychoanalytic perspective', *Journal of Social Work Practice*, 15: 161–80.

Price, T.L. (2003) 'The ethics of authentic transformational leadership', *Leadership Quarterly*, 14: 67–81.

Prince, L. (2005) 'Eating the menu rather than the dinner: Tao and leadership', *Leadership*, 1,1: 105–26.

Pritchard, C., Deem, R. and Ozga, J. (1998) 'Managing further education: is it still men's work too?'. Paper at Gender, Work and Organisation Conference, UMIST and Manchester Metropolitan University, January.

PWC (Price Waterhouse Coopers) (2002) *Leadership and Management in Further Education and Work-based Learning: Final Summary Report to the Department for Education & Skills.* London: PWC.

Randle, K. and Brady, N. (1997a) 'Managerialism and professionalism in the "Cinderella service"', *Journal of Vocational Education and Training*, 49: 121–40.

—— and Brady, N. (1997b) 'Further education and the new managerialism', *Journal of Further and Higher Education*, 21: 229–38.

Reason, P. and Rowan, J. (ed) (1981) *Human Inquiry: A Source Book of New Paradigm Research.* Chichester: John Wiley.

Reh, F.J. (2006) 'How to manage'. Available online: management. about.com/cs/people/a/HowtoManage0600.htm. Accessed 6 November 2006.

Richman, J.D. (2001) *Quantum Mechanics.* Course notes for Physics 115a, winter 2001. Available online: hep.ucsb.edu/people/richman/ph115a_syllabus_winter2001.htm. Accessed 3 October 2006.

Richmon, M.J. and Allison, D.J. (2003) 'Toward a conceptual

framework for leadership inquiry', *Educational Management and Administration*, 31, 1: 31–50.

Rodgers, H., Frearson, M., Gold, J. and Holden, R. (2003) *International Comparator Contexts*. London: LSRC.

Rogers, C. and Freiberg, H.J. (1993) *Freedom to Learn* (3rd ed), New York: Merrill.

Rubenstein, H. (2004) 'Ethical Leadership: The State of the Art'. article in the CEO Refresher Archives. Toronto: Refresher Publications. Available online: www.refresher.com/!hrrethical.html. Accessed 6 November 2006.

Russell, M. (2004) 'The importance of the affective domain in further education classroom culture', *Research in Post-Compulsory Education*, 9, 2: 249–70.

Ryan, J. (2006) *Inclusive Leadership*. San Francisco, CA: Jossey–Bass.

Sachs, J. (2003) Keynote speech, presented to the British Educational Research Association Annual Conference, Heriot-Watt University, Edinburgh, 11–13 September.

Salo, F. (2002) *Leadership in Education: Effective UK College Principals*. McClelland Centre, Hay Group.

Schön, D.A. (1983) *How Professionals Think in Action*. New York: Basic Books.

—— (1987) *Educating the Reflective Practitioner*. San Francisco, CA: Jossey-Bass.

Sedgmore, L. (2002) 'Learning excellence: towards a learning skilled age', *People and Organisations*, 9, 3: 1–12.

—— (2003) Transformational Leadership, in *Human Resources*.

Senge, P.M. (1990) *The Fifth Discipline: The Art and Practice of the Learning Organisation*. London: Random House Business Books.

—— (1998) 'The practice of innovation', *Leader to Leader 9*. Available online: www.leadertoleader.org/knowledgecenter/L2L/summer98/senge.html. Accessed 14 January 2007.

—— (1999) *The Dance of Change*. New York: Currency Doubleday.

—— Kleiner, A., Roberts, C., Ross, R., Roth, G. and Smith, B. (1999) *The Dance of Change: The Challenges of Sustaining Momentum in Learning Organizations*. A Fifth Discipline Resource. London: Nicholas Brealey Publishing.

Shain, F. (1999) 'Managing to lead: women managers in the further education sector', paper presented at the British Educational Research Association Annual Conference, University of Sussex at Brighton, 2–5 Sept.

—— and Gleeson, D. (1999) 'Under new management: changing conceptions of teacher professionalism and policy in further education', *Journal of Education Policy*, 14, 4: 445–62.

Shelton, C.D. and Darling, J.R. (2001) 'The quantum skills model in management: a new paradigm to enhance effective leadership', *Leadership and Organizational Development Journal*, 22, 6: 264–73.

—— McKenna, M.K. and Darling, J.R. (2002) 'Leading in the age of paradox: optimizing behavioural style, job fit and cultural cohesion', *Leadership and Organization Development Journal*, 23, 7: 372–9.

Siegrist, G. (1999) 'Educational leadership must move beyond management training to visionary and moral transformational leaders', *Education*, 120: 297–303.

Simkins, T. (1999). 'Values, power and instrumentality: theory and research in education management', *Educational Management and Administration*, 27, 3: 267–81.

—— (2000) 'Education reform and managerialism: comparing the experience of schools and colleges', *Journal of Education Policy*, 15, 3: 317–32.

—— (2003) Reform, accountability and strategic choice in education', in *Strategic Leadership and Educational Improvement*, M. Preedy, R. Glatter and C. Wise (eds). London: Paul Chapman: 215–32.

—— (2005) 'Leadership in education: "What works" or "What makes sense"?', *Educational Administration and Leadership*, 33, 1: 9–26.

—— and Lumby, J. (2002) 'Cultural transformation in further education? Mapping the debate', *Research in Post-Compulsory Education* 7, 1:9–25.

Skyrme, D.J. (2002) 'The 3Cs of Knowledge Sharing: Culture, Co-opetition and Commitment', I^3 Update/*Entovation International News*. Main feature monthly briefing article. Available online: www.skyrme.com/updates/u64_f1.htm. Accessed 12 January 2007.

Smith, C., Gidney, M., Barclay, N. and Rosenfield, R. (2002) 'Dominant logics of strategy in further education colleges', *Research in Post-Compulsory Education*, 7, 1: 45–61.

Smithers, R. (2005) 'Review calls for tougher sanctions against failing colleges', *Guardian Unlimited*, 15 November. Available online: education.guardian.co.uk/further/story/0,,1642535,00.html. Accessed 6 November 2006.

Spears, L.C. (ed) (1998) *Insights on Leadership: Service, Stewardship, Spirit, and Servant-leadership*. New York: John Wiley.

—— (2005) *On character and servant-leadership: ten characteristics of effective, caring leaders*. Indianapolis, IN: The Robert K. Greenleaf Center for Servant-Leadership. Available online: www.greenleaf.org/leadership/read-about-it/Servant-Leadership-Articles-Book-Reviews.html.

Stanton, G. and Morris, A. (2000) 'Making R&D more than research plus development', *Higher Education Quarterly*, 54, 2: 127–46.

Sternberg, R.J., Kaufman, J.C. and Pretz, J.E. (2003) 'A propulsion model of creative leadership', *Leadership Quarterly*, 14: 455–73.

Stogdill, R.M. (1948) 'Personal factors associated with leadership. A survey of the literature', *Journal of Psychology*, 25: 35–71.

Storey, J. (2005) 'What next for strategy-level leadership research?', *Leadership*, 1, 1:89–104.

Stott, C. and Lawson, L. (1997) *Women at the Top in Further Education*. Coombe Lodge, Bristol: Further Education Development Agency.

Summerhayes, P. (2005) *Hints and Tips: Career Insights from Successful Leaders in the Learning and Skills Sector*. London: Careers Development Service, CEL.

Tenbrunsel, A.E. and Messick, D.M. (2004) 'Ethical fading: the role of self deception in unethical behavior', *Social Justice Research*, 17, 2.

TES (*Times Educational Supplement*) (2006) *Eword event and website*. Available online: www.tes.co.uk/fefocus/Eword/. Accessed 4 November 2006.

Thompson, L., Aranda, E. and Robbins, S.P. (2000) *Tools for Teams*. Boston: Pearson Custom Publishing.

Tomlinson Committee Report (2004) *Final Report of the Working Group on 14–19 Reform. Report 0976, Great Britain*. Department for Education and Skills (DfES). Annesley: DfES Publications.

Torbert, W.R. (1981a) 'Why educational research has been so uneducational: the case for a new model of social science based on collaborative inquiry', in *Human Inquiry: A Sourcebook of New Paradigm Research*, P. Reason and J. Rowan (eds). Chichester: John Wiley and Sons.

—— (1981b) 'Interpersonal competence', in *The Modern American College*, A.W. Chickering and Associates. San Francisco, CA: Jossey-Bass.

—— (1991) *Power of Balance: Transforming Self, Society and Scientific Inquiry*. London: Sage Publications.

Trevino, L.K., Brown, M. and Hartmann, L.P. (2003) 'A qualitative investigation of perceived executive ethical leadership: perceptions from inside and outside the executive suite', *Human Relations*, 56, 1: 5–37, Tavistock Institute.

Tuckman, B.W. (1965) 'Developmental sequence in small groups', *Psychological Bulletin*, 63: 384–99, reprinted in *Group Facilitation: A Research and Applications Journal*, 3. Available online: www.dennis learningcenter.osu.edu/references/GROUP%20DEV%20ARTICLE. doc. Accessed 6 November 2006.

—— and Jensen, M.A.C. (1977) 'Stages of small group development revisited', *Group and Organizational Studies*, 2: 419–27.

Turner, F. (2005) 'Poor ethics in organizations – how to avoid fleas coming back'. Research report in *LeaderValues* online leadership resource centre. Available online: www.leader-values.com/Content/detail.asp?ContentDetailID=966. Accessed 6 November 2006.

Vaill, P.B. (1989) *Managing as a Performing Art: New Ideas for a World of Chaotic Change*. San Francisco, CA: Jossey-Bass.

—— (1996) *Learning as a Way of Being*. San Francisco, CA: Jossey-Bass.

Vecchio, R. (2002) 'Leadership and gender advantage', *Leadership Quarterly*, 13:643–71.

Waters, T., Marzano, R.J. and McNulty, B. (2003) *Balanced Leadership: What 30 Years of Research Tells us about the Effect of Leadership on Student Achievement*. Information Analysis Report, Aurora, CO: Mid-Continent Regional Educational Lab., available from ERIC Clearing House on Educational Management.

Watson, G. and Crossley, M. (2001) 'The strategic management process: an aid to organisational learning in further education?', *Research in Post-Compulsory Education*, 6, 1: 19–29.

Watts, D.J. (2004) *Six Degrees: The Science of a Connected Age*. London: Vintage.

Wenger, E. (1998) *Communities of Practice: Learning, Meaning and Identity*. Cambridge: Cambridge University Press.

Wheatley, M.J. (1999) *Leadership and the New Science: Discovering Order in a Chaotic World* (2nd ed). San Francisco, CA: Berrett-Koehler.

Wren, H.D. (1999) *A profile of community college presidents' leadership styles*. Dissertation Abstracts International. Mississippi State University, 36.

Wright, P. (1996) *Managerial Leadership*. London: Routledge.

Yammarino, F.J., Spangler, W.D. and Bass, B.M. (2003) 'Transformational leadership and performance: a longitudinal investigation', *Leadership Quarterly*, 4, 1: 81–102.

Yukl, G. (1999) 'An evaluation of conceptual weaknesses in transformational and charismatic leadership theories', *Leadership Quarterly*, 10, 2: 285–305.

—— (2002) *Leadership in Organizations* (5th ed). Upper Saddle Creek, NJ: Prentice-Hall.

Zaleznik, A. (1990) 'Managers and leaders: are they different?', in *Harvard Business Review* on leadership. Boston, MA: Harvard Business School Publishing.

Appendix One
Finding out more

Glossary

ACL – Adult and Community Learning (a.k.a. Personal, Community & Development Learning)
AE – Adult Education
ALI – Adult Learning Inspectorate
BME – Black and Minority Ethnic
DCLG – Department for Communities and Local Government
DfES – Department for Education and Skills
DWP – Department for Work and Pensions
E2E – Entry to Employment
EI – External Institutions
EMA – Education Maintenance Allowance
ETP – Employer Training Pilot
FE – Further Education
GFEC/TC – General FE College
GFEC/TC – General FE and Tertiary College
HEFCE – Higher Education Funding Council for England
HEI – Higher education institution (.a.k.a. university)
ILR – Individualised Learner Record
ISC – Independent Schools Council
LSDA – Learning and Skills Development Agency (now QIA and LSN)
LSN – Learning and Skills Network
LLDD – Learners with learning difficulties and/or disabilities
LSC – Learning and Skills Council
NEET – Not in education, employment or training
NESS – National Employer Skills Survey
PCDL – Personal, Community and Development Learning

PI – Performance Indicator
PLASC – Pupil Level Annual School Census
PSA – Public Service Agreement
QCA – Qualifications and Curriculum Authority
QIA – Quality Improvement Agency for Lifelong Learning
RDA – Regional Development Agency
SFC – Sixth Form College
SSC – Sector Skills Council
SSF – School Sixth Forms
UfI – University for Industry
WBL – Work-based

Useful journals with research articles relating to FE:

Journal of Educational Management and Administration (sometimes has articles on FE/PCET)
Adults Learning (exclusively has articles on adult learning)
Association for Learning Technology Journal (ALT-J) (sometimes has articles on FE)
Journal of Access Studies (dedicated to access issues – often directly linked to FE)
Journal of Further and Higher Education (frequently has articles on FE)
British Journal of Educational Technology (sometimes has articles on lifelong learning)
British Journal of Sociology of Education (sometimes has articles on areas relating to FE)
British Educational Research Journal (sometimes has articles on FE)
Research in Post-Compulsory Education (exclusively has articles on post-compulsory education)

Useful websites relating to FE, including leadership, management and policy issues:

- The Learning and Skills Council:
  http://www.lsc.gov.uk
- http://www.dfes.gov.uk/index.htm DfES

- http://www.becta.org.uk/start/bectasite.html   British Educational Communications and Technology Agency
- http://education.guardian.co.uk/further/   Guardian FE Focus
- http://www.bbc.co.uk/education/asguru/ BBC
- http://www.lsn.org.uk/home.asp The Learning & Skills Network
- http://www.lifelonglearninguk.org/ Lifelong Learning UK
- http://www.niace.org.uk/ National Institute of Adult Continuing Education
- http://www.nln.ac.uk/ National Learning Network
- http://www.qca.org.uk/index.asp Qualifications & Curriculum Agency
- The Vocational Learning Support Programme National Resource Databank
  http://www.vocationallearning.org.uk/databank/
- Bath Spa University College (Jim Crawley):
  http://www.itslifejimbutnotasweknowit.org.uk/
- De Monfort University (James Atherton):
  http://www.doceo.co.uk/

Appendix Two
Survey on Leadership in the Learning and Skills Sector, 2006

Results Summary

2. Senior leadership evaluation

1. Senior leaders (senior management team) give staff a clear vision of the direction the institution is headed, in the organization I work for.

	Response Percent	Response Total
Strongly disagree	5.3%	4
Somewhat disagree	7.9%	6
Neutral	2.6%	2
Somewhat agree	21.1%	16
Strongly agree	60.5%	46
Not applicable to my situation	2.6%	2
Total Respondents		76
(skipped this question)		3

2. I am satisfied with the strategic direction planned by senior leaders in the organization I work for.

	Response Percent	Response Total
Strongly disagree	4%	3
Somewhat disagree	6.7%	5
Neutral	6.7%	5
Somewhat agree	24%	18
Strongly agree	58.7%	44
Not applicable to my situation	1.3%	1
Total Respondents		75
(skipped this question)		4

3. Senior leaders in the organization I work for seem willing to invest in the development of new team members at all levels of the organization.

	Response Percent	Response Total
Strongly disagree	6.9%	5
Somewhat disagree	9.7%	7
Neutral	5.6%	4
Somewhat agree	37.5%	27
Strongly agree	38.9%	28
Not applicable to my situation	1.4%	1
Total Respondents		72
(skipped this question)		7

4. Senior leaders in the organization I work for are 'authentic leaders' (i.e. genuine and truthful in serving the purposes of the organization).

	Response Percent	Response Total
Strongly disagree	5.5%	4
Somewhat disagree	5.5%	4
Neutral	8.2%	6
Somewhat agree	27.4%	20
Strongly agree	53.4%	39
Not applicable to my situation	0%	0
Total Respondents		73
(skipped this question)		6

5. Senior leaders in the organization I work for seem willing to accept mistakes made by their staff in the process of trying new things.

	Response Percent	Response Total
Strongly disagree	8.3%	6
Somewhat disagree	18.1%	13
Neutral	6.9%	5
Somewhat agree	47.2%	34
Strongly agree	20.8%	15
Not applicable to my situation	0%	0
Total Respondents		72
(skipped this question)		7

6. Senior leaders in the organization I work for understand staff at all levels and the problems we can face in our jobs.

	Response Percent	Response Total
Strongly disagree	9.7%	7
Somewhat disagree	23.6%	17
Neutral	4.2%	3
Somewhat agree	**48.6%**	**35**
Strongly agree	13.9%	10
Not applicable to my situation	0%	0
Total Respondents		**72**
(skipped this question)		7

7. Overall, upper management (Heads of Dept and above) in the organization I work for do a good job and treat me with respect.

	Response Percent	Response Total
Strongly disagree	4.2%	3
Somewhat disagree	9.9%	7
Neutral	7%	5
Somewhat agree	32.4%	23
Strongly agree	**43.7%**	**31**
Not applicable to my situation	2.8%	2
Other (please elaborate on any of the above)	0%	0
Total Respondents		**71**
(skipped this question)		8

8. Overall, how satisfied are you with the job being done by your immediate supervisor in the organization you work for?

	Response Percent	Response Total
Very dissatisfied	7%	5
Somewhat dissatisfied	9.9%	7
Undecided	5.6%	4
Somewhat satisfied	16.9%	12
Very satisfied	45.1%	32
Not applicable to my situation	15.5%	11
Total Respondents		71
(skipped this question)		8

9. Most leaders at senior and middle levels in my organization visibly demonstrate a commitment to high-quality provision for learners.

	Response Percent	Response Total
Strongly disagree	2.9%	2
Somewhat disagree	0%	0
Neither agree nor disagree	4.3%	3
Somewhat agree	28.6%	20
Strongly agree	65.7%	46
Not applicable to my situation	0%	0
Total Respondents		70
(skipped this question)		9

10. Overall, would you rate the senior managers in the organization you work for as effective leaders?

	Response Percent	Response Total
Strongly disagree	2.8%	2
Somewhat disagree	16.9%	12
Somewhat agree	38%	27
Strongly agree	39.4%	28
Not applicable to my situation	2.8%	2
Total Respondents		71
(skipped this question)		8

11. I would describe the leadership and management of the organization I work for in the following way:

View	Total Respondents	55
	(skipped this question)	24

3. Leadership across the learning and skills sector

12. Overall, I have strong confidence that the majority of leaders in the learning and skills sector are performing very well in the following areas:

	Strongly disagree	Somewhat disagree	Neutral	Somewhat agree	Strongly agree	N/A	Response Average
National LSC	13% (8)	25% (15)	31% (19)	26% (16)	2% (1)	3% (2)	2.78

Local LSC	10% (6)	26% (16)	19% (12)	34% (21)	8% (5)	3% (2)	3.05
My institution - governance	2% (1)	6% (4)	12% (8)	47% (30)	31% (20)	2% (1)	4.02
My institution - principal/CEO/head	2% (1)	8% (5)	3% (2)	29% (18)	46% (29)	13% (8)	4.25
My institution - senior managers	2% (1)	10% (6)	8% (5)	34% (21)	45% (28)	2% (1)	4.13
My institution - middle managers	5% (3)	5% (3)	5% (3)	59% (37)	27% (17)	0% (0)	3.98
My institution - academic/teacher leaders	0% (0)	13% (8)	6% (4)	54% (34)	24% (15)	3% (2)	3.92
My own line manager	5% (3)	6% (4)	6% (4)	22% (14)	41% (26)	19% (12)	4.10
LSC sector union leaders	6% (4)	19% (12)	24% (15)	21% (13)	3% (2)	27% (17)	2.93
LSC sector external business leaders	8% (5)	8% (5)	34% (21)	27% (17)	2% (1)	21% (13)	3.08
Other informal leaders I know	2% (1)	5% (3)	27% (16)	28% (17)	10% (6)	28% (17)	3.56
						Total Respondents	65
						(skipped this question)	14

13. Evidence from research indicates that learning and skills sector leadership is insufficiently diverse and that there are not enough female, black and disabled leaders. How important do you think this issue is?

	Response Percent	Response Total
This is without doubt the most important challenge for the sector	4.6%	3
This one of the most important challenges for the sector	27.7%	18
This is quite important, but there are many other issues we need to consider	52.3%	34
This issue is over-emphasised and is not that important	12.3%	8
View Other (please elaborate if you wish to re, any answer above)	10.8%	7
Total Respondents		65
(skipped this question)		14

14. In your view, what are the most important qualities needed, now, to develop good leadership in the learning and skills sector?

1. Business focus visionary - able to see it through to implementation.

2. Innovative leaders who understand the needs and demands of customers, and the sector who serve them, 20-year vision, ability to inspire and motivate, business sense, not ideology.

3. Honesty and integrity to listen and act on what being told.

4. Sharing of peer practice but also recognition that there are good lessons to learn from outside the sector. Stability at national LSC level would be very helpful.

5. Stamina, vision and drive and a believe in social justice, a head for data and networking skills.

6. Commitment, stamina and drive commitment to excellence and continual improvement passion for education and students.

7. Good communication skills, good knowledge of the sector and its customers.

8. People-centredness. Consensus management techniques. Organic, inclusive, collegial, empowering leadership models.

9. Empathy comes in part from common ground (or common back-ground). Multiculturality and age/sex 'diversity' etc are very important otherwise what ensues is but a mirror reflection of a largely excessively distanced white, able-bodied, middle class leadership.

10. Commitment and time to listen to all staff, articulate shared values and then implement them.

11. Listen to the practitioners.

12. Flexibility, Interpersonal capabilities, Inspiration, Doggedness.

13. Identification with the effects of decisions at the 'chalkface'. It is not effective to put in new initiatives without the gift of time or some other reward to enable them at lecturer and curriculum management level. The standard of many of our practitioner level people far exceeds that of industry in my experience but we do not get the best out of them because they are often exhausted.

14. Thorough understanding of the national and local political demands that impact upon FE. Excellent interpersonal skills, a high standard of leadership and management skills, the ability to manage a team but also be a team player. Effective analytical skills, good communication skills.

15. Clear vision, good communicator, listening skills, decision maker, able to prioritise, able to empathise with those on the ground and willing to roll up sleeves and lead by example at appropriate times.

16. Visionary, Participative, Supportive leaders must have followers!!

17. Vision, positive thinking, less negative approach.

18. Experience, understanding of the sector especially learning and teaching. Good business sense, tenacity, stickability and being an optimist. Probably a hint of insanity - who in their right mind would want to do the job!!!!

19. Understanding of changing student needs and business sector strategies.

20. Commitment to becoming more consultative.

21. We need bodies like the LSC and the other 64 Foster agencies to trust the leaders and staff in colleges, especially large GFEs. We are tired of the sixthformism that dominates policy. We are often the only agencies able to transform difficult lives. This sector is undervalued and underfunded.

22. Empathy with followers, Clarity of what needs to be done, Humility, Willingness to do what needs to be done and having the 'bottle' to see it through.

23. Vision, creative ability, problem solving, good communication, empathy & tolerance. Leading by example and being willing to demonstrate what needs to be done then roll up our sleeves and get on with it.

24. Experience gained within the education sector, a focus on learner success and financial acumen.

25. People skills (emotional intelligence) to motivate a whole staff to give their best.

26. Value staff input, listen, action, awareness of staff roles and responsibilities, good awareness of their impact on the organization.

27. The capacity to relate to the external world and to continually connect to the fact that we are public servants , not neo-business folks. Good communication skills , a sense of adventure, to talk as educational leaders not as management moaners caught continually in power struggles . To be well educated themselves , with a cultural hinterland of their own which contributes to them making meaning to others of the world we find ourselves in as it relates to our tasks and values. To be an example.

28. Emotionally intelligent and transformational approach allied to decisive and rational planning.

29. Consistency of approach and listening to all levels of management.

30. Listening to managers.

31. People management/coaching. Staff need to be encouraged to develop at all levels and in all jobs.

32. Understanding of the pressures staff are under to meet requirements.

33. Clarity of vision and values, An uncompromising commitment to excellence A real focus on the success of students The guts to drive through change in every college by tackling the "difficult bits". A willingness to really engage with the staff in following this through so that it impacts on every teaching and learning session, every hour, every day!

34. The ability to motivate diverse groups of staff, to provide vision, strategy and, above all, optimism and energy.

35. Knowledge and understanding of the sector in balancing the needs of both customers(employers)and clients (students/trainees), Clarity of direction Dtermination and strength of leadership Recognition of teamwork.

36. Vision, flexibility, empathy, commitment to learners and to excellent teaching.

37. A balance of a strategic and hands-on approach. Its seems to be either leaders who are too concerned with policy/strategy, are too remote & non-involved, or those who are very hands-on and involved locally but do not invest enough time in keeping abreast of changes/new directions. * Innovation & standardisation which leads to raising quality - Its seems that many services have been left to their own devices, & quality is too varied.

38. Target setting should be a working tool, rather than a 'benchmark' plucked at random out of thin air. Leaders who maintain regular contact with learners and staff are in a better position both to decide on priorities and to set targets accordingly. Good leaders are trusted by - and put their trust in - the staff under them. This usually holds true for middle management, but not for senior management where distrust on both sides appears the norm. This must change.

39. .

40. Vision, clarity, wisdom, inspirational.

41. Institutional leadership is impossible in the managed market state that we have nowadays.

42. Vision and a willingness to be innovative even if this leads to short term 'pain'. This then needs to be coupled with an ability to persuade others of the validity of this vision by allowing - and listening to - open debate and constructive challenge to such innovations from those expected to implement change. Courage to follow through on 'painful' decisions.

43. Stop the unwitting racism and prejudice and inequality in education, recruitment, selection and management of the learning and skills sector.

44. A good role model and team player. To inspire others by example. Encourages other to reach their full potential. There is also a need for additional funding to enable staff to attend training on leadership issues.

45. Vision, empathy with front line staff, experience of the sector, willingness to get involved with front line activities (especially students) on a regular (preferably frequent) basis. Political nous and clout. Ability to survive in a poorly led, politically ineptly led, poorly planned sector.

46. Vision, fairness, influence, depth and breadth of understanding of the sector and deprivation factors, ability to communicate effectively to people at all levels and effective strategist. There must be enthusiasm for the future and for social justice. There must be support for ways of working which are less bureaucratic so that resources are well targeted at the needy.

47. Willingness to change Communication skills Integrity Honesty Being able to spot good managers.

48. Effective delegation from senior management. Effective management of the institution's culture which then values the knowledge, skills and contribution of all staff.

49. Clear grasp of the landscape of F.E followed through into a robust strategic direction which is effectively communicated to staff at all levels and facilitated through effective performance management with clear lines of accountability and reporting.

50. A realistic understanding of what the people in the colleges can do. The establishment of meaningful priorities would help us enormously.

51. Better management of people at all levels.

52. The courage to speak out against ill-conceived government policies and initiatives that are top-down and continually target driven.

	View	Total Respondents	52
		(skipped this question)	27

15. What changes would you like to see in the overall leadership of the learning and skills sector?

| View | Total Respondents | 46 |
| (skipped this question) | | 33 |

4. General leadership issues

16. Some people describe leadership using metaphors. They talk of leaders being guardians, fighters, etc. Others view leadership as distributed, not individual. How do you think about leadership? Can you find a metaphor to describe it? (e.g. good leadership lights up a room; poor leadership crashes and burns). Please write down any metaphors you find useful about leadership below.

| View | Total Respondents | 39 |
| (skipped this question) | | 40 |

17. 'Transformational' leadership (visionary, inspiring) is sometimes contrasted with 'transactional' leadership (getting tasks done). Do you know of examples of inspiring leaders in the sector who transform organizations effectively? OR is this mostly just rhetoric, or worse, excessive self-promotion?

	Response Percent	Response Total
Transformational leadership is just rhetoric: nothing ever really changes	0%	0
Transformational leadership is mostly rhetoric, but there are also a few effective leaders	12%	6
No idea either way	6%	3
Transformational leadership is problematic and can lead to excessive self-promotion, but there are some good leaders who do get tasks done.	8%	4
Transformational leadership is much more than just rhetoric: some very effective, inspiring leaders do transform organizations	**50%**	**25**
Transformational leadership works well through many outstandingly inspiring & effective leaders: we can develop more - the way to do so is clear	10%	5
Other (please specify)	14%	7
Total Respondents		**50**
(skipped this question)		29

18. How would you rate management in the organization you work for according to Blake and Mouton's (1978) four profiles for management (re: management concerns for people, tasks and/or teams)?

	Response Percent	Response Total
Impoverished management - low concern for both tasks and people	2%	1
Authority-compliance management - high concern for task, but low concern for people	34%	17
Middle-of-the-road management - moderate concern for task, moderate concern for people	16%	8
'Country club' management - low concern for task, but high concern for people	0%	0

Team management - high concern for outcomes, high concern for people	42%	21
Other (please specify)	6%	3
Total Respondents		50
(skipped this question)		29

View

19. Can you name one example of a person or institution in any sphere of public life whose leadership qualities inspire you? Why?

View **Total Respondents**	36
(skipped this question)	43

20. Can you name one example of a person or institution in any sphere of public life whose poor leadership has disappointed or upset you? Why/how?

View **Total Respondents**	29
(skipped this question)	50

5. Your role

21. Please pull down the menu to select your main job role in the organization you mainly work for:

	Response Percent	Response Total
Full-time Lecturer	2%	1
Part-time Lecturer	0%	0

Answer Options	Response Percent	Response Count
Researcher	2%	1
Administrator	2%	1
Technician	0%	0
Librarian or Learning Resources Officer	2%	1
Counsellor/Advice Worker	0%	0
Programme Leader	5.9%	3
Head of Department	25.5%	13
Other middle manager	9.8%	5
Administrative senior manager	2%	1
Other senior manager	5.9%	3
Professor	0%	0
Dean	0%	0
Director	3.9%	2
Vice Principal	3.9%	2
Principal/Chief Executive	27.5%	14
Vice Chancellor	2%	1
Governor	0%	0
Business contact	0%	0
Other (please specify)	5.9%	3
Total Respondents		**51**
(skipped this question)		28

Index

This index covers all chapters excluding chapter summaries.